Co-operative Process Management

Cognition and Information Technology

EDITED BY

YVONNE WÆRN

Linköping University, Sweden

TAYLOR & FRANCIS
ALERE FLAMMAM
1798 – 1998

UK   Taylor & Francis Ltd, 1 Gunpowder Square, London EC4A 3DE
USA   Taylor & Francis Inc., 1900 Frost Road, Suite 101, Bristol, PA 19007

British Library Cataloguing in Publication Data

A catalogue record for this book is available from the British Library.

ISBN 0-7484-0713-8 (paperback)

Library of Congress Cataloging Publication Data are available

Cover design by Amanda Barragry

Typeset in Times 10/12pt by Graphicraft Typesetters Ltd., Hong Kong

Printed by T. J. International Ltd, Padstow, U.K.

Management

Contents

Preface

This book has emerged from a project within the Co-operation Scientifique et Technologique (COST) action called "Co-operative Technology", COST-14. It has been a most exciting exercise getting to grips with the ideas and seeing how difficult it is to bring various perspectives together.

But first, how did it all start? The COST-14 action was approaching its second period. Some people had gathered in Brussels to bring their interests and ideas to the table, including Sture Hägglund, Roel Popping, Kalle Lyytinen and the present author, all of whom were interested in knowledge, its storage and use. After we had presented our ideas, the board (with Professor Albert Kündig as a chairman) withdrew to reflect. We chatted and drank coffee. The board returned, and Albert gave us his verdict: knowledge storage was indeed an interesting topic, but why did we not consider dynamic systems? Here, interaction between the knowledge of various people would be even more at stake! This was the time when a chemical plant in Switzerland had collapsed and emitted a lot of poisonous chemicals into the Rhein river. Albert Kündig was worried, as every good citizen should be, and he passed on to us his worry and concern.

A couple of us started to define a computer-supported co-operative process management project, which eventually came to be called COPROM. I want to quote the following from the very first description.

BRIEF DESCRIPTION

The domain is characterized as follows:

- computer based representation of an ongoing process
- expertise is distributed (in terms of competence as well as time and place)
- cooperation for process management is time critical
- problem is complex
- organizational learning (feedback from error management)
- multiple representations of process exist.

MOTIVATION

The problem has great economical and societal impacts. The area is rich in complex and diverse group behaviour. Experience of IT use in this domain already exists, but the co-operative aspects have to a great extent been neglected. This work group can build upon previous work and benefit from working within computer-supported co-operative work (CSCW). At the same time it gives an opportunity to furnish CSCW with new and important domains.

OBJECTIVES

- Identifying key features of collaborative process management (where "management" includes control but also refers to planning, action, diagnosing, remediation and learning in case of errors).
- Identifying critical needs in the domain of collaborative process management.
- Identifying and analyzing opportunities for integrating CSCW into existing computer support for process management.

Ideas have changed during the process. This book is the result. I have learned a lot and I hope to inspire more people to approach this important and intriguing research domain.

I want to thank all involved in the COST-14 action, above all Albert Kündig, who started all this, and Kjeld Schmidt, who continued despite all unexpected difficulties – organizational difficulties as well as personal illness. I want to thank Rolf Speth, who made the COST-14 action possible, and Peter Wintlev-Jensen, who continued it. Both are at Commission of the European Community (CEC).

It is impossible to mention everybody who has been involved in some way, but the following particularly deserve a mention. Christian Heath has inspired me enormously with his conscientious research into work place conversations. Janine Rogalski and Renan Samurçay have performed pioneer work within this area and they, together with Bernard Conein and Jacques Thereau, contributed to a workshop in Paris discussing, among other things, how to conceptualize "dynamic". During workshops in the USA I met Patricia Jones and Christine Halverson, who contributed to an understanding of the difficulty of providing a knowledge store during a dynamically developing situation. Liam Bannon and Pierre Falzon have contributed with their ideas on collective knowledge or information stores, in workshops as well as otherwise. Carla Simone followed our work nearly to the end, but was not able to finish her joint chapter with Kjeld Schmidt. I miss their approach to co-ordination mechanisms!

Since the project has been a European one, we have suffered through and been inspired by one another's language differences. I want to thank our always patient language checkers, i.e. Ivan Rankin and Alan Dixon. A book can never leave the ground if there is not somebody to take care of the last details on the manuscripts: I want to thank the diligent Charlotte Lodens at the Department of Communication Studies for these services.

Last, but not least, I want to thank the authors for their co-operation. I am happy to have been able to bring their ideas together. The present texts might seem diverse and even diverging. However, we need them all in order to understand this important and intriguing domain of co-operation in process management.

Yvonne Wærn
EACE (European Association for Cognitive Ergonomics)
Department of Communication Studies, Linköping University, 1997

PART ONE

Analyses

CHAPTER ONE

Background

YVONNE WÆRN

1.1. INTRODUCTION

Situations where people have to manage complex processes are increasingly being mediated by Information Technology. Examples of situations that involve co-operation between people, computers and machines are emergency management, military command and control, control centres for traffic control (air, rail, road, water) and rescue services, stock exchange, dealing rooms, grid control, intensive care and industrial plant control.

The above situations are demanding both on people and on machines. As situations develop, people have to get information on their state, to act on the state and to observe the effects of the actions. As the situations get complex, more people are required for information gathering and actions. Therefore, co-ordination between people is essential. Information technology is designed to support information gathering as well as control. Therefore, it is essential to understand the interaction between people and information technology with regard to the situations to be controlled. Consequences of failures of controlling the situations include uncontrolled releases, injuries, poisoning, and single deaths, all of which it is highly desirable to prevent.

Because of their importance, these situations have long been a focus of research, both from technical and from human points of view. However, the considerations have been very much domain dependent. There are characteristics that are common to domains, and insights from one domain can inform development in others. In particular, new technological developments are aimed at solving general problems, to some extent independent of domain. At the same time, new technology leads to more complex situations and therefore necessitates new research. The emerging complexity of the systems to be controlled as well as the controlling systems requires new considerations as to how to control the dynamic systems. The indispensability of human beings in situations that could not be predicted by designers of automated systems has been acknowledged. Therefore, the adaptation of automated system characteristics to human requirements is accepted as an important way to increase the whole system safety. In particular, two new requirements for the human part of the chain are increasingly stressed: complex cognitive functioning and collaboration.

The complexity of the present problem requires the collaboration of several disciplines. Design disciplines and human disciplines, as well as experts within particular fields, have to contribute their knowledge. Within the design approach, dynamic characteristics and their control have to be analyzed and solved, as well as problems of knowledge representation and the interaction with human beings. Within the human approach, problems of organizational and task analysis have to be attacked, as well as problems related to cognitive, communicative and collaborative functioning.

The aim of this book was to have people with different backgrounds and different approaches meet to discuss issues related to human co-operation in dynamic situations, with particular emphasis on existing or possible computer support.

The perspectives covered are as follows:

- human factors with controlled studies
- field studies in complex environments
- information science
- computer science.

1.2. HUMAN FACTORS PERSPECTIVE

The human factors perspective to be considered concerns the design of information technology support with respect to particular tasks as well as the organization of work for managing dynamic situations. Various issues of automation are considered, mainly related to the information needs of the situation to be controlled. The human factors perspective has often concerned anthropometric issues (body characteristics) and cognitive issues (such as attention and perception), where the emphasis has been on single individuals as actors and information processors.

Issues directly related to co-operation have not been as frequently researched within the human factors approach. Due to the complexity of the present problems, a need to consider such issues was found to exist. However, existing studies do not give a univocal account of such issues. Some laboratory and experimental studies have shown that people have difficulties in co-operating due to various social psychological factors such as "groupthink" or "social loafing" (Janis, 1972). Other studies have suggested that proper team organization and training may lead to a higher performance than the work of combined single individuals. In particular, critical teamwork behaviour has been suggested to be related to giving suggestions or criticisms, co-operation, communication, team spirit and morale, adaptability, co-ordination and acceptance of suggestions or criticism (Morgan *et al.*, 1986).

For human factors, a situational or task analysis is important in order to understand the requirements on human beings (this kind of analysis is here presented by Yvonne Wærn and Rob Stammers). Human factors research also aims at modelling human behaviour (this kind of approach is here represented by Erik Hollnagel). In order to study the characteristics of human beings, the field of human factors has a research tradition in performing controlled experiments in the laboratory or in so-called microworlds (a perspective represented here by Henrik Artman, Berndt Brehmer and Peter Svenmarck).

1.3. FIELD STUDIES

Field studies are performed for several purposes and with various methods. One objective is concerned with understanding work in as much detail as possible, without any concern with changing it or evaluating it. This objective is most common in the ethnography tradition, which unfortunately could not be represented here. Another objective is concerned with identifying crucial factors which may affect the performance of the team. This approach is often used in an exploratory way, and is here represented by the studies by Henrik Artman. Field studies may also be used as input to design considerations (this approach is here represented by the studies by Esa Auramäki and Mikko Kovalainen). Further, quasi-field studies can be performed in a simulated setting, with the objective of identifying factors influencing human processing in dynamic situations as well as their performance (such studies are here presented by Henrik Artman, Leena Norros and Kristiina Hukki).

1.4. COMPUTER SUPPORT

In the computer support perspective the objective is to design some artifact which can serve people in their work situation. This perspective thus includes both an analysis phase and a design phase. This book gives three approaches to the issue of "support". One is concerned with storing temporary information about the dynamic system, and is here represented by the studies by Esa Auramäki and Mikko Kovalainen. A second aims at supporting a complex process of simulating a real world dynamic situation for learning purposes: this approach is here represented by Rego Granlund, whereas John Dowell and Walter Smith compare different systems aiming at training for emergency management. A third perspective is related to storing "long-term knowledge", i.e. knowledge about the processes which can be used independent of the particular situation. This approach is here represented by the analyses of Sture Hägglund and Roel Popping.

1.5. VARIOUS DOMAINS

Dynamic situations are found in different domains, as was pointed out above, and our analyses pertain to a range of such domains. First we have a domain related to industrial process control: one concerned with paper and pulp production. Then we have a domain related to the managing of big vessels. This domain is to some extent similar to industrial process control, however; there is no product, but only a process (navigation and steering). This process is highly automated, like many modern plant processes, and requires the intervention of people only in certain critical moments. The third kind of domain is concerned with co-ordination centres and comprises air traffic control, rescue services, military command and control as well as an emergency co-ordination centre. In this domain, people are co-operating closely and managing situations in real time without any computer control of the process.

These three types of domain may seem quite different, but there are some similarities which we want to point out. First, the domains all require processes with different time-scales. That is, short-term processes have to be considered as well as long-term processes. The short-term processes are concerned with production (in the process control cases) and action (in the navigation and emergency service situations). The long-term processes are concerned with planning and supervising the short-term processes as well as reflecting on these afterwards. Much work has been concerned with fault and error analyses, an example of long-term, *post hoc* analysis. We will see that the organizing of the long-term processes as well as the interactions between the long-term ones and the short-term ones will be among the main issues of handling dynamic systems.

Secondly, all domains require some kind of social consideration, i.e. a consideration of what kind of information co-operating people may need and what kind of information people may offer one another. We'll see that the social requirements are attended to in different ways in the different domains, but they are always present.

Thirdly, all domains contain an element of learning, which is heeded to a greater or lesser degree in the studies to be presented. Some studies (emergency management, military command and control) have learning as their main topic; others attend to learning through a computer artifact aimed at storing some kind of "collective" or "organizational" memory.

1.6. THE STRUCTURE OF THE BOOK

The book starts with analyses of the situations considered. Then field studies are presented, within three different domains, i.e. military command and control, navigation, and an emergency co-ordination centre. Microworld studies are presented in the third part; training issues are considered in the fourth part. Computer support is treated in the fifth part, with some reflections on repositories for use in short-term and long-term perspectives. The final chapter summarizes current knowledge and future issues to be considered.

1.7. REFERENCES

JANIS, I.L. (1972). *Victims of Groupthink*. New York: Houghton-Mifflin.
MORGAN, B.B., GLICKMAN, A.S., WOODWARD, E.A., BLAIWES, A.S. and SALAS, E. (1986). *Measurement of Team Behaviours in a Navy Environment*. Technical report NTSC TR-86-014. Orlando, FL: Naval Training Systems Center.

CHAPTER TWO

Analysis of a generic dynamic situation

YVONNE WÆRN

2.1. INTRODUCTION

A situation where people control a spontaneously changing situation will here be regarded as consisting of two systems: one a target system (the system to be controlled) and the other a controlling system (comprising people and artifacts whose goal is to control the target system). These two systems are tightly linked, and may be regarded as two sides of a coin. Current analyses tend to concentrate on one or other of the sides, and so it can be advantageous to separate them.

When we say that the "target system" is dynamic, this means that it spontaneously (autonomously) changes its states over time and without any intervention on the part of the controlling system. The controlling system thus has to cope both with these spontaneous changes and with the effects of actions on the system.

Of course, the target system may vary in character from a linearly developing and easy-to-predict process to a highly unstable process with a high degree of uncertainty. It may also vary in terms of the number of processes which have to be controlled simultaneously and the relationships between them. It is easy to see that control is more difficult in situations where there are several interacting events (a complex system), when the development is nonlinear, and when the states of the system can be predicted only with some uncertainty (a probabilistic system).

2.2. SITUATION ASSESSMENT

Efficient performance in coping with dynamic situations is dependent on people's ability to notice, diagnose and react appropriately to the situation, as well as on their ability to combine and co-ordinate their perceptions, interpretations and actions.

Let us start by considering the requirements of the situation. In general, a dynamic situation will require an information intake which is revised as the situation changes. One has to have some idea of how to cope with the changing situation, to perform actions and subsequently observe the feedback resulting from the actions. The activities involved in getting to grips with the situation have been covered to varying degrees by the concept of "situation assessment", which gives rise to a "situation awareness" (see special issue of *Human Factors*, 1995). As an adaptive cycle, situation assessment can be depicted as a feedback loop (Fig. 2.1).

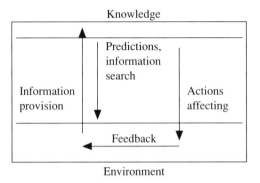

Figure 2.1. The feedback loop involved in situation assessment.

Fig. 2.1 indicates that knowledge is part of the environment, but can still be separated from it. The environment is spontaneously providing input (the arrow pointing upwards), which may change currently active knowledge. This knowledge is used for predicting the course of the target system and in order to direct further information search (the left-hand downward pointing arrow). When actions are performed (the right-hand downward pointing arrow) they give rise to changes in the environment, which then feed back as new information.

Note that in Fig. 2.1 there is no particular concept covering "situation awareness". Situation awareness can be regarded as the changing result of situated assessments, and should be treated as a conceptual entity belonging to the researcher rather than to the operator (see Flach, 1995). This concept involves a normative element, i.e. a "good" or "adaptive" situation awareness implying that the assessment gives a result which is "close" to the situation to be controlled. As Endsley (1995) points out, a relevant situation aware-ness is necessary but does not guarantee a successful performance. Flach points out that we should be careful not to confuse the performance (for instance an accident or a breakdown) with the postulated concept of "situated awareness". In that case, we might run in conceptual circles, proposing that a loss of a situation awareness leads to mishaps at the same time as we infer that situation awareness was lost due to the inappropriate human response.

Let us therefore talk about the process of assessing the situation and suggest that this process contains a perception of the situation, an interpretation of the situation as well as some prediction of the future states of the target system (Endsley, 1995). There is one theoretical difficulty related to this conceptualization, i.e. that concerned with the place of action in the situation assessment, and thus with the place of feedback. This difficulty is particularly acute when it is a question of controlling a dynamic target system. The feedback will contain information about the actions' results as well as information about the autonomous changes. How can these be separated from one another in the situation assessment? The situation is depicted in Fig. 2.2.

It is easy to see from Fig. 2.2 that the feedback from the action is confounded by the spontaneous change of the target system. Thus, predictions have to take into account both the spontaneous changes and the possible effects of actions. The situation assessments

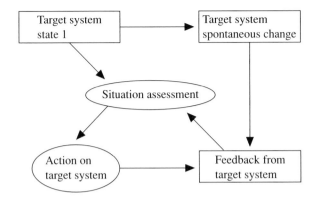

Figure 2.2. Situation assessment is an activity that takes initial information from the target situation as well as information from changes in the target system as input in order to decide what actions to take on the target system.

have to be concerned with long-range strategies of handling the target system as well as with short-term operations of coping with immediate changes. So, for instance, in forest fire fighting a strategy has been developed which involves making a clearance in the forest by burning or chopping down some of the forest. This strategy might lead to undesired consequences in the short term (having to lose some more forest) but may turn out to have desirable consequences in the long run (preventing the fire from spreading beyond the clearance line). Whenever the target system is changing fast, there will always be this need to look beyond the current situation to some prediction of future states, as well as to future actions and their possible effects.

This overview of the situation shows that in all situations, even the most unpredictable ones, people benefit from some overall knowledge or model of the system to be controlled. As pointed out by Conant & Ashby (1970), a model of the target system is essential for any regulator. For people, it serves by enabling them to solve the routine parts of the problem while their attention is directed to other parts of the problem (see Rasmussen, 1985). It enables people to think ahead of the situation and attend to what is relevant in the situation instead of getting bogged down in the overflow of information resulting from a quickly changing situation.

The "think ahead" requirement shows the importance of planning. Planning is involved in the link between situation assessment and action. It involves "instructions", which might be linked to observations of the current state or to observations of change. The "instructions" may also involve intentions: "If you want to accomplish goal X, then take actions Y and Z."

Such instructions may be worked out by particular people in the controlling system, or they may be a common activity of the team. The instructions may be worked out either far in advance or as the situation unfolds. The main idea of "planning", however, is that these "instructions" are worked out in advance of the actual events in the situation. When the situation develops, people can choose to follow these instructions in detail, to follow just the gist of the instructions or to act without considering the instructions, and react only on their immediate observations of the situation. We cannot take it for granted that plans will be followed; rather we should consider the way in which plans are used as an issue in its own right (see Suchman, 1987).

During the development of a dynamic situation, it is probable that detailed planning, based on a particular state, will not be very helpful once some time has passed. Planning based on changes may be more fruitful, as could alternative plans coupled to predictions concerning the effects of alternative courses of action.

Another aspect of planning concerns the direction of attention. In order to be able to act quickly enough, attention should be directed to what will happen instead of to what has already happened. It has been shown, for instance, that people who communicate their intentions are a greater help to other people in their actions than people who only report their current actions (Brehmer, 1994).

These insights show that planning is essential, but that it must involve the opportunity of having several plans and of adapting plans and actions according to changes in the current situation assessment.

Unfortunately, the more we analyze the situation, the more conceptual entities will be involved: entities which are not readily observable, i.e. "model of target system" and "situation assessment", which may be expanded to "perception, interpretation, prediction and planning". There are no ready measures of these entities (see Endsley, 1995).

We will see below that the need to track the changing states of the system has led to proposals of various kinds of recording procedures. The computer supports to be suggested are mostly concerned with such records of temporary states as well as with modelling knowledge of the target system.

2.3. RECORDING ACTIONS

In order to keep track of actions, people in all dynamic situations have a tradition of recording their actions, be it in a log of activities as in ship navigation, in flight strips for air traffic control or on sheets of paper for emergency control. It has also been found natural to computerize the recording procedure.

Recording actions naturally requires additional resources. When the same person is recording and acting, recording conflicts with actual actions. If some people record and other people act, using the record as an informative device, these people have to communicate and co-ordinate their activities.

Recording has several functions beyond keeping track of actions. It is also a way of preparing for an expansion of resources. A record enables additional people to know what decisions have been taken and what actions have been performed, and this information helps them to understand more quickly what has to be performed when they enter the scene. We should note that keeping a record for the use of other people requires recording to be performed in a way that takes account of other people and other contexts.

A stored report of activities can be utilized for following up of possible errors made and for learning from mistakes. Legal prescriptions might require recording, even when formulating decisions and actions may be perceived as interfering with actual actions in the current, quickly changing situation.

The record of ongoing activities can be regarded as a "collective memory" for temporary activities as well as a more long-lasting repository to be used for other purposes. Fig. 2.3 shows a general overview of the processes of long-term and short-term recording during a certain time-frame.

In Fig. 2.3 the arrows on the time-line delimit the time-frame considered in a single unit of the short-term record. Several activities may have been performed during the time-frame, and some or all of them are noted in the record. The unit of the time-frame may differ, depending on who does the recording and on competing activities. People at a higher time-level may use a longer time unit for recording than people actually performing the actions.

The recording of an activity requires that the physical action of handling the dynamic system be formulated (usually verbalized) in some way. The short-term record is used and interpreted during the handling of a complex event. A complex event may involve several recording points, thus several time-frames. An "event" may for instance consist of a patient, an emergency situation or an incoming aeroplane.

The long-term record is based on general knowledge which may be expressed in terms of principles or cases, depending on the representation of knowledge (see Chapters 15 and 16). The long-term record can be used during the handling of an event, but then it needs interpretation and adaptation to the particular event.

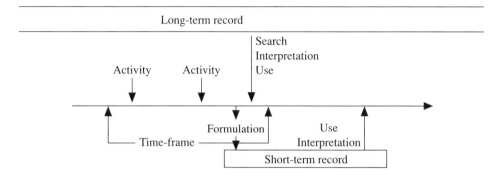

Figure 2.3. Recording and retrieving processes during a particular time-frame.

When each particular event is of immediate importance to the participants involved, it will be the subject of communication between them and may be related to other cases or principles. Some of this discussion may also be recorded. The event is met by several actions which may take more or less time, some of which may be discontinued while others may be initiated during the event. These actions are depicted as downward-pointing arrows in Fig. 2.3. The actions are influenced by, and in turn affect, the short-term record (through immediate recording) and the long-term record (after the event).

Both the long-term record and the short-term record can be regarded as "resources" which are used during the processing of the event. However, it should not be assumed that individual people always agree concerning the interpretation of the data in these resources, or that the same individual will produce a consistent interpretation in different contexts.

Within the long-term record there has traditionally been a differentiation between two kinds of stores, i.e. the episodic one and the semantic one. The episodic store is related to "cases" and consists of "stories" or "narratives" relating to these cases. The "semantic" store or the "abstract" store relates to the general propositions that may be formulated as general rules about events, or as general characteristics of objects. The long-term store develops through abstractions and generalizations from cases as well as from the application of a general semantic memory to specific cases. One of the most difficult issues in utilizing a collective store is concerned with the categorization of cases and with the terminology involved in how to distinguish cases as well as concepts.

The short-term record evolves on the one hand through the event itself and the actions taken upon this event, and on the other hand through the communication and discussions about it among the people involved, either in formal meetings or by spontaneous interventions. Sometimes, the discussions are noted in the records (such as in the patient records in medicine or records of plant status for shift transitions; see Chapter 13).

If we take one event at a time it seems useful to have this kind of record of it, since it is a record which may be collectively put together and collectively used. However, when several events go on simultaneously, problems of ordering and structuring the events arise. It is not obvious how the events should be separated and described in order to be easily accessed for immediate use. It also seems to be the case that the need for short-term use is different from the need for more long-term access (see Visser & Perron, 1996).

Several researchers have pointed out (see Bannon & Kuutti, 1996) that a repository model may not always be appropriate for conceiving the collective management of events. For instance, stored solutions may be hard to index and thus difficult to retrieve. Further, interpretation of the elements stored may be problematic as the context changes between the time when data were stored and the time when they are accessed.

The main concern with the concept of "store" is that the content of the store is not material but rather conceptual. Even when we store a description of an event for our own purposes we take it away from its context. When we retrieve it in another context, we have to re-interpret its meaning to understand what happened and the actions taken. Even for ourselves, this may be difficult if the contexts are different, and if we do not remember the first context. A record made for the use of other people will run into decontextualization and recontextualization problems which are much greater, since both situational and personal contexts will be lacking.

Despite these arguments against repositories, throughout the history of writing people have believed in the usefulness of texts (and pictures) to serve as holders for event descriptions as well as for reflections. Although their usefulness might be less than enthu-siastic computer science proponents maintain, computerized repositories should not be more difficult to interpret than non-computerized ones. An insightful analysis, such as the one provided by Bannon and Kuutti (1996), should in fact make it possible to design computerized stores that allow for recontextualization and reinterpretation to a greater extent than we are accustomed to from our acquaintance with books. Some further sug-gestions will be provided in Chapters 14, 15 and 16.

2.4. CO-ORDINATION ISSUES

Having covered the requirements for handling the dynamics of the target system, we now have to return to the problem of co-ordinating people and artifacts with respect to this task.

2.4.1. Team, group or distributed cognition?

First, I would like to point out that the situations I am going to approach are most ade-quately described by the concept of "team". By a team is meant "a distinguishable set of two or more people who interact dynamically, interdependently, and adaptively toward a common and valued goal/object/mission, who have each been assigned specific roles or functions to perform, and who have a limited life span of membership" (Salas *et al.*, 1992).

This definition differs somewhat from the definition of "group", which usually is con-sidered as a more tightly-knit collection of people. The participants in a group, moreover, do not seem to be characterized by having "specific roles" or "different windows on the world".

levels and between different aspects of the same part task, the drawbacks of which have been amply shown in the problems with a bureaucratic organization.

2.4.3. Efficient co-ordination?

Let us now turn to what is required if co-ordination is to be regarded as "efficient". The following requirements for efficient co-ordination have been suggested:

1. shared model, shared situation awareness (shared understanding of goals, shared understanding of situation); shared = overlapping but not necessarily the same

2. sharing resources – dividing resources among the participants (if one resource can be used by only one person)

3. co-ordination of action – temporal and spatial integration of team action with respect to the controlling system goals

4. shared mental model (of co-ordination) – common understanding of which team member is responsible for which task and what the information requirements are

5. mutual understanding – cognitive empathy – an individual's understanding of the other person's understanding.

To simplify the reasoning, let us go through these requirements one by one, although they are of course interdependent.

2.4.4. Shared situation awareness

It may seem self-evident that people who are responsible for a common task (such as fighting a fire, fighting an enemy or steering a ship) have to have a shared situation awareness. But what does "a shared understanding" actually mean? Does it mean that everybody should understand the target system to the same degree of detail? Or does it only mean that they trust that their combined competence provides a sufficient model of the target system to be useful for the continual situation assessment?

Does the shared understanding imply that everybody should agree on a common goal? To some extent this is probably the case, but it should also be noted that people may have to have varying and to some extent conflicting goals in order to cope efficiently with different aspects of the problem, such as both long-term and short-term aspects of the target system (see the example of "clearances" above). The nature of the team implies that people have different competencies and interests. A rescue team, for instance, may involve the conflicting interests of ambulances wanting to rescue people and fire-fighters wanting to shield new people from the danger of entering the burning area.

Does a shared understanding mean that everybody should have the same interpretation of the situation, the same predictions and the same suggestions as to actions to be taken? To some extent a common understanding is helpful, but to some extent, again, it might be better to approach the target system from different perspectives, to check on one another's interpretations and to be able to argue about various solutions.

There are other arguments against a total common understanding. In particular, it has been found that people who are tightly coupled to one another in a joint mission may fall prey to a phenomenon called "group-think" (Janis, 1972). This phenomenon occurs when people do not complement one another but rather fall into the same common trap of misjudging the situation, clinging to nonfunctional hypotheses, not searching for contrary evidence and "risky shifts". The phenomenon is attributed to group dynamics, i.e. a tendency for people to follow one another at the price of losing independent judgment. Reports suggest that detrimental group dynamics have existed in several accidents, the Chernobyl catastrophe being one of the best known. It is possible that these effects are stronger in tightly coupled groups than in teams, where the participants should contribute with their varying degrees of competence.

2.4.5. Sharing resources and co-ordination of action

Sharing resources and co-ordinating actions imply similar kinds of problems, i.e. the ordering of individual activities over time and space. When the same resource (e.g. an artifact or a restricted space) has to be shared by several people in the same time slot, conflicts will emerge. In order to prevent such collisions in space and time, the work is usually organized in some way.

There are in principle three ways of organizing the process of work (see also "Co-ordination architectures" below) in order to avoid conflicts. The first works by issuing commands concerning who is to do what and when. The second works by planning the activity by proper task allocation. The third works by local co-ordination. Each of these has advantages and drawbacks.

The advantage of commanding is that the participants commanded will not have to reflect, only to act. This will then make each activity independent of the others and dependent only on the commander's orders. A good commander may further be able to issue orders which do not require complex activities by the commanded. As we will see later, a system with independent and simple elements will function most efficiently in all kinds of situations. The drawback is that the organization will suffer a "bottleneck" problem. The commander is the bottleneck, since he or she will have to assess the situation as well as issue commands. If the commander does not get support in these activities, the system will be stifled when the commander reflects.

The advantage of plans made in advance is that people know what to do and when, that they do not need to communicate while acting, and that they do not interfere with one another, given of course that the plan is good. A plan can be embedded in an organization, such as in a Taylor type of organization or in the modern organization known as "work flow". However, it has been pointed out by several researchers (see Robinson & Bannon, 1991) that a plan may become too rigid to be functional. People need to "articulate" their work with respect to one another, not only because they like to do so, but also because circumstances change.

Finally, co-ordination problems may be solved locally. People who have activities bordering on one another may communicate and negotiate their activities with respect to both the use of common artifacts and tight space restrictions. The drawback here is that it may be too late to communicate actions after these have been performed. All participants in a situation involving local co-ordination need to be able to predict actions of the others. For this reason, it is helpful that participants communicate their intentions to act and not only their current actions.

2.4.6. Shared co-ordination model and cognitive empathy

In order to co-ordinate understanding and action, people not only have to know what they themselves need to do, but they should also have some kind of understanding of what other people are expected to do. They should know so much of the other people's tasks that they can predict when to expect information from them. In this way they may monitor the incoming information for the information they need, although they may not need it exactly at the time it is provided. They should also be able to provide others with the information they need, preferably when they need it. This means that they should monitor not only their own information intake but also other people's need for information.

This may be called a "shared co-ordination model" and may be built into the system by the task allocation. It may also be built upon a "cognitive empathy", i.e. an intuition about what information the various participants need at different points in time. This concept is further covered in Chapter 3 and we shall see one example of it in Chapter 6.

2.4.7. Co-ordination architectures

One question that arises is how the various sub-tasks of a controlling system should best be allocated to different roles. From a system point of view, the parts included in the system should be as independent of each other as possible, as well as being as simple as possible. The reason for this is that each interaction between elements results in a loss (of energy or information) in the system as a whole (see Fig. 2.7). Complex elements, on the other hand, imply increased effort for each element. Thus the cost of interactions as well as of handling complexity should be minimized.

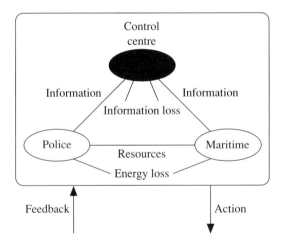

Figure 2.7. An example of interactions between an SOS control centre and some agents involved.

This idea of independence can now be used for designing the controlling system. If people act upon the same object from different perspectives, they have to communicate about their actions. If people perform interdependent actions, they also need to communicate. Tasks which require several interdependent actions are therefore better handled by a single person than distributed over several persons (i.e. maximizing intra-task organization, see also Chapter 3). In controlling a dynamic system, where the time lag between information collection, planning and action has to be short, it thus seems that vertical organization is efficient in the immediate situation. This is exemplified in Fig. 2.7 by the police and maritime crews.

As to reducing complexity for each element, it can be said that a minimum complexity is achieved by each element performing only one basic task repeatedly rather than continuously shifting between different tasks. The shift between tasks will imply increased complexity if the tasks require conflicting attention or actions.

Taking an emergency and its control as an example, it follows from the independency and complexity principles that it is more efficient to install a control centre than to have the active agents (police etc.) co-ordinating their actions themselves. Although there is some information loss between the control centre and the active agents, the complexity of the tasks at each point is lower.

Similar reasoning can be applied to the need for distributing planning and action to different people. It has been shown (Brehmer, 1991; Brehmer & Svenmarck, 1995) that a task allocation according to different time-scales is efficiently used in the military as well as in hospitals. Planning refers to a slower time-scale than acting and can thus, to some extent, be performed independently of the physical activities. Horizontal organization is applied to different time-scales.

The principle of independency conflicts, however, with another principle, i.e. that of redundancy. In a complex and time-demanding task, redundancy of resources and information is required. There are at least two reasons for redundancy: the risk that some element will fail, and the need for expansion. People may fail when their attention gets overloaded; communication between people may fail when there is too much "noise" in the situation (physical or virtual). In a situation where more events will occur and greater time pressure arises, people have to split their activities. In these situations, redundancy is a resource which can be used to enable the team to undertake more tasks. This extension is facilitated if all participants have some knowledge of the unfolding situation as well as of actions already taken.

Examples of how to allocate tasks to take these different task allocation considerations into account are given in Chapter 3.

2.5. SUMMARY

This chapter gives a general frame of reference for the chapters to follow. Two sections of the chapter are devoted to issues involved in handling the dynamic system, while one section is devoted to issues concerned with co-ordination between people involved in the dynamic management process.

The concept of *situation assessment* was found to be useful in promoting an understanding of the dynamic system, in predicting its future states as well as possible alternative actions to take in order to control the system. Although there is no general agreement on how to define the concept, most researchers seem to agree that it involves perception of the situation as well as some prediction as to its future progress.

Recording of system states and actions was suggested as a useful way of providing continuous situation assessment, for preparing new participants and for later reflections on events and their handling. Recordings are common activities in all dynamic situations. It is evident, however, that the activities of recording itself and of using the record have to be considered carefully in order not to conflict with the actions that must be taken. Further, it is important to consider the possible problems occurring when a record is used in a context which differs from the one in which it was originally formulated.

Co-ordination issues are concerned with how to share information about the situation and the activities performed, how to distribute tasks and how to share common resources.

The concept of team and distributed cognition was introduced to characterize the situation when people have different tasks, but still have to be aware of what information other participants in the team can offer or may need. It seems to be the case that participants have to possess some common knowledge, both about the general characteristics of their topic and about the particular situation. However, in order to be efficient they should also be able to act independently of each other. Organizational issues in this context pertain to how to spread information as well as to how planning and actual actions are to be managed. Different co-ordination architectures may be chosen. It seems that a hierarchical organization, where people allocate tasks according to different time levels, is beneficial for the handling of a dynamic system.

The following chapters consider most of the above issues, but cannot of course give a full account of the complexities, nor can they provide solutions to all problems. Some further insights will be gained, however, from the studies and analyses.

2.6. REFERENCES

BANNON, L.J. & KUUTTI, K. (1996). Shifting perspectives on organizational memory: from storage to active remembering. *Proc. of the 29th IEEE HICSS*, vol. III, Information Systems – Collaboration Systems and Technology. Washington, DC, IEEE Computer Society Press, 1996, 156–167.

BREHMER, B. (1991). Modern information technology: timescales and distributed decision making. In: J. RASMUSSEN, B. BREHMER & J. LEPLAT (Eds), *Distributed Decision Making. Cognitive Models for Co-operative Work*. Chichester: Wiley, 193–200.

BREHMER, B. (1994). *Distributed decision making in dynamic environments*. Uppsala University, Sweden, Foa Report.

BREHMER, B. & SVENMARCK, P. (1995). Distributed decision making in dynamic environments. Time scales and architectures of decision making. In J.-P. CAVERNI, M. BAR-HILLEL, F.H. BARRON & H. JUNGERMANN (Eds), *Contributions to Decision Making – 1*. Amsterdam: Elsevier.

CONANT, R.C. & ASHBY, W.R. (1970). Every good regulator of a system must be a model of that system. *Int. J. Systems Sci.*, vol. 1, No. 2, 89–97.

ENDSLEY, M.R. (1995). Measurement of situation awareness in dynamic systems. *Human Factors*, vol. 37, 65–84.

FLACH, J.M. (1995). Situation awareness: proceed with caution. *Human Factors*, vol. 37, 149–157.

Human Factors (1995). Special issue: Situation Awareness, vol. 37, 3–157.

JANIS, I.L. (1972). *Victims of Groupthink*. New York: Houghton-Mifflin.

RASMUSSEN, J. (1985). The role of hierarchical knowledge representation in decision making and system management. *IEEE Transactions on Systems, Man and Cybernetics*, SMC-13, No. 2, 234–243.

ROBINSON, M. & BANNON, L. (1991). Questioning representations. In L. BANNON, M. ROBINSON, and K. SCHMIDT (Eds), *ECSCW '91. Proceedings of the Second European Conference on Computer-Supported Co-operative Work*, 24–27 September 1991, Amsterdam, Kluwer Academic Publishers.

SALAS, E., DICKINSON, T.I., CONVERSE, S. & TANNENBAUM, S.I. (1992). Toward an understanding of team performance and training. In R.W. SWEZY & E. SALAS (Eds), *Teams: Their Training and Performance*. Norwood, NJ: Ablex.

SUCHMAN, L.A. (1987). *Plans and Situated Action*. Cambridge, MA: Cambridge University Press.

VISSER, W. & PERRON, L. (1996). Goal-oriented categorisation: the role of task, daily activity, expertise and problem attributes. In: T.R.G. GREEN, J.J. CAÑAS and C.P. WARREN, Cognition and the Worksystem. *Proceedings from the European Conference of Cognitive Ergonomics*, 8, University of Granada. Le Chesnay Cedex: EACE, 109–114.

CHAPTER THREE

Task analysis and its relevance for team work

ROB STAMMERS

3.1. INTRODUCTION

One of the problems with the description of task analysis methodology in the ergonomics literature is that how it is carried out, and what it is used for, is not explained in detail. Some of those who have come more recently to task analysis activities from, for example, a concern with human–computer interaction or from the co-operative work area have criticized things that they have assumed that ergonomists do. For example, they may comment on the use of inappropriate underlying theory or they may assume that ergonomists take a very mechanistic view of the people in the system. It is appropriate therefore to explain how ergonomists actually work. Task analysis methodologies have not been widely reported in academic journals. They are often buried away in reports or book chapters that are not widely known to the other disciplines. Task analysis can be seen as a stage in some activity, usually a design activity, but that might, for example, mean design of a training programme. In a sense, task analysis is a tool to do a job rather than an end in itself. By focusing not on this, but on the elegance and the theoretical strength of task analysis, it is possible to miss some of the point of what it is there for. Task analysis is, in many ways, a transition phase that is gone through and then put aside when one moves on to another activity.

A range of influences have led to various task analysis approaches. There have been informal influences from work study, and formal influences from ways of representing activity in networks or information flow diagrams. There have been influences from systems approaches, with attempts to represent complex entities as systems with interacting elements. Influences have also come from behaviourism, and although there is a tendency to want to dissociate ourselves from this particular field of psychology, it has been of some assistance by focusing on what the objectives of activities are. Skill psychology and information processing theory have been important in developing a view about how humans work as information processing systems, and that has matured into cognitive psychology approaches. There are also influences from linguistics that look at ways in which tasks can be expressed in terms of such things as grammars of activity. Additionally, artificial intelligence has had an impact, with attempts at capturing human activity in a programmable form. Then there is ethnography, with its focus on observing and recording human activities in naturalistic settings. With all of these influences, it is perhaps not surprising that there is a lot of confusion in the field. There are different influences, different objectives and different professions all examining human activity. To illustrate the problem of terminology in the area, Singleton (1974) put forward one set of terms for describing activities, i.e. elements, skills, tasks, job, occupation, role. Then there is a second set of terms for describing the stage of the work that is being carried out, i.e. study, description, analysis and specification. The suggestion is that every permutation of these two sets of terms could be used at some time, by a variety of researchers, to describe what they are doing.

3.2. HIERARCHICAL TASK ANALYSIS

An approach that has been widely used in ergonomics is hierarchical task analysis (HTA). It has been used both in its specific form as the technique put forward by people who have worked with it (Stammers and Shepherd, 1995) and in the form of a general approach of analyzing tasks and representing them as hierarchies. HTA represents tasks in terms of a series of elements called operations that are hierarchically organized. There is a progressive re-description of a complex task by breaking it down into more and more detail and expressing it in these terms as instructions to carry out the task. It is very functionally oriented, in terms of what the person is trying to do in relation to the system's objectives. It also includes what are called plans. These are sets of rules for how and when operations are carried out. The hierarchy on its own functions as an index to what goes on in the task; the plans say how those elements are sequenced, selected and co-ordinated. The hierarchical representation does not really capture the essence of what the approach is trying to do: the plans are also important. There is, however, a representational problem of how to include plans within the overall analysis. Another feature of HTA that is not widely understood is that the analysis on its own is simply an overview of the detail the analyst wants to record. One way of recording detail is in a table, where there is a numerical index in one column and further description of the task in another column. Comments and notes can be put in other columns. The problem of documentation does not go away, but it is possible to provide more detail about the task elements in a table and this can be very flexible. Advocates of the approach try not to be dogmatic about how to represent a task analysis, as they feel it is necessary to adapt the analysis for the specific purpose.

There are three stages in the task analysis process when a system is being examined in relation to how it is controlled:

- data collection stage
- task description stage
- task analysis stage.

The objective may be to produce a new controlling system, to produce training for that system, to reduce error in that system, to redesign and improve the user interface for that system. Initially, varying amounts of task data are available for examination from the system. A common misconception is that collecting information is all that is involved in task analysis: in fact it is only the first stage. There is a range of approaches for collecting information which can be simplified to: questioning, observing, or using existing documentation.

When information has been collected, there is then the representational phase, i.e. putting information in a form that is communicable to those that are working with it. This is the description stage. The people carrying out the task can be shown the analyst's view of their task. They can comment on it, and help with its revision.

The information can then be interpreted in the analysis phase. This is where information is analyzed for the objective in hand. Task analysts are never going to have as detailed an understanding of the task as the people doing that task, but they are trying to capture something of it so as to be able to carry out the design process. It can be shown to those with whom the analyst is working, e.g. system designers, trainers, human reliability specialists. They can then utilize the information on the task which has been represented.

One feature of HTA that is worth commenting on is that it is quite compatible with our general way of thinking about complex things. That is, it is a convenient way of communicating with people and sharing knowledge about a complex entity, i.e. a set of tasks. Although it is simplified and artificial in many ways, it is something of which we can share an understanding.

3.3. TEAM ACTIVITIES

Difficulties arise when tasks are examined that are shared between two or more people. These situations have been called collaborative tasks, team tasks, group work, etc. When the author first began to look at team tasks a number of years ago (Stammers & Hallam, 1985), there was a search for some theoretical context for examining tasks allocated among team members. In studying that work again, in the light of more recent experience, one interpretation is that tasks are, in many ways, artificial creations that are imposed on something that is there within the work that people do (Schäl & Shapiro, 1992). It is not a major issue until the way in which tasks are allocated between people is examined. Task organization can be seen as the different types of linkage that there could be between sub-tasks and the way they are shared between people. It turns out that it is possible to differentiate between intra-task organization and inter-task organization. Intra-task organization refers to the linkages between the tasks that individuals are themselves performing. Inter-task organization involves linkages of information flow between individuals.

As an example, it is possible to envisage an abstraction of some details from a real-world task that exists in military ships, where information comes in and is processed through various stages. It is called a picture compilation task. It is then possible to look at the different sub-tasks and the links between them. For example, a piece of information arrives and it has to be identified. It then has to be associated with other pieces of information. Thus three sub-tasks are formed. If those three sub-tasks are given to one person, then the links between those task elements, the information that is carried across, is the intra-task organization. If those sub-tasks are split between two people, the links between them are called inter-task organization.

In laboratory experiments, the various ways in which teams can be configured were examined, together with varying levels of task loading. One form of team structure was serial organization. Information came in and the first person (X) carried out sub-tasks A and B, then the information was transferred to the second person (Y). Person Y carried out sub-task C and then passed the information on. So the links between sub-tasks A and B were intra-task organization but the links to sub-task C were inter-task organization.

Another way of doing this task is a parallel team organization. Information comes in, but the input flow is divided between X and Y and they do all three tasks. It is possible to divide up the information flow in this way, with half of the items coming in going to person X, half going to Y. This is a way of sharing the mental workload that arises. For example, the items of information to be processed can be shared in this way, based on a geographical split, with everything coming from the north of the ship's position going to one person and everything coming from the south going to the other person. Thus each team member gets approximately half of the information load, but carries out all the sub-tasks. In one study, perhaps not surprisingly, the parallel form of organization produced faster and more accurate performance under higher workload. The serial organization produced queuing in the system; the performance of the second person in the series was determined by the information flow from the first person.

It is also possible to explore the problems that arise when there is a need for inter-task communication. In the first study everything conveniently stayed in the north or in the south and did not cross over. Once the information sources cross the sector there was the need for transfer of information between team members and when this was done, under different levels of workload, the efficiency of the parallel organization began to deteriorate. Studying team tasks in experimental settings is one way of looking at shared mental workload. It is also possible to examine these concepts by field studies of real-world teams. The author has been involved with work of this nature.

3.4. BALANCING WORKLOAD BY TEAM ORGANIZATION IN AIR TRAFFIC CONTROL

An earlier programme of work in air traffic control (ATC) came about because the limits of reducing workload had been reached by division of labour, i.e. by splitting the tasks up between controllers (e.g. Whitfield *et al.*, 1980). For example, the picture on a radar screen can represent a geographical sector for which just one controller is responsible. Aircraft are flying into this region, usually in air lanes; there are perhaps two air lanes, with aircraft going in both directions. But as air traffic demands increase, that area can become too much for one person to handle. One solution is to divide the sector up in various ways. Thus part of the sector would be handled by one controller, and another part by a second controller. This also gives rise to the need for intercommunication between the team members and this passing of messages adds to the controllers' work-loads. Workload may be reduced in one way but then added to in another. With a continued growth in air traffic demand, followed by even more splitting up of sectors, a point can be reached where every time the sector size is reduced it gives rise to increased communication. The gains can be outweighed by the losses. At that point the questions can be asked of the form: "how else can we reduce mental workload?", "can we have some form of computer assistance?". That was the task we took on: to look at future system design, and examine how the mental workload of controllers might be reduced by sharing the task with computers.

This programme of work went through several phases, but an interesting, serendipitous, result emerged. A colleague and myself both carried out task analyses of the same control room, but with a separation of a few years. When we had occasion to compare these analyses at a later date we found that some of the tasks had changed, but not others.

In the original arrangements two controllers worked in series, one carrying out planning activities and the other controlling activities. They were controlling aircraft arriving at and departing from an airport. In this particular airport, separate runways were used for arriving and departing aircraft. The planning activities of the first controller had to do with sorting out an optimum sequence of departures and with determining the arriving sequence of aircraft. A second controller dealt with all airborne and on-runway aircraft, it being felt important to keep all this information under one person's control. However, this gave rise to one job – the planner's – having a low workload at all times. The second job had very high workload on many occasions.

A reorganization of these positions gave rise to two new task allocations to controllers that gave more balanced workloads. One controller dealt with all departing aircraft, both their planning and controlling demands. Similarly, the other controller dealt with all aspects of arriving aircraft. What seems to have happened, in the terms that were developed in the experimental programme described above, is that the informational links between the tasks associated with the separate streams of arriving and departing air-craft have been given to separate controllers. This maximizes intra-task organization and minimizes the links between controllers, the inter-task organization. There are occasions when the controllers do have to co-ordinate, e.g. when a landing aircraft does not land but flies on and may end up close to departing aircraft. In these rare but critical circum-stances there is a need for inter-task organization, but such events, being infrequent, do not justify a permanent poor balancing of load between the controller roles.

In contrast to this, we found that two other ATC jobs had not changed over the time between the two analyses. These jobs were concerned with controlling aircraft taxiing on the airport. Here again there was a planning job and a controlling job. The planning job had a very low load, and the controlling job had a very high one. However, it was not possible to separate the departing from the arriving aircraft as they all used the same areas of the airport. All of the information had to be "in one person's head". So this situation remained as it was: two ill-balanced loads persisted as it was impossible on the grounds of safety and of coherency of tasks to separate the control of arriving and depart-ing aircraft.

It is worth describing another situation in this context that demonstrated that some-times the information links between people are very subtle. It involves the highly loaded person controlling the taxiing aircraft. They had help from another person in the team who had a more minor role, the air traffic control assistant. These are less qualified people who do subsidiary tasks for controllers. They do not actually control aircraft, but they get information and they fit flight strips into the holders and put them into the racks. The assistant operated a lighting control panel, listened to what the controller was saying to aircraft and set up a pattern of lights, defining a path for an aircraft to follow.

This person is following what the controller is doing via the radio and observing the situation on the airport. On one occasion the author observed a situation where an aircraft called, asking for some directional information. The controller looked at the assistant and by a facial gesture indicated that he did not know the location of the aircraft. The assistant looked around and then pointed to where this aircraft was located. There were no words exchanged between them, but it was very clear that vital information had been exchanged. This sensitivity to another team member's information needs under high workload has also been observed by the author in military command and control teams. It is particularly interesting if it occurs when the voice channel is occupied, as in the ATC example. Here the system personnel have expanded on their communication channels with this non-verbal communication. They use a form of communication that is more usually associated with social interaction in everyday life, in a noisy room or at a party.

It would be easy to destroy inadvertently the possibilities for this form of communica-tion in the way a control room was arranged. There is a need to identify such activities in a task analysis. This sensitivity to another person's workload could be termed cognitive empathy. It is related to social cognition, situation awareness or shared mental models, but all of these terms warrant closer examination and study (see also Chapter 2). It would be easy to reduce the possibilities for this very human type of communication by, for example, putting people in remote locations. Then we would have to think about ways in which we might use technology to compensate for those changes. One example can be found in a military command and control system where people were physically separated, but often needed to consult one another about their displayed information. In this system they had the facility on their screen for using a big arrow and a tracker ball to point to a particular piece of information and say such things as "keep an eye on this one". They used a physical pointing gesture that cuts through complex message transmission and identification issues. It is possible to enhance the possibilities for more direct form of communication by good design.

It is hoped that this brief description has illustrated that task analysis is not just the recording of observable actions and information sources, etc. It should also involve a sensitivity to how highly skilled and experienced people have evolved patterns of work. This understanding must be brought to the design activity, and ways must be sought to exploit these uniquely human characteristics and not to restrict them.

3.5. REFERENCES

SCHÄL, T. & SHAPIRO, D. (1992). What's wrong with tasks: objections in the large and in the small. In: *Proceedings of the International Conference on Task Analysis*. Austria, Schärding.

SINGLETON, W.T. (1974). *Man–machine Systems*. London: Penguin.

STAMMERS, R.B. & HALLAM, J. (1985). Task allocation and the balancing of load in the multi-man machine system: some case studies. *Applied Ergonomics*, vol. 16, 251–257.

STAMMERS, R.B. & SHEPHERD, A. (1995). Task analysis. In: J.R. WILSON & E.N. CORLETT (Eds), *Evaluation of Human Work: A Practical Ergonomics Methodology*, 2nd Edn. London: Taylor & Francis, pp. 144–168.

WHITFIELD, D., BALL, R.G. & ORD, G. (1980). Some human factors aspects of computer-aiding concepts for air traffic controllers. *Human Factors*, vol. **22**, 569–580.

CHAPTER FOUR

Context, cognition and control

ERIK HOLLNAGEL

There never comes a point where a theory can be said to be true. The most that one can claim for any theory is that it has shared the successes of all its rivals and that it has passed at least one test which they have failed.

A.J. Ayer (1910–89), British philosopher. *Philosophy in the Twentieth Century*, ch. 4 (1982).

4.1. THE NEED FOR MODELS OF HUMAN BEHAVIOUR

Although the sophistication of technology has increased dramatically during the latter half of the 20th century, the importance of the human operator has not diminished. On the contrary, the uneasy symbiosis between people and machines often creates situations where operator performance is the only defence against unwanted consequences. A growing number of essential technological systems rely on the interaction between people and machines to accomplish their purpose, so they depend on adequate human performance. The proper specification of the man–machine interaction (MMI) is therefore a central issue in man–machine systems (MMS) design, and this has created a need to improve the underlying concepts and models.

The study of cognition has traditionally focused on the cognition of the individual – as either the user or the operator. Over the past decade or so, however, it has been realised to an increasing degree that there is a need to study cognition in the context in which it occurs, and that this context is constituted not only by the technological environment but also – and most importantly – by the organization and the people in it. Thus, rather than studying the detailed "mechanisms of the mind" or cognitive functions *per se*, the focus should be on how a person or a group of persons can maintain control of a situation, thereby enabling them effectively to control the processes or systems with which they work. The control depends on the knowledge of the situation, and that knowledge is to a significant extent provided by communication.

4.1.1. Maintaining control

The importance of communication in maintaining control of a situation can be illustrated by considering Fig. 4.1, which depicts the general paradigm for situation understanding, based on Neisser's (1976) notion of the perceptual circle. As the relations of the figure indicate, the current understanding directs or controls observation – and also action. These produce an outcome, which constitutes the input information or feedback to the person. That information modifies the current understanding, either by reinforcing it or changing it more or less drastically, thereby closing the loop.

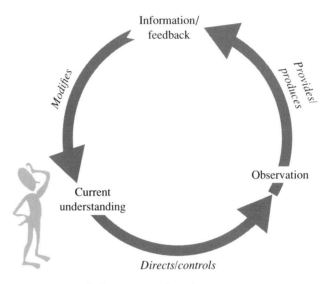

Figure 4.1. Maintaining control: the perceptual circle.

Fig. 4.2 shows how the general paradigm can be extended to cover the case of two or more people working together. For each individual the general paradigm can be used to describe how control of the situation is maintained. The two "individual worlds" are, however, joined by the fact that work is carried out in a common environment, and by the communication that takes place between people. This communication may itself effectively modify the current understanding, either independent of or in addition to observations and actions.

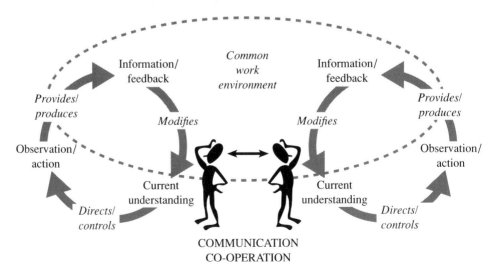

Figure 4.2. Maintaining control: the role of communication.

This view of how control and performance are linked helps to answer two important questions for human performance modelling, relating to the *purpose* and the *contents* of the model. The first refers to what the model should enable us to do, while the second concerns what should be modelled. The two questions are, of course, related: if we know what the model should enable us to do, then we are in a better position to specify what should be modelled.

The answer to the question of what the model should enable us to do is that it should provide better *predictions* of the developments that may occur, and hence help the design of specific solutions and to assess possible risks. An example is the analysis of possible error modes due, for example, to communication or procedures. Explanation and understanding, which otherwise are typical purposes of models, are less relevant here since the ability to explain something after the fact has limited practical value in system design. A preliminary answer to the question of what should be modelled is that it should help us to *describe* the overall performance characteristics rather than focus on detailed modelling of specific cognitive functions and cognitive mechanisms.

4.1.2. Requirements of modelling

A person's control over a situation is inseparable from the ability to predict correctly the developments of the situation (see. Figs 4.1 and 4.2). In a familiar situation it is easy to predict what will happen, hence easy to maintain – or regain – control. The effectiveness of the predictions can be enhanced by training and experience, and in many cases large groups of functions can be automated, thereby internalizing the predictions in the system itself. In unfamiliar situations, and in particular in emergencies, predictions are more difficult to make. Many, if not all, of the system's automatic functions may be defeated and proper operator actions are consequently more important because they may be the only means to prevent serious damage. Conversely, inappropriate operator actions may further jeopardize the safety and integrity of the system. Similarly, not doing anything, such as the two hours and twenty minutes of inaction during the TMI accident (Perrow, 1984), may be harmful because the dynamics of the system may take it further away from the region of normal conditions. There are several reasons why an operator is unable to maintain control in an emergency, including the following.

■ The process can be in an unknown state that nevertheless is clearly abnormal or dangerous, hence recognized as an emergency. If the state is unknown, then operators by definition do not know what to do. The situation may either be one where there is a lack of information (Hollnagel, 1988) or, paradoxically, one where there is too much information (Miller, 1960). In the latter case the problem is often to isolate the relevant information from the rest (e.g. an avalanche of alarms).

■ The operator may recognize the state and have established a goal (well defined or vaguely defined), but not know how to achieve it. If the situation is partly conflicting with design assumptions, then available support, procedures, etc. will be inadequate. The problem is therefore to produce a plan or procedure for what to do, either by generating one anew or by retrieving and adapting an existing one.

■ The operator may know both what he wants to do and how it could be done, but recognize that the required resources (in particular time) are inadequate. Since there is more to do and less time to do it in, the increased demands for fast and correct performance may produce a greater workload and lead to errors (De Keyser, 1994). The problem here is either to establish the required resources or to adapt the procedures so that they are executable within the given restrictions.

In either case time is spent either doing nothing or planning what to do, thereby leaving less time to carry out the actions. Psychologically speaking, the passing of time may lead to a conceptual deadlock; although the awareness of time limitations may, in the words of the illustrious Dr Johnson, "concentrate the mind wonderfully", it may also cause a complete loss of control. Models of cognition should therefore be able to account for: (1) how control is maintained, (2) how it can be lost, and (3) how it can be regained. In general it must be assumed that the impact of the existing conditions (the situation) will eclipse the impact of specific cognitive processes. It is therefore more important that models of cognition comply with empirical evidence, the requisite variety (Ashby, 1956), than that they are based on a set of "first principles of cognition" (like the basic laws of physics) – quite apart from the fact that we do not at present have sufficient strong "first principles" of cognition to support such an approach. In particular, models of cognition must acknowledge that control is based on an understanding of the situation and that this is established and shared through communication.

4.1.3. Flowchart models

It must be a fundamental assumption for the study of cognition at work that human behaviour is orderly, in the sense that it can be described as if it were guided or directed by something – whether this is called a goal, a purpose, a plan, a rule or an intention. Behaviour – as far as anyone can tell – is essentially purposive. There are several ways in which this fundamental trait can be accounted for, and the classical information processing approach is not necessarily the most appropriate. Information processing models usually take the form of the flowchart description of cognitive functions. The virtues of the flowchart description were strongly argued by Miller *et al.* (1960), and the approach is, indeed, very powerful, not only for human action but for functions in many different types of system. In cognitive psychology it has led to the ubiquitous representation of cognitive functions as a set of "elementary" steps or stages linked in various ways that correspond to a representative flow of action. As an example, consider the typical representation of decision-making shown in Fig. 4.3.

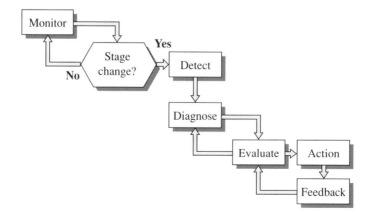

Figure 4.3. A typical information processing model.

Models of human action that accord with the view of the mind as an information processing system will only be orderly when cognition is treated as a hypothetical process that occurs within the human mind. Unfortunately, the kind of orderliness that is expressed by these models comes from their *structure* and therefore does not necessarily correspond to the orderliness that is observed in practice. In such models the interaction with the environment takes place at well-defined points and in an orderly fashion, and the performance is basically a set of pre-defined reactions to external events. Humans are, however, proactive as well as reactive and performance never occurs in isolation. This can be demonstrated by considering the notion of diagnostic strategies. The psychological literature provides a number of diagnostic strategies with evocative names such as topographic, symptomatic, hypothesis driven, data driven, etc. However, these are idealized descriptions of what performance *could be* like and rarely correspond to what performance *is* like (for example Hollnagel *et al.*, 1996; Jones *et al.*, 1995). The models can only hope to match actual performance if the conditions are sufficiently restrained, as for example in an experimental or tightly controlled setting. The experience from observing performance at work is that humans tend to combine strategies or switch between them rather than adhering to a single strategy. Even the notion of switching assumes that the assumption of identifiable "pure" strategies is reasonable. Following the information processing approach therefore creates the problem of explaining the "switching", which is difficult to predict from the models. It might be simpler to recognize that human performance is orderly in the sense that it usually achieves the goals efficiently and also in the sense that there are characteristic patterns that occur frequently. The objective therefore becomes how to describe this orderliness without making too many assumptions about the "mechanisms" of the mind. Put differently, human performance is orderly relative to the purpose of performance rather than to the characteristics of an internal "mental mechanism".

4.1.4. Orderliness and control

It is part of human nature, or at least our second nature, to try to *control* a situation so that actions taken will achieve the desired goal. The preconditions for purposeful or orderly behaviour in a task are knowing what the goal or objective is and being able to assess how much remains to be done before the goal is reached. In practical terms we should be interested in finding out how we can make it easier for people to achieve control of their work situations. In theoretical terms we should be interested in how we can model, and hence explain, and control the orderliness of actions.

Orderly performance can only be achieved if there is sufficient feedback about the results of actions (Mackay, 1968). The information processing approach emphasizes that performance is controlled by feedback, but makes less of the fact that performance is also controlled by feedforward, i.e. expectations or predictions of what will happen. Whereas feedback enables an operator, and more generally a system, to achieve a goal state, feedforward enables the operator to do it efficiently. The feedforward can be used to determine a course of action, in anticipation of future system states (Gregory, 1987). This relieves the operator from constantly monitoring the feedback, hence enables smooth and efficient performance. In the extreme case where the understanding of the environment is perfect, performance can be completely feedforward driven. On the other hand, if the expectations are incorrect, unexpected events are bound to occur. These will produce unexpected information that requires attention and takes time to recognize and understand, thereby increasing the overall demands on the operator. In order to be proactive, there must be sufficient time to develop an understanding of the situation and to plan ahead. If the orderliness of performance begins to break down, the situation may quickly deteriorate (Miller, 1960). There will be more unexpected information and less time to try to absorb it, hence possibly an increase in the unexpected information, etc. As illustrated by Fig. 4.4, this may constitute an evil circle that competes, so to speak, with the "normal" circle of understanding–action–feedback.

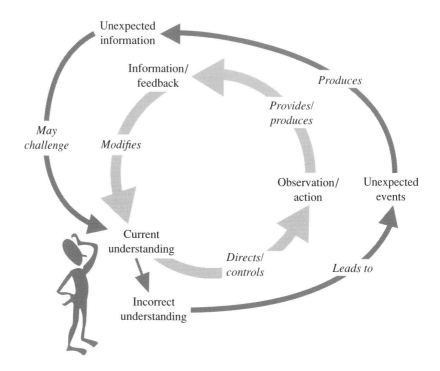

Figure 4.4. The evil cycle of incorrect understanding.

To illustrate this, consider the difference between driving a car on the daily route from home to work and driving a car while trying to find your way through an unknown city. In the first case the environment is highly predictable. Although there may be the occasional disturbance and traffic jams, the environment is stable in the sense that traffic signals and landmarks are in their usual positions, and changes in direction therefore can be planned and executed smoothly. In the second case the environment is essentially unknown, and driving therefore becomes somewhat unpredictable. Instead of planning ahead the driver must constantly look for landmarks, street names, etc., and relate them to a map. Quite often turns are missed and it becomes necessary to turn back. The average speed goes down and driving becomes less smooth – often to the irritation of the driver behind. Similar examples can be found in areas of work, such as flying a plane or controlling a process. In each case performance will be orderly and controlled to the extent that developments in the system or the environment can be predicted, i.e. to the extent that the operator(s) understand the system correctly. Conversely, performance cannot be accounted for only as responses to events, hence as feedback driven. The explanations, and therefore also the models, must include concepts such as situation understanding, planning and feedforward.

When cognitive systems engineering was developed in the early 1980s (Hollnagel & Woods, 1983), a cognitive system was defined as: (1) being goal oriented and based on symbol manipulation; (2) being adaptive and able to view a problem in more than one way; and (3) operating by using knowledge about itself and the environment, hence being able to plan and modify actions based on that knowledge. This definition clearly bears the mark of its time, which was characterized by a rising enthusiasm for expert systems, knowledge representation, and the like. Today, in 1997, a better definition is that a cognitive system is able to *control* its behaviour using information about itself and the situation, where the information can be prior information (knowledge, competence), situation specific information (feedback, indicators) and constructs (hypotheses, assumptions). The control can be complete or partial and depends to a considerable extent on the ratio of unexpected information to expected information.

4.2. CONTROL AND COGNITION

The essence of efficient control is the ability to predict, and to predict correctly, which is tantamount to having a correct understanding or model of the situation. A model can in this respect be seen as a schematic description that accounts for the known or inferred properties of a system. When the model is about humans at work, it must address the characteristics of cognition. When the model is about systems where people and technology interact to achieve a specific goal, the model must address the salient features of the joint system in a way that achieves the goals of the design. Modelling in joint systems must therefore focus on how control is maintained or re-established, both for the human and for the system as a whole.

Being able to anticipate the consequences of actions requires a set of *constructs*, i.e. expressions or representations of what is known or believed about the world, where these constructs are used to select appropriate actions. If a system can achieve that, it will be in control of the situation. Conversely, if a system cannot do that, it will have lost control. On the practical level the loss of control means that the predicted events do not match the actual events, in other words that the consequences of actions are unexpected or surprising.

The term "construct" is used as a neutral reference to the temporary information that is required to maintain control. In other contexts this has been called knowledge or mental models. These terms, however, usually carry with them quite specific connotations that may be unnecessary for the purpose of describing the orderliness of performance. At the present stage, the term "construct" seems less burdened. The information is furthermore temporary, in the sense that it may change over time, either as a consequence of learning or because it is correct only for a certain time or a certain set of conditions. For instance, when I leave a hotel I have no longer any need of remembering the room number. In fact, it may become a problem at later hotel visits if I cannot forget it. Similarly, much of the information we use during work is of a temporary nature, and need not be remembered. In principle the argument may be extended to the point that very little information needs to be permanent, such as one's name, date of birth, and immediate relatives. Other information is temporary to various degrees, such as place of living, profession, etc. although information that is consistent over longer periods usually is treated as permanent. From an empiristic point of view there may indeed be no permanent information at all.

Even without going to such philosophical extremes, it is probably not necessary for cognitive modelling to assume that any information is permanent, but only that some of it is stable for the duration of a given situation. In terms of the model, it may therefore suffice to consider all information as constructs and none of it as universal. For the purpose of understanding control and co-operation it is also important to acknowledge that many constructs must be shared between the members of a team or a group. Shared information, in turn, is established by means of communication.

4.2.1. Inner worlds and outer worlds

The traditional approach to description and analysis of human performance makes a strong distinction between two entities. One is an "inner" world or a "cognitive mechanism". This is the brain or the mind, commonly described as an information processing system. The other is the "outer" world, i.e. the environment or the context. In the traditional view the two are linked by the exchange of input and output described, for example, as information vectors or as events and actions – or even as stimuli and responses. The classical description is that of the general automaton (Arbib, 1964), described as a quintuple:

$$A = (I, O, S, \lambda, \delta)$$

where   I is a finite set of inputs

O is a finite set of outputs

S is a finite set of internal states

$\lambda: S \times I \to S$ is the next-state function

$\delta: S \times I \to O$ is the next-output function

The description of the general automaton makes a clear distinction between the external world, represented by the inputs and outputs, and the internal world, represented by the set of internal states. Although the typical information processing model is less explicitly described, it corresponds in all essentials to the principles of the general automaton. The general conception of information processing models is that the inner world is different from the outer world, almost as a form of representational dualism. Furthermore, the emphasis in psychology has been on describing the inner world, while the outer world has been reduced to the input/output parameters. This corresponds to a perfect mechanistic or deterministic description of psychology.

Humans have often been modelled as information processing systems that are decoupled from the context, where the only exchange is via input/output. This adherence to a sequential information processing model has created a number of problems that have been difficult to solve. Chief among these is how to account for the influence of performance shaping factors, how to describe the selection of and switch between strategies, how decisions are made, how and why performance levels may change, etc. (see Hollnagel, 1983). These problems remain unsolved not because of a lack of trying, but rather because the problems are artifacts of the underlying theory.

In accordance with the principles of cognitive systems engineering, any attempt to model cognition must start by acknowledging that cognition is always *embedded* in a context or a situation. Thus, cognition is always "cognition in the wild" (Hutchins, 1995; Miller & Woods, 1996) – even under laboratory conditions. The context includes demands and resources, physical working environment, tasks, goals, organization, social environment, etc. A model of cognition must therefore account for how cognition depends on the *context* in a broad sense rather than on the *input* in a narrow one. What we perceive depends on what we expect to see which in turn is determined by the context, as described by the "perceptual cycle" (see Fig. 4.1). The modelling of cognition must therefore abandon the notion of input information as something that has a value in itself, independently of the context.

4.2.2. The sequentiality of cognition

Descriptions, but not predictions, of human performance must necessarily refer to what *has* happened. Accounts of human performance therefore describe a sequence of actions and events, but the orderliness of this sequence is illusory. Any description that is organised in relation to time must be well-ordered and sequential, simply because time is directed and one-dimensional. Human performance appears to be sequential when viewed in retrospect, but this orderliness is an artifact of the characteristics of time. This is illustrated in a rather primitive way by Figs 4.5 and 4.6, which show how the "same" development may look in the "future" and in the "past". Fig. 4.5 shows some of the possible sequences of cognitive functions that could occur in the immediate future, using the limited set of [observation, identification, planning, action] that is part of the simple model of cognition (Hollnagel & Cacciabue, 1991). Initially the person makes an observation, for example notices a change in the system. That will in turn lead to another cognitive function but it is impossible in advance to determine which, even when the set is limited to only four.

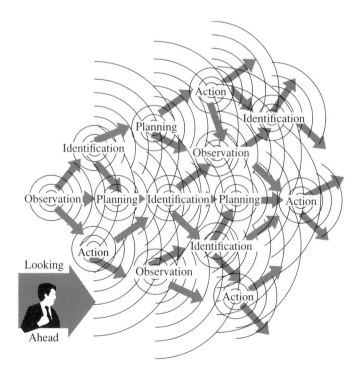

Figure 4.5. Performance in the "future".

In contrast, Fig. 4.6 shows the sequence of events *after* they have occurred. In this representation the cognitive functions did occur in an orderly way, although this specific sequence was impossible to predict. Since the sequence of events achieved the desired goal, it is tempting to see it as the result of a rational process. The example shows, however, that it is a mistake to assume that an orderly underlying process or "mental mechanism" by itself produced the observed sequence of actions. In practice, people usually prepare themselves for the most likely development of events, whether they are planning to fly a mission over enemy territory (Amalberti & Deblon, 1992) or are going for an important meeting with their boss. Yet the actual sequence of actions will be the result of a coupling between the person's control of the situation and the conditions that exist at the time.

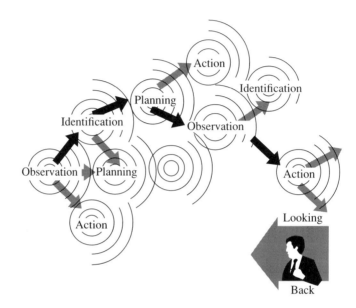

Figure 4.6. Performance in the "past".

Because the sequential ordering of performance is an artifact of time, it is unnecessary that models or explanations of cognition contain specific prototypical sequences. In other words, models of cognition need not describe cognitive processes as a set of steps or stages that are executed one by one. This means that the seemingly disorder or complexity of actions – jumps, disruptions, reversals, captures – need not be explained as *deviations* from an underlying sequence or from the well-ordered flow of cognition that is a consequence of human information processing models. Instead, models of cognition must be able to account for human actions in general, regardless of what the outcome of the actions is.

4.3. MODELLING APPROACHES

The information processing approach uses a set of elements or structures of the human information processing system as the basic building blocks for models and theories. Thus elements such as short-term memory, long-term memory (knowledge base), attention capacity, etc. are common primary components. Such *structural approaches* are attractive because they provide an apparently objective frame of reference where human information processing is a reflection of information processing in the machine. Their disadvantage is that they refer to an information processing mechanism in near splendid isolation that is triggered by events in the external world. Cognition thereby becomes a kind of higher level information processing that occurs entirely within the human mind, and the holy grail of cognitive science is to unravel the mechanisms of pure cognition. Although information processing in some disciplines can be described as an abstract process, it makes little sense to speak of basic human information processes in the same manner. While the information processing metaphor is useful in helping to understand some fundamental features of human thinking, it does not mean that the mind *is* an information processor or that cognition is computation.

In the late 1980s many people began to realize that cognition actually occurs in a context, as illustrated by the notion of situated cognition and naturalistic decision making (e.g. Zambok & Klein, 1996). This view, however, implicitly maintains a distinction between cognition and context by describing them as two separate entities. If this distinction is abandoned it becomes meaningless to describe cognition separately from the context. From the perspective of cognitive systems engineering (Hollnagel & Woods, 1983) it is self-evident that there is no cognition without a context: there can be no being, of either natural or artificial cognitive systems, without being in a context or in a situation. Even in extreme conditions, such as can be created in laboratory experiments or found in moments of quiet introspection, there is still a context because a person exists in a world. The view of pure or context-independent cognition is therefore a category mistake in the Rylean sense and the "discovery" of situated cognition is accordingly superfluous.

The alternative to a structural approach is to describe the regularities of performance rather than the details of human information processing. This *functional approach* is driven by the requisite variety of human performance rather than by hypothetical conceptual constructs. The observed regularities of human behaviour by definition exist only in a given context, and actions occur in anticipation of events as well as in response to them. Functional approaches avoid the problems associated with the notion of pure mental processes, and in particular do not explain cognition as an epiphenomenon of information processing. In a structural approach it is necessary to account for the context separately from the processes of the mind; in a functional approach this problem disappears. The advantages of that should be obvious.

4.3.1. Procedural prototypes

In terms of models of cognition the structural and functional approaches correspond to a distinction between *procedural prototype models* and *contextual control models*. A procedural prototype model emphasizes the sequential nature of cognition and is a *normative* description of how a given task should be executed. It implies that one sequence of actions represents a more natural way of doing things than others, or that a certain sequence or ordering is to be preferred. A contextual control model, on the other hand, views cognition as being determined by the context rather than by inherent sequence relations between actions. A contextual control model concentrates on how the *control*, or the choice of next action, takes place and fully acknowledges that this is determined by the nature of the situation.

The difference can be illustrated by considering a common form of the procedural prototype model (see Fig. 4.3). The procedural prototype model contains a basic set of functions that is carried out time after time. Since this rarely corresponds to practice, the models require the introduction of a number of embellishments to account for alternative paths, bypasses, and short-cuts. Changes in the environment are described as changes in the input to the model, but have no effect on how the steps are ordered. The bypasses may skip one or more steps but the underlying step-by-step progression is immutable.

Although this kind of modelling is appealing on a conceptual level, it presents serious practical problems. In the simple version, control is an integral part of the model: when a step has been completed, the person goes on to the next, until the overall objectives have been achieved. In the more elaborate versions the control issue is complex and basically unsolved. The procedural prototype model describes the task as if the person attempted a rational progress through the various phases. Since this rarely is the case, the model matches only poorly the variety of human action and other solutions must therefore be found.

4.4. COMPETENCE, CONTROL, AND CONSTRUCTS

Human performance is determined, largely, by the situation. People can do many things and achieve their objectives in many different ways. The selection among the possible actions is not determined by normative characteristics of the action elements (as components), but by the current needs and constraints – that is, by the demand characteristics of the situation. Due to the regularity of the environment there may be frequently recurring patterns or configurations of actions, but this is not evidence for procedural prototypes. The challenge of cognitive systems engineering is to provide a reasonable account of how this regularity can occur without making too many assumptions about human cognition or about the capabilities of an internal information processing system. A contextual control model is based on three main concepts: *competence*, *control*, and *constructs*.

4.4.1. Competence

Competence represents the set of capabilities for what a person can do in a given situation. It describes what a person is able to do and includes various functions ranging from elementary actions to composite types of behaviour such as decision-making, problem solving, planning, etc. The competence should not be described in terms of elementary actions, such as one would find at the bottom of an action hierarchy, but rather in terms of what a person is capable of doing. What may be a single action for a skilled person can be a series or complex of multiple actions for an unskilled person. The definition of what constitutes single or complex actions in the model, the *activity set*, thus depends on the situation and on the person's background and experience. The extent of the set of possible actions mainly depends on the level of detail or the granularity of the analysis that is used for the model, and is potentially not denumerable. The possible actions are the set from which the actual actions are chosen; consequently, the person cannot do something that either is not available as a possible action or cannot be constructed or aggregated from the available possible actions. Possible actions may exist on different levels of aggregation as a mixture of simple and composite actions. The only thing common to them is that they can be used in the context.

The competence also includes a set of recurrent patterns or specific relations between two or more actions which in a given situation can determine the order in which they are executed. Such groupings, the *template set*, are necessary for human action to be efficient; if every action was the result of an explicit choice or decision, very little would be accomplished in practice. At most we would, as a child who has just learned to walk, be able to do only one thing at a time. Templates may be plans, procedures, guidelines, heuristics, strong associations or anything else that can serve as a guide for performance.

The distinction between the template set and the activity set makes it easier to account for how a person can be involved in several lines of actions at the same time, and how a new goal can be established. It can also be used to describe how rigid performance can come about (as strict compliance to a template), how mistakes are made (strong associations between actions which may override a plan or procedure), how random performance can be modelled (by unsystematic choice among plans or even choice among actions without consideration of plans), and how dominant phenomena can be modelled (leading to frequent error modes). The distinction provides a way of modelling very diverse phenomena with a few simple principles.

4.4.2. Control

Control describes how we do things and how actions are chosen and executed. Control can be described in a number of ways, where the granularity of the description and the mode of functioning are important issues. The modelling of cognition must reflect a pragmatic definition of the variety (or variability) that needs to be modelled (Ashby, 1956). The nature and range of this variability – but not its origin – will prescribe what the model of control should be able to do. From the practical point of view, it is sufficient to match only the requisite variety.

The essential part of the control is planning what to do in the short term, within the person's time horizon (e.g. Amalberti & Deblon, 1992). This planning is influenced by the context, by knowledge or experience of dependencies between actions, and by expectations about how the situation is going to develop – in terms of, for example, resources, constraints, and demands. The outcome prescribes a certain sequence of the possible actions but, as argued above, the sequence is *constructed* rather than *pre-defined*. In this view frequent patterns or characteristic distributions of actions reflect a relative constancy (regularity) of the environment as well as the constituent features of human cognition rather than the constraints of the performance model.

Control can obviously occur on several levels or in several modes. Although the levels of control that a person – or a joint system – can have over a situation can vary continuously, it is useful to make a distinction between the following four characteristic control modes.

- *Scrambled* control mode: the choice of next action is apparently irrational or random. The person is in a state where little, if any, reflection or cognition is involved but rather a blind trial-and-error type of performance. This is typically the case when people act in panic, when cognition is paralyzed and there accordingly is little or no correspondence between the situation and the actions. The scrambled control mode includes the extreme situation of zero control. While performance is unpredictable from the person's point of view it may, paradoxically, be relatively easy to predict from an observer's point of view, due to the limited variability.

- *Opportunistic* control mode: the choice of next action is determined by the salient features of the situation. There is limited planning or anticipation, perhaps because the context is not clearly understood or because the situation is chaotic. Opportunistic control is a heuristic that is applied when the constructs (knowledge) are inadequate, due to inexperience, lack of knowledge, or an unusual state of the environment. The resulting choice of actions may not be very efficient and may give rise to many useless attempts. In this type of situation the person will often be driven either by the perceptually dominant features of the interface or by those which, due to experience or habit, are the most frequently used, e.g. similarity matching or frequency gambling heuristics (Reason, 1990).

■ *Tactical* control mode: this is characteristic of situations where performance more or less follows a known procedure or rule. The person's time horizon goes beyond the dominant needs of the present, but planning is of limited scope or limited range and the needs taken into account may sometimes be *ad hoc*. If a plan is used frequently, performance may seem as if it was based on a procedural prototype – corresponding to, for example, rule-based behaviour (Rasmussen, 1986). Yet the underlying basis is completely different.

■ *Strategic* control mode: the person uses a wider time horizon and looks ahead at higher level goals. The choice of action is therefore less influenced by the dominant features of the situation or the interface. Strategic control provides a more efficient and robust performance than the other modes. The attainment of strategic control is influenced by the knowledge and skills of the person, and although all competence can be assumed to be available, the degree of accessibility may vary greatly between persons, and hence be a determiner of their performance. At the strategic level the functional dependencies between task steps and the interaction between multiple goals will also be taken into account in planning.

The scrambled control mode is clearly the least attractive, while the strategic is the most attractive – seen in relation to efficacy and reliability of performance. In practice, people will usually be working in what corresponds to an opportunistic or tactical control mode. Most cases of controlled flight into ground, for instance, correspond to the pilots being in an opportunistic mode. Although the strategic control mode is the optimal one, it is not often achieved. Consider, for instance, all the situations when you afterwards, i.e. in hindsight, realize what you should have done or said. Whenever this occurs, it is a good indication that you acted in a tactical or opportunistic way. On the other hand, preparing for the contingencies that may arise is a way of guarding against having to function in an opportunistic mode.

4.4.3. Control modes and attention

It is natural to consider the relations between the control modes and the level of attention, particularly since the lack of attention may easily lead to the loss of control. For three of the control modes there will always be a reasonable, and possibly even a high, level of attention. Strategic control is the deliberate and careful planning of actions, hence it cannot be achieved without paying attention. Opportunistic control is less methodical, but still the person will be attending to what is being done – in particular to the outcome, since that determines the further developments. In scrambled control the attention is also high, not in the selection of actions but in the sense that the person's attention is dominated by a single goal or concern, possibly to the extent of hyperattention.

In the tactical control mode it is, however, reasonable to distinguish between an attended and an unattended form. The attended form is the meticulous and careful execution of procedures and plans (templates), either pre-defined or made for the occasion. This is characteristic of situations that are slightly unfamiliar, or where the performance conditions are tightened so that greater care is required. The unattended form is the familiar situation where people know what to do but may not bother to follow it in detail, for instance because the situation is very familiar or because there seems to be plenty of time available. Yet these are often the conditions where performance failures appear. Good examples can be found in, for instance, familiar household chores such as cooking and cleaning (see Reason & Mycielska (1982) for many excellent examples of these kinds of failure). The corresponding cases in work are those where people have a false sense of security in what they do.

Both the level of attention and the control mode are hypothetical intervening variables that are used because they facilitate an understanding of the characteristics of human performance. In order to provide a more tangible illustration of the control modes, it is necessary to refer to performance variables that have a reasonably clear relation to observable performance characteristics. Two such dimensions are the familiarity of the situation and the subjectively available time. Although both refer to subjective aspects, there is clearly a strong correlation with objective descriptors. The familiarity of the situation is strongly related to how common the situation is, i.e. how often it has occurred. (It is also related to other factors, such as the level of training and experience of the operator.) The subjectively available time is strongly related to the objectively available time that, for instance, can be reliably estimated by process experts. The degree of familiarity and the available time are both important determinants of performance, and the relation between these and the control modes can be illustrated as shown in Fig. 4.7. However, the illustration does not imply that the two dimensions also must be parameters of the model.

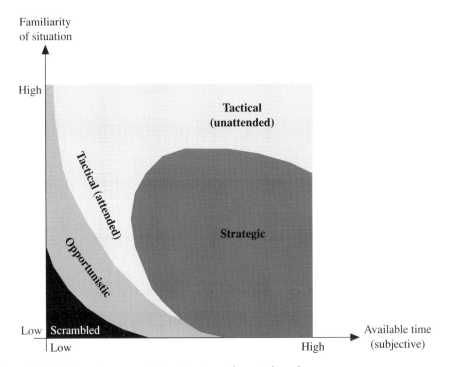

Figure 4.7. Main performance determinants and control modes.

In agreement with the definitions of the control modes, scrambled control is expected to occur when the situation is very uncommon (unfamiliar) and when the available time is very limited. If there is an increase in the familiarity of the situation or in the available time, the control mode changes from scrambled to opportunistic. In both cases the change means that performance demands are reduced, thereby providing the person with some opportunity to consider what actions should be taken – although mainly in a fragmentary manner. As the familiarity of the situation and/or the available time continues to improve, the tactical and strategic control modes can take over. As indicated by Fig. 4.7, the strategic control mode will come into play in situations that are in the medium to low range of familiarity, but where there is sufficient time to reflect on them. The tactical control mode dominates in situations that are of medium to high familiarity. If, furthermore, there is ample available time, then the tactical control may be of the unattended kind.

The characteristics of the four main control modes can also be described in writing, as shown in Table 4.1. In addition to listing the characteristic values of the dimensions of familiarity and available time, the corresponding characteristics for the level of attention are also included. Further details of the possible parameters of contextual control model will be given in the following.

Table 4.1. Characteristics of the control modes

	Available time (subjective)	Familiarity of situation	Level of attention
Strategic	Abundant	Routine or novel	Medium–high
Tactical: attended	Limited – adequate	Routine, but not quite familiar – or task is very important	Medium–high
Tactical: unattended	More than adequate	Very familiar or routine, almost boring	Low
Opportunistic	Short or inadequate	Vaguely familiar, but not fully recognized	High
Scrambled	Very limited	No recognition	Full – hyperattention

4.4.4. Constructs

Constructs, finally, refer to what a person knows or assumes about the situation where the action takes place and are thus equivalent to the person's knowledge about something. If the person does not have (or cannot remember) a construct about something, action will not be possible except in a random fashion based on guesses, i.e. shallow *ad hoc* constructs. This corresponds to performance in the scrambled or opportunistic mode of control. Information processing psychology uses terms such as knowledge representation, frames, (mental) models, etc. The term implies that constructs are both temporary and artificial, in the sense of being constructions or reconstructions of salient aspects of the situation. Constructs are similar to the schemata of Neisser (1976) in that they serve as the basis for selecting actions and interpreting information.

Constructs can deliberately be temporary, such as where the car is parked, the weather forecast for the next two days, or the value of a measurement five minutes ago. In such cases constructs are only placeholders for information, and it would be detrimental to performance if they were permanent. In other cases constructs are of a longer duration, such as the operating instructions for a machine, knowledge about how a specific device works, and the way to the office. Some constructs are like hypotheses, some are more like beliefs, and some represent general or "universal" knowledge. Constructs, as well as competence, can change as a consequence of learning.

Constructs are intrinsically linked with competence, the difference being that competence always includes the ability to *do* something. (From a formalistic point of view, competence may easily be seen as a special form of constructs.) Knowing the characteristics of a hydraulic or electronic system may be a construct, but the ability to make use of, diagnose, or maintain the system is a competence. Knowing what happens when the system is in use is a construct, although that construct is also part of the goal (goals-state) of the competence.

4.4.5. Interaction between competence, control, and constructs

All attempts at modelling human performance contain some distinction between the various ways in which a plan or an action can be carried out, corresponding to different levels of performance – such as automated or skill-based and deliberate or knowledge-based. It therefore seems sensible to distinguish clearly between control and competence in the models, and in particular to develop ways of describing how control is accomplished. This emphasizes the *principles* that govern behaviour and separates them from specific exemplars or *prototypes* of performance. A good model should not prescribe a sequence of actions but rather provide the means to describe how sequences are planned and how specific actions are chosen.

There is clearly a strong coupling between the different modes of control, the level of competence, and the nature and contents of the constructs. Here concepts such as feedback driven and feedforward driven behaviour are important. Information processing models typically focus on feedback driven behaviour, although any student of human behaviour knows that it is open loop as well as closed loop. The characteristics of open loop behaviour require something that is functionally equivalent to knowledge or constructs, and which can be used to anticipate changes in the environment. The level of control depends on what happens, which in turn depends on what the person expects to happen. Yet what a person expects to happen is, in terms of modelling of cognition, determined mainly by the constructs and the competence. If, for instance, a work shift goes by with no untoward events, i.e. nothing unexpected happens, then it is reasonable to expect that the operators will remain in full control. Conversely, if something goes wrong in the process, an operator can only maintain control if the requisite knowledge and competence are available.

In the functional approach to modelling, the four modes of control are not absolute categories but rather represent regions in the control space. They allow the model of cognition to replicate the dynamic selection of actions, the various modes in which this can take place, and the influence of internal and external information such as the operator's current interpretation of the state, previous actions, time and resource constraints, competence, constructs, and external factors (communication).

4.5. ISSUES IN CONTEXTUAL CONTROL MODELS

In order to be more than a loosely formulated set of principles, it is necessary that the functional approach be expressed as models that are useful in practice, for instance as a basis for simulations, for analyses, etc. First and foremost it is necessary to provide a description – and preferably a set of operational principles – which can account for how control depends on the context, and which accordingly can describe how performance is shaped by the events. There are in particular two aspects of such models that must be accounted for: (1) how the transition between control modes takes place, and (2) the characteristics of performance in a given control mode.

A functional model must be able to explain how control can be lost, how it can be regained, and how it can be maintained. It is easy to find instances where a person loses control of the situation, typically when something unexpected occurs (e.g. Sarter & Woods, 1995; Wiener, 1989), and we can easily corroborate that by personal experience. The same goes for regaining or maintaining control, which is very important in high-risk, high-impact systems. This aspect has been captured by one of the most famous simplifications of human performance characteristics, the time reliability correlation or TRC (Hall *et al.*, 1982), which states that the probability of not responding to an event decreases as a function of time. In other words, if more time has elapsed, then it is more likely that the person will respond – and respond correctly. (The TRC is thus of little comfort for situations where time is at a premium.) In terms of a functional model this corresponds to regaining control. The main complication is that for identical circumstances one person may lose control while another may maintain control. Or the same person may behave differently at different times! This requires a closer study of the personal and interpersonal (situation) parameters that determine the type of response.

The second important aspect of the model is how to account for the performance characteristics in a control mode. It is a basic assumption that the quality of performance depends on the degree of control a person has over the situation. Thus, a person who is in an opportunistic control mode behaves differently from a person who is in a tactical control mode, and the latter is expected to do better. The model must, however, provide a description of the specific characteristics of performance at a given level of control. This description not only should correspond to the general experience and potential specific empirical data, but should also serve as a blueprint for implementing the model in software. Part of that description must be an account of the interaction between competence and control. It is common sense that a higher level of competence makes it more likely that control is maintained – and, if lost, regained – but this should also be expressed in terms of the model's parameters.

4.5.1. COCOM parameters

The proposed contextual control model (COCOM) can be described in terms of some basic model parameters and model characteristics. This will follow the principles of the functional approach, hence it will not rely on the traditional assumptions about the nature of human information processing. Structural models have naturally depended on the parameters of the basic information processing elements, such as short-term memory span and decay rate, attention span, depth of knowledge, etc. In a functional model, such as COCOM, the parameters rather reflect the main characteristics of human performance and should ideally be as few and as simple as possible. The current version of COCOM requires only two parameters (number of goals and subjectively available time) and two "functions" (choice of next action and evaluation of outcome). Together these account for how actions are chosen and carried out, i.e. for control. The two other main components of the model, competence and constructs, need only be referred to on a general level, although some of the requirements as to their description can be derived from the characteristics of how the control component is assumed to function.

One type of parameter that can be found in many models and theories has to do with the subjective task demands in a situation. Through the years a number of different terms have been tried, such as workload, mental load, cognitive workload, information input overload, performance requirements, etc. Common to them is the notion that a person in a given situation may have more to do that can easily (or possibly) be accomplished, given the existing conditions and constraints. In COCOM the preferred term for this parameter is the *number of goals*.

There are several reasons for using this term. One reason is that it is possible to make a reasonably objective assessment of the number of goals or required activities under nominal conditions, for instance through a cognitive task analysis (Kirwan & Ainsworth, 1992; Hollnagel, 1993). Another is that it is in accordance with the functional approach to describe performance as being driven by goals or intentions, as well as by events. In COCOM, the goals may furthermore be seen as a special type of construct. Finally, the number of goals is a simple parameter whereas workload is a composite.

Subjective available time has already been mentioned in the discussion of Fig. 4.7. The subjectively available time can be seen as another facet of workload, since experienced workload clearly depends on how much time is available. Again, it is reasonable to assume a rather strong correlation between objectively available time and subjectively available time. The former can usually be reliably estimated, including upper and lower boundaries, hence it can serve as a good approximation to subjectively available time. There is also a considerable amount of research relating to how time may affect performance (e.g. Decortis & Cacciabue, 1988; De Keyser, 1994).

In order to make COCOM as simple as possible, the *choice of next action* follows a single principle in all control modes. The difference in the result, i.e. the quality or appropriateness of the chosen action, can be explained by how competence and constructs are used to different degrees, i.e. the depth of search or matching depends on the control mode. According to the general principle for choice of next action, the first step is to screen for apparent or superficial action characteristics that correspond to the goal. This is followed by checking that the primary or immediate effects of the action do match the current goals, that the preconditions for the action are fulfilled, that the necessary resources are available, and finally that the side effects are not inconsistent with the goal or goals of the following actions. At the same time the person may possibly consider other current goals, either with the purpose of selecting the one that is most relevant at the moment or in order to assess dependencies between goals and actions. This principle is proposed as a possible function – or micro-code – of the model that will enable a different outcome depending on the control mode.

The *evaluation of outcome* also takes place according to a single principle regardless of the control mode. The difference in the result, i.e. whether the evaluation leads to success or failure, is due to the degree of elaboration of the evaluation depending on the control mode. In line with the principle for choice of next action, the first step of outcome evaluation is to check whether the outcome appears to be a success or a failure, i.e. whether the goal for the action has been achieved. This is followed by distinguishing between whether the outcome actually corresponded to the expected feedback from a previous action or whether it must be classified as a new event. In the former case it is checked whether the outcome matches the goal(s) of the action, firstly looking at the immediate outcome of the action but possibly extending that to include protracted or delayed effects. The latter clearly requires that the person can either just wait for the required time or remember that this needs to be done while doing something else. Finally, the evaluation may also consider possible secondary effects and long-term consequences.

4.5.2. Functional relations in COCOM

The overall configuration of COCOM is shown in Fig. 4.8. The diagram is composed of "boxes and arrows" in order to show the functional relations between the various elements of the model, but this should not be construed as a structure of COCOM. The difference between the grey and the black arrows is that the former indicate a direct effect of one model parameter or function on another, while the latter indicate an indirect or potential effect. For example, the choice of next action leads to the next action, but also affects the way in which the evaluation of the outcome will be made by anticipating that certain events or changes will occur. That, however, only becomes effective when the next event occurs; if the next event is delayed or does not manifest itself, the potential change in the evaluation of the outcome will not be realized.

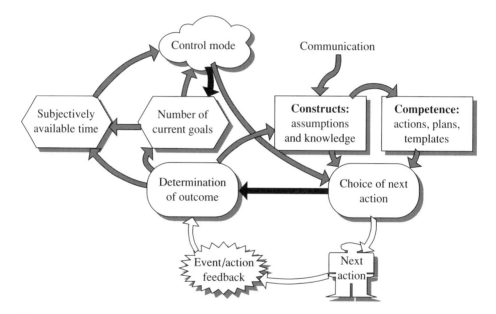

Figure 4.8. Functional relations in COCOM.

Fig. 4.8 contains an additional element, called the control mode. Unlike number of goals and available time, the control mode is a purely hypothetical model parameter that is unlikely to correspond to any simple or single measurable attribute of the situation. The control mode is used to determine how many goals can be considered at the same time, and also indirectly the subjectively available time. It also determines the extensity of the choice of next action and the determination of outcome. If, for instance, the control changes from tactical to opportunistic because the outcome of the previous action failed, then this means that fewer goals can be considered. A consequence of that may be that a goal is "lost" or "forgotten", which at a later stage may further deteriorate the situation. (This corresponds to impoverished situation understanding in the terms of Fig. 4.4.) In the opportunistic control mode the choice of next action will also be more shallow, as will the determination of the outcome. The control mode corresponds to the fact that people can have a feeling of being more or less in control of a situation, and that the loss of control characteristically is seen as a precursor of accidents (e.g. Casey, 1993). The control mode is perhaps best seen as an abstraction of the state of the model, and is of a different quality than the two other parameters. It may nevertheless be useful to treat it as a single parameter in an actual implementation of the model.

A summary of the characteristics of the four main control modes in terms of the two COCOM parameters and two functions is provided in Table 4.2. An outline of the relations has been given in the text, and further details can be found in Hollnagel (1997). When evaluating the model it is important to remember that it has not been proposed as a candidate explanation of how the human mind actually functions, but rather as a basis for developing practical tools and methods for, for example, joint system design, performance simulation, or performance analysis. It is strongly believed that a model specified according to these principles will be able to reproduce some of the fundamental characteristics of human performance, in particular the orderliness of human action and how this depends on the context.

Table 4.2. Main characteristics of the control modes

	Number of goals	Subjectively available time	Choice of next action	Evaluation of outcome
Strategic	Several	Abundant	Prediction based	Elaborate
Tactical (attended)	Several (limited)	Limited, but adequate	Plan based	Normal
Tactical (unattended)	Several (limited)	More than adequate	Plan based, but unreflective	Normal, but imprecise
Opportunistic	One, or two (competing)	Short or inadequate	Association based	Cursory
Scrambled	One	Very limited	Random	Rudimentary

4.5.3. How does context affect control?

One reason for proposing a contextual control model is to make it possible to account for how performance depends on the context, and specifically on how control depends on the context. Unfortunately this cannot be done in a simple manner, since there is no single input called "context" and no single function called "control". The context is rather a combination of the situation understanding or the constructs (e.g. Fig. 4.2) and the developments of the worksystem, i.e. the events that happen in the environment and affect the people who are working in it.

The situation understanding determines what goals are considered by the person as well as the criteria that are applied in the selection of actions and evaluation of results. Corresponding to the situation understanding certain developments and events will be expected, while others will not. The set of expected events is therefore an important indicator of the situation understanding. The match between actual and expected developments and events determines the level of control, and in that sense the two become coupled (see Fig. 4.4). The critical parameter in all of this is time. For any given physical process or control task there will be a limit on the amount of time that can be used to think before something has to be done, referred to as time allowed. In some cases, such as aviation, the limit is very low, in the order of seconds. In other cases the limit can be in the order of minutes, tens of minutes, or even hours. A set of values from different types of process is given in Table 4.3.

Table 4.3. Characteristics of various process types (Alty *et al.*, 1985)

Process type/domain	Number of information points (variables) in process	Main frequency of operator actions	Time allowed for operator action
Power distribution networks	~100–200,000	1/hour (usually clustered)	<1 minute
Power generating stations	10,000–20,000	1/hour (usually clustered) More during start-up	10–30 minutes
Process industries	2,000–10,000	5–6/hour (sometimes clustered)	<1 minute
Rolling mills	<100	1/second	Direct
Aeroplanes	100–300	1/minute (landing) 2–3/hour (cruising) 1/second (manual flight)	Direct

If situation understanding, and therefore also the match between expected and actual events, is good then little time will presumably be needed to evaluate process developments. The situation will not be challenging, control can easily be maintained, and there will correspondingly be time to do other things such as looking ahead, planning, etc. In this sense the context, as the union of situation understanding and developments in the worksystem, determines control. Conversely, if the match between expected and actual events is insufficient, then it will take longer to evaluate developments and changes and there will be less time to spare. Inadequate situation understanding leads to imprecise predictions, hence to a loss of control. The critical limit is reached when the evaluation takes as long as, or longer than, the time allowed. In this case the person lags behind the process, and control is likely to deteriorate. The relations described above can be illustrated as in Fig. 4.9.

Fig. 4.9 tries to illustrate how the time needed to evaluate events depends on the adequacy of situation understanding, and what may happen when this time becomes longer than the time allowed. In the case where the match between expected and actual events is good, there is time available for other things, and in general it can be assumed that this will sustain or improve the situation understanding. As the match gets worse, the point is reached where the time needed for the evaluation is as large as the time allowed. At that point the person can just manage to keep up with the process, but there is no spare capacity and the situation may therefore easily degrade. As this point is approached the person is likely to resort to various strategies to cope with the information input overload (Miller, 1960). If these are not successful a condition will eventually be reached where the time needed is greater than the time allowed, which means that the situation clearly has got out of hand.

Fig. 4.9 also shows how the various control modes relate to the amount of available time. In the scrambled control mode there is insufficient time and the person lags seriously behind the events. This will generally make the situation even worse unless serendipity

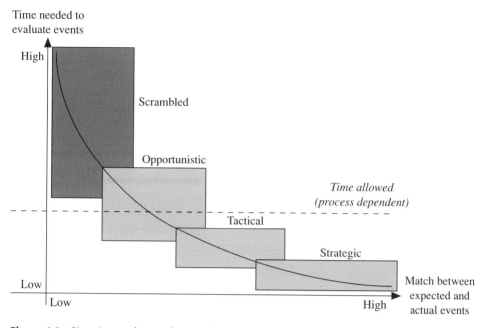

Figure 4.9. Situation understanding and control modes.

intervenes or the process state otherwise changes so that there is more time available to consider (which in Fig. 4.9 means that the horizontal broken line moves up). The opportunistic control mode characterizes the region around the point when there is just about enough time to keep track of events – possibly somewhat too little, possibly some slack. In this case the planning and selection of actions cannot afford to be very thorough, since that will take time that is not available. In the tactical and strategic control modes there is sufficient time to keep track of events. As more and more time becomes available, the person can afford to spend efforts to analyze the situation, to plan and to think ahead. (Note the difference between Fig. 4.9 and Fig. 4.7. Since Fig. 4.9 does not include the aspect of familiarity, it cannot be used to make a distinction between the tactical attended and tactical unattended control modes. This emphasizes that such diagrams show only one or a few salient characteristics of the context/control coupling, and that a more detailed description probably is beyond the range of simple graphical means.)

4.6. CONCLUSION

People are willy-nilly forced to use technology and work together with machines, and that creates a necessity for modelling the orderliness of human action. Cognitive systems engineering tries to account for how people interpret the states of the system and how they decide to act: in short, what constitutes the fundamentals of regulation or control in human performance. Cybernetics has taught us that a controller of a system must be a model of the system that is controlled (Conant & Ashby, 1970). The systems to be controlled are designed to be orderly and predictable, if not completely then at least to a significant degree. The system that controls must reflect that orderliness; in particular, it must be able to predict the future states of the target system. Otherwise the controlling system will not be able to make the right choices.

When it comes to humans, there are few good descriptions or models with which to work. Information processing models are limited because they really only have one state, i.e. they are "flat". The functions always work in exactly the same way, the only difference being the path taken through the various steps or stages. The models therefore cannot function in ways that are qualitatively different, because the execution of a function (e.g. decision, observation) is state independent. In contrast, COCOM introduces the notion of state dependent functions, i.e. the extensity of a function basically depends on the situation as it has developed through previous actions, represented as the control mode or state of the model. This makes the model more flexible than the standard information processing models.

The purpose of COCOM is to provide flexibility in modelling by proposing a few principles that can be used with different temporal and spatial resolutions. In other words, it is not necessary to have one sub-model for, for example, skilled performance and another for problem solving, or to have different "knowledge bases". Contextual control modelling makes the assumption that the underlying competence is the same and that performance differences come about because the competence is used to a different degree, depending on the current situation. Performance is determined by the events that occur, by how they are interpreted, and by the general level of control. This is a simple and powerful but very general approach that helps to make the model simpler.

The notion of the control modes carries with it a strong normative aspect. It is clear from the definitions that the scrambled and opportunistic control modes generally are less desirable states than the tactical and strategic control modes. It also seems reasonable to assume that the tactical attended mode will be better than the others in terms of, for example, performance accuracy or reliability. So far these are hypotheses, but it is not difficult to subject them to an empirical test. This requires two things: a method for determining the control mode during performance (or rather from a performance protocol), and a measure for performance quality. In the case of performance quality numerous measures and indicators have been used, and for any given investigation there are few problems in devising an appropriate measure. In the case of identifying the control mode the situation is in many ways the same as in the search for diagnostic strategies, workload, stress, etc. It is usually possible to devise a set of data, a set of criteria, and a method by means of which the identification can be made, although inevitably a considerable residual of interpretation is involved. Work to achieve this is under way in several places.

The design of a joint cognitive system should strive to sustain an appropriate level of control, given the performance conditions. Given the assumptions underlying Fig. 4.7 this should, for normal situations, be the middle region consisting of a mixture of the tactical attended and the strategic control modes. If for some reason the situation developed in unexpected ways, then a shift towards a strategic control mode should be the aim. According to the principles of Fig. 4.7 this would require the time pressure to be reduced, hence favouring design features that had that effect. Similarly, Fig. 4.7 suggests that the design of the interaction should be such that the operator was prevented from drifting into the tactical unattended region. This approach differs from the notion of forcing the operator to work on a specific, model-defined level of behaviour (e.g. Vicente & Rasmussen, 1992), and underlines the importance of providing the right context. This can be achieved if the significant goals of the system are easy to see, and if the operators are supported by adequate supported facilities for, for example, resolving them into sub-goals, evaluating the consequences, planning on a long range, etc. The technological details of the solutions are in many cases readily available. The difference will be that the solutions are used in the proper spirit of cognitive systems engineering, to amplify rather than to substitute for human tasks and functions.

4.7. REFERENCES

ALTY, J.L., ELZER, P., HOLST, O., JOHANNSEN, S. & SAVORY, S. (1985). *Literature and User Survey of Issues Related to Man–Machine Interfaces for Supervision and Control Systems.* Kassel, Germany: Gesamthochschule Kassel, Fachbereich maschinenbau.

AMALBERTI, R. & DEBLON, F. (1992). Cognitive modeling of fighter aircraft process control: a step towards an intelligent onboard assistance system. *International Journal of Man–Machine Studies*, vol. 36, 639–671.

ARBIB, M.A. (1964). *Brains, Machines and Mathematics.* New York: McGraw-Hill.

ASHBY, W.R. (1956). *An Introduction to Cybernetics.* London: Methuen.

CASEY, S. (1993). *Set Phasers on Stun.* Santa Barbara, CA: Aegean Publishing Company.

CONANT, R.C. & ASHBY, W.R. (1970). Every good regulator of a system must be a model of that system. *International Journal of Systems Science*, vol. 1(2), 89–97.

DE KEYSER, V. (1994). Time in ergonomic research. Recent developments and perspectives. Keynote address: *12th Congress of the International Ergonomics Association*, Toronto, Canada, 15–19 August.

DECORTIS, F. & CACCIABUE, P.C. (1988). Temporal dimensions in cognitive models. *4th IEEE Conference on Human Factors and Power Plants*, Monterey, CA, 5–9 June.

GREGORY, R.L. (Ed.) (1987). *The Oxford Companion to the Mind.* Oxford: Oxford University Press.

HALL, R.E., FRAGOLA, J. & WREATHALL, J. (1982). *Post Event Human Decision Errors: Operator Action Tree/Time Reliability Correlation* (NUREG/CR-3010). Washington, DC: U.S. Nuclear Regulatory Commission.

HOLLNAGEL, E. (1983). What we do not know about man–machine systems. *International Journal of Man–Machine Studies*, vol. 18, 135–143.

HOLLNAGEL, E. (1988). Information and reasoning in intelligent decision support systems. In E. HOLLNAGEL, G. MANCINI & D.D. WOODS (Eds), *Cognitive Engineering in Complex Dynamic Worlds.* London: Academic Press.

HOLLNAGEL, E. (1993). *Human Reliability Analysis: Context and Control.* London: Academic Press.

HOLLNAGEL, E. (1997). Modelling the orderliness of human action. In R. AMALBERTI & N. SARTER (Eds), *Cognitive Engineering in the Aviation Domain.* Hillsdale, NJ: Erlbaum.

HOLLNAGEL, E. & WOODS, D.D. (1983). Cognitive systems engineering: new wine in new bottles. *International Journal of Man–Machine Studies*, vol. 18, 583–600.

HOLLNAGEL, E. & CACCIABUE, P.C. (1991). Cognitive modelling in system simulation. *Proceedings of Third European Conference on Cognitive Science Approaches to Process Control*, Cardiff, 2–6 September.

HOLLNAGEL, E., DRØIVOLDSMO, A. & KIRWAN, B. (1996). Practical insights from studies of operator diagnosis. *Proceedings of 8th European Conference on Cognitive Ergonomics* (ECCE-8), Granada, Spain, 9–13 September.

HUTCHINS, E. (1995). *Cognition in the Wild.* Cambridge, MA: MIT Press.

JONES, L., BOREHAM, N. & MOULTON, C. (1995). Social aspects of decision-making in a hospital emergency department: implications for introducing a computer information tool. In L. NORROS (Ed.), *5th European Conference on Cognitive Science Approaches to Process Control* (VTT Symposium 158). Espoo, Finland: Technical Research Centre of Finland.

KIRWAN, B. & AINSWORTH, L.A. (Eds) (1992). *A Guide to Task Analysis.* London: Taylor & Francis.

MACKAY, D.M. (1968). Towards an information-flow model of human behaviour. In W. BUCKLEY (Ed.), *Modern Systems Research for the Behavioral Scientist.* Chicago, IL: Aldine Publishing Company.

MILLER, J.G. (1960). Information input overload and psychopathology. *American Journal of Psychiatry*, vol. 116, 695–704.

MILLER, G.A., GALANTER, E. & PRIBRAM, K.H. (1960). *Plans and the Structure of Behavior.* New York: Holt, Rinehart & Winston.

MILLER, T.E. & WOODS, D.D. (1996). Key issues for naturalistic decision making researchers in systems design. In C. ZAMBOK & G. KLEIN (Eds), *Naturalistic Decision Making.* Hillsdale, NJ: Lawrence Erlbaum Associates.

NEISSER, U. (1976). *Cognition and Reality.* San Francisco, CA: W.H. Freeman.

PERROW, C. (1984). *Normal Accidents: Living with High-risk Technologies.* New York: Basic Books.

RASMUSSEN, J. (1986). *Information Processing and Human–Machine Interaction: An Approach to Cognitive Engineering.* New York: North-Holland.

REASON, J.T. (1990). *Human Error.* Cambridge: Cambridge University Press.

REASON, J.T. & MYCIELSKA, K. (1982). *Absent-minded? The Psychology of Mental Lapses and Everyday Errors.* Englewood Cliffs, NJ: Prentice-Hall.

SARTER, N. & WOODS, D.D. (1995). "How in the world did we ever get into that mode?" Mode awareness and supervisory control. *Human Factors*, vol. 37, 5–19.

VICENTE, K.J. & RASMUSSEN, J. (1992). Ecological interface design: theoretical foundations. *IEEE Transactions on Systems, Man, and Cybernetics*, SMC-22, 589–596.

WIENER, E.L. (1989). *Human Factors of Advanced Technology ("Glass Cockpit") Transport Aircraft* (BASA CR-177528). Moffet Field, CA: NASA Ames Research Centre.

ZAMBOK, C. & KLEIN, G. (Eds) (1996). *Naturalistic Decision Making.* Hillsdale, NJ: Lawrence Erlbaum Associates.

PART TWO

Field Studies

CHAPTER FIVE

Team decision-making and situation awareness in military command and control

HENRIK ARTMAN

5.1. INTRODUCTION

This chapter describes the co-operative work within two teams of a command and control unit, i.e. a military staff unit at battalion level which has the task of ensuring that its company units can control the enemy forces. Its work is to plan and transmit orders to its subordinates and artillery units, and also to have an overall picture of the situation at the front in order to be able to direct and co-ordinate action between troops and companies, as well as forecasting what the enemy will do next and how best to utilize its own forces both at the present moment and in the near future.

Enemy forces are complex dynamic, autonomous systems in the same sense as forest fires, air traffic, etc., which have been defined by Brehmer & Svenmarck (1994) as systems which change both autonomously and as a consequence of actions by the controlling unit. Control of the system has to occur in real-time and it is difficult, or impossible, to conceive a complete current state of the system because the dynamics of, and the relations within, the system are not clearly visible. Furthermore, the organization is characterized as being geographically distributed, which means that no single person has a complete view of the system to be controlled. The staff must have knowledge about how their own units change as a consequence of both enemy action and their own decisions, and also about how the enemy forces change as a consequence of both their own decision-makers' decisions and the action taken by them. The team thus has to have a model of the whole battle front which includes both its own forces and the enemy forces.

Brehmer & Svenmarck (1994) have investigated how geographically distributed decision-makers, together considered as a team, manage to control a dynamic system. They compared a hierarchical architecture and a so-called fully connected architecture where all can communicate with all, and found that the hierarchical condition managed to control the system better, but only marginally. However, in Brehmer's experiments (Brehmer & Allard, 1991; Brehmer, 1992) the formal leader works on two time-scales at the same time: he or she operates on the system and also tries to get an overall picture of the other operators in the system and orders them to go to specific places. In order to avoid having such a double work load the military, like other management systems, delegates a team to work on the second time-scale and work strategically with a larger time horizon than the actors at lower levels.

We can easily see that the task of command and control is too great for one individual to grasp cognitively. After all a battalion is divided into five to seven companies, with several subunits such as platoons and troops who are able to communicate with the staff; also the enemy forces might be as big or bigger. In order to handle this complex system the task has to be distributed even at battalion staff level; as Conant and Ashby (1970) so aptly put it, "Every good regulator of a system must be a model of that system". The military has therefore divided the task into at least two tasks for the real-time control, one person being responsible for handling the companies and their information processes and another person being assigned to control enemies. The former mainly co-ordinates actions that have to be performed in conjunction with several units and keeps track of where the forces are, while the latter mainly tries to control the enemy by using the artillery forces which the battalion and the brigade have at hand.

5.2. TEAM DECISION-MAKING

In the recent research field of team decision-making, several researchers (Klein & Thordsen, 1989; Orasanu & Salas, 1993; Duffy, 1993; Human Factors, 1995) argue that research in teams differs from general group research in that the members explicitly have different roles and tasks, and thus attend to different items of information in the decision process, while members of groups in group decision-making often are fully involved in the decision process (see also Brehmer (1994) for a critical discussion). In group decision research the emphasis is on how a group reaches consensus. This is not as important in team decision-making, as all the members of the team have well-defined roles and tasks and the goal is more one of merging the information under a common goal than of making a decision that all accept. In the team one member may concentrate on gathering information and another on analysing the information, but these may not have to communicate about the actual decision since this is another person's responsibility. The different configuration of the collection of people in the team decision-making process might not be as sensitive to many of the well-known findings of group decision-making such as risky shifts, group pressure, group-think, etc. (see McGrath (1984) for review) as all team members are not equally involved in the decision process and do not attend to the same information. Nor is team decision-making a typical group problem-solving situation as the product does not rely on the most able member but on the co-ordinated work of the team with individual tasks (Brehmer, 1994; McGrath, 1984). Yet the members of the team depend on the timeliness and quality of work of each member in order to fulfil the goal and task of the team, and the team's decision may have the same consequences as a group decision. To consider each member's work as an individual island would definitely corrupt the image of the team decision process: as Hutchins (1990, p. 211) puts it, "if the distribution of labor was fixed, the system would surely fail whenever one of its components failed". The team decision process does not depend only on task allocation but also on several tacitly and socially organized practices which Heath & Luff (1992) have elegantly shown in the London Underground Line Control Room, where individual tasks are carefully co-ordinated with those of others and where the members of the team monitor each other's work in order to fulfil the team task in a concerted manner.

Research on team decision-making is in its infancy and has not yet yielded any immediate results allowing greater generalization (see Brehmer (1994) for a recent review). Even so, two similar frameworks for understanding team decision making have been developed by Klein & Thordsen (1989) and Duffy (1993). Klein & Thordsen propose a perspective called the team mind which asserts that the team process can be treated analogously to the mind of the person in a general way. They distinguish between three levels: the behavioural, the collective conscious and the subconscious levels. The behavioural level is what members of the team do in the form of action (excluding talk). The conscious level is what is said out loud for all to hear. Finally, the subconscious level is what is held by one person and not shared with others. Duffy is more specific and proposes an information-processing perspective in order to understand biases and errors. Both are examples of treating the team as a unit for analysis, where the explicit information-processing is highlighted more than the tacit practices of the team members. Hutchins (1995) has captured the question for team decision-making in the following quote: "If groups can have cognitive properties that are significantly different from those of the individuals in them, then differences in the cognitive accomplishments of any two groups might depend entirely on the differences in the social organization of distributed cognition and not at all on differences in the cognitive properties of individuals in the two groups." (p. 177). Furthermore Hutchins argues that "The arrangement of equipment in a workplace might seem to be a topic for traditional, noncognitive ergonomics. However, it has an interpretation in terms of the construction of systems of socially distributed cognition. The interaction of the properties of the senses with the physical layout of the task environment defines possibilities for the distribution of access to information." (ibid, p. 197). We will here look at two configurations that emerged in two military commander teams. The configurations emerged spontaneously, without our intervention, during training in a simulator, and are originated from a very small change in the technology. This minor alteration may have major consequences.

5.3. RESEARCH QUESTIONS

First and foremost this case study is supposed to be hypothesis-generating. We wanted to start from a work situation where actual practitioners used their ordinary methods in order to be able to work out hypotheses which we can test in an experimental situation. The research questions concern team decision-making and particularly how practitioners organize their work given the kind of artifacts they have at hand. What interaction patterns do different uses of the technology imply? How is co-ordination within the team accomplished? What agency do the mediating tools have that the team uses in order to process information? What difference do different interaction patterns imply for the shared mental model within the team?

5.4. METHOD

The present study has used video–audio recordings and computer logging as the main data collection resource. We video-recorded a full battalion staff training session. A full battalion staff consists of two teams working in shifts. The training was divided in two parts, the first lasting from 0830 to 1930 hours and the second from 0800 to 1100 hours: 14 hours in all. One of the teams used about two-thirds of the time. We could not operate in the control room because of a lack of space and the possible disturbance factor. Instead we observed the sessions from a monitor connected to the video, and could ask other officers what the teams were doing.

We have transcribed 4 hours of sampled chunks of the video recording. There are 71 messages which concern all members of the team. We used this as the first sampling criterion. We randomly sampled 8, and transcribed half an hour backwards from that point. By this procedure we covered 28 of the 71 (39.4%) messages as well as other forms of situations. These 28 messages were divided 20 and 8 between the teams, and reflect the proportion of time the teams used in the session.

The transcriptions include what is said, who is talking to whom (or to "the room"), actions such as gestures, and other comments about certain things such as how to use the different representations, etc. The analysis started by looking at how the teams differed in respect to co-operative work. It was evident that the two teams chose to work in different ways. The teams used the technology differently and one team seemed much more stressed than the other. We traced the information-processing and analyzed how the mediating tools and interactions made the work co-ordinated. The different work patterns that emerged for this analysis elicited several questions and we furthermore analyzed some breakdowns in the teams' work to show how the technology might enforce different situation awareness states within the teams.

5.5. THE CONTROL ROOM

The room where the staff is housed is a small tracked vehicle, identical to the kind used in an actual combat situation. It is about 6 metres by 2.5 metres in area, with a big table in the centre where the staff keep all their artifacts. The staff consist of four people, two signallers and two officers. The signallers sit at each end and the officers in the centre (see Fig. 5.1).

Figure 5.1. The control room setting. The signaller (S1) at the rear, the co-ordinator (C) in the middle and the artillery leader (A) up front. The other signaller (S2) sits just under the camera.

5.5.1. Staff and responsibilities

The signallers (S1 and S2) each have a small computer for which they are responsible. They write and receive messages from other geographically distributed units. They also have a small printer on which they print out the messages, and they distribute these to the officers within the team.

Each officer has specific tasks connected to his rank and formal competence. We call them here the co-ordinator (C) and the artillery leader (A) respectively. The co-ordinator is responsible for the co-ordination and communication with the distributed forces, as well as for the accurate updating of the map. His main task is to gather, analyze, update the map and distribute relevant information (orientation, orders, etc.) to appropriate units. The artillery leader's task is to decide how the artillery resources are to be used and by whom. This means that he has to analyze, prioritize, order and inform the units about when and how much artillery they might use, as well as to order the artillery units where and when to fire. To make decisions he uses the information the co-ordinator has gathered and organized. Together the officers are responsible for the planning and for predicting how the dynamic system could change.

5.5.2. Artifacts

As can be seen in Fig. 5.1, there is map in front of C and A as well as a voice-radio system. The map is the main mediating tool combined with verbal communication for C and A. The map looks like an ordinary map with a co-ordinate grid and general signs (there might be special details for military purposes) of the area for which the battalion is responsible. As noted above, C is responsible for updating the map with symbols relating the movement of his/her own forces and the enemy forces; for this he/she uses different standard colours and symbols. This map has two general purposes. First, it is used as an overview of the battalion and the enemy forces about which they have information. It is from this information that they decide about movements of the forces and the use of artillery. Second, it is used as a tool for discussing and hypothesizing about what the enemy is up to and what can be done with their forces to hinder the enemy. In this sense it can metaphorically be seen as a chessboard, although they do not have complete information about the enemy, so they can only make inferences based on what they know from the chart.

The team receive all new information by a voice-radio or by e-mail, and occasionally via other members of the battalion. The voice-radio console includes two radiophones to contact distributed units. One phone has loudspeakers so everyone in the room can hear what the persons at the other end are saying. This is of course very important, as it provides the members of the team with a common ground on which to discuss and decide about further actions. This loud-speaker system is mainly used by C to seek and receive information from the distributed units. The other phone is a "private phone", which means that the other team members do not hear what the other person is saying. This phone is connected to a tracked vehicle where the battalion major is situated. To keep track of what is said on the phone they also have a logbook where all spoken messages by radio are to be entered.

In the Swedish army the commanders and control units have recently been equipped with a new, complementary, tool for communicating with distributed units. It is called DART. In simple terms it can be described as a notebook computer designed for handling electronic mail. Each commander and control unit have two such systems, one for each signaller. Each DART has a printer and also has a memory in which messages can be stored. The DART can be programmed with certain formats to standardize message writing and make it easy. If a programmed formula is not wanted messages can be sent in "clear", which is comparable with an ordinary e-mail.

The printed messages are then given to the officers, who take care of them and put them on pins for incoming or outgoing messages, thus providing a chronological logbook of the messages they have received and sent. Thus can be regarded as a collective memory of what has been done. This is useful if C has not updated the map properly or if they have to check specific messages again.

5.5.3. Procedures that must be accomplished

The battalion's overall goal is to delay and prevent the enemy from invading the territory. In order to do this the team has to co-ordinate its forces and the brigade artillery. As noted above, the team members have quite distinct work assignments, though the outcome is dependent on the team's collective achievement. We will try here to describe schematically what the team has to do.

The command and control unit receives a message from the subordinates, either by the radio or the e-mail system. If the message is received by e-mail it is confirmed by one of the signallers, who then prints it out and gives it to C. If the message is received via radio the co-ordinator takes care of it. In both cases C evaluates the message and transforms the information onto the map. When the information is on the map it constitutes, together with other information, a second time-scale with respect to where the information was gathered.

If the message is of importance for the artillery (for example if a company or troop calls for artillery fire), C gives A the message; otherwise he sticks it on the incoming pin.

When A has received the message, he reads it and evaluates what if anything the artillery can do. Often there are several messages calling for artillery fire and then A has to prioritize. When he has decided on artillery fire he must send a message to the artillery (subordinate, ordinate, or both). He tells one of the signallers to prepare for such a message and then dictates it to the signaller, who transmits it to the originator of the request.

Every now and then A and C have to confer about what the enemy is doing and how they can plan in order to be one step ahead and delay or stop them.

As we will see, *how* these procedures are carried out in the teams correlates with how the DARTs are connected, i.e. the technology architectures. Before we can discuss the direct work we must, therefore, have some idea of how the technology can be configured.

5.6. TECHNOLOGY ARCHITECTURES

The two DARTs can be connected to other units in at least two different configurations. One of the architectures lets one of the DARTs be connected to subordinates (companies) and the other to ordinates (brigade) (see Fig. 5.2). The other architecture lets both DARTs be connected to the subordinates and only one to the ordinates (see Fig. 5.3). It is possible at any time to shift between the two architectures. In both cases it is possible to send messages between the machines via the so-called local link. The rationale for having these two structures is that if the S1-DART breaks down all messages can be still be received by the team.

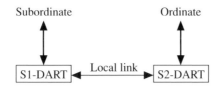

Figure 5.2. The technology architecture when one computer is connected to each of the lower units.

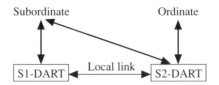

Figure 5.3. The technology architecture when both computers are connected to the lower units.

5.7. INTERACTION PATTERNS

As we have seen, the technology can be configured in two different architectures, which give rise to different demands on the team and different information flows. We call these two interaction structures serial and parallel respectively, depending on how the information is processed. Under normal circumstances (e.g. when both DARTs work), the teams are taught, they should work by using the serial technology architecture. Despite this the teams chose to organize their work differently: one team worked with the sequential architecture while the second worked with the parallel one.

We follow the information flow within the team and highlight the stages when the information is transformed into different representation states. Bear in mind that we are concerned here only when the information is received via the e-mail system, and not via the phone, as this is the more frequently recurring situation.

5.7.1. Serial work organization: team 1

This team is less stressed than the other team. They work calmly and methodically through all incoming information. The culture of this group seems to be quite socially oriented, i.e. they talk quite a lot with each other and try to resolve most problems collaboratively. If we follow any average message, the serial organization would work like the following:

S1 one monitors his DART to see when an incoming message is received. When the DART tells him that a new message is received he prints this message on a small printer (Fig. 5.4; stage 2). When the message is transformed into a paperstrip it is more easily handled within the team, and can constitute a buffer of information as S1 lays it in front of C, who then can deal with it as soon as he has time (Fig. 5.4; stage 3). S1 is repeatedly told also to tell C when the message seems to be an urgent one, and he also sends an acknowledgement to the originator of the message.

C then picks up the strip of paper and evaluates it. Often this is done aloud, as if he is talking to himself. Sometimes A is then able to hear what the message is about and then promptly helps him out and prepares his own task with respect to this message. C transforms the message to symbols and colours on the map. When the information is

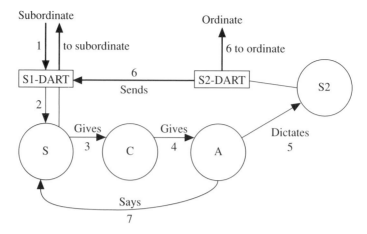

Figure 5.4. The serial interaction pattern when the normal technology structure is used. The numbers denote the stages of the information processes.

on the map it is potentially accessible to all members and constitutes a second time-scale, in respect of where it originated, and from this time-scale the team members can read out possible ways of reacting to the situation.

After C has noted the information on the paperstrip he lays it down or gives it to A, who evaluates the message in accordance with what he can read from the positions and symbols on the map (Fig. 5.4; stage 4). This evaluation is often done quietly. If there are several messages he also has to prioritize the order in which they should be handled. C and A could start to interpret the message together, interrupting the fluent information flow (see Section 5.8). Whatever the content of the message he has to send an acknow-ledgement to the originator, and so he dictates a message for S2, who converts it into electronic form (Fig. 5.4; stage 5). When this is done S2 sends the message via the local link to S1 and to the ordinates (Fig. 5.4; stage 6). In order for S1 to know what to do with it (and not just print it out automatically), A tells him to resend (or let it through) to the subordinate originator, as S2 does not have access to the subordinates (Fig. 5.4; stage 7). Then the decision sequence for this particular message is covered, and several sequences have started.

In this serial processing procedure, A becomes quite central as he relies on information from C and S1 on his left, and must also tell S1 to resend the message going back to the originator. "A" thus has to monitor incoming and outgoing messages. The information is redundant at several levels but cannot be dealt with in parallel as the organization is sequentially organized. As this procedure is serially organized it would not happen, except by mistake, that A would get information before C and that he then would make a decision on information (e.g. the map) that is not properly updated. C will always update the map before A gets this particular information. In that way this organization is error-free but the information-processing also takes time, and time is of the essence in controlling dynamic systems.

5.7.2. Parallel work organization: team 2

The other team is working calmly, but this team is working hastily and under pressure. They try to process the information as quickly as they can and use the technology as efficiently as possible. One of the bottlenecks in the serial processing team is how they use the technology. When A has made a decision they write a new message and send this to the orginator. This team instead re-use the information in the electronic message they received, and so save some minutes per decision made. They also switch between the two technology architectures described above. Their information-processing procedure started as it did in the other team, but when A had made a decision he told S1 to send the message received via the local link to S2. A and S2 could then elaborate the message on their side of the room. When they are ready A switches over to the parallel technology architecture, which enables them to send the message directly to the originator, without sending it via S1. Thus the team make use of the fact that electronically held information can be modified at any stage. The procedure is depicted in Fig. 5.5.

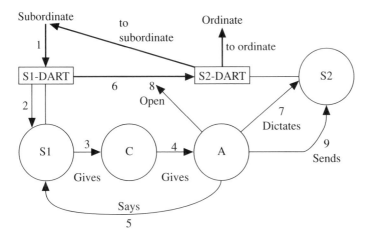

Figure 5.5. The interaction pattern when alternating between the two technology architectures. The numbers denote the stages of information-processing.

In order for this cycle to continue, the team has to switch between the two technology architectures every time a message is sent. In fact, on almost every occasion they forgot to change over the technology architecture to serial. This initiated a new form of inter-action structure, which the team adopted after a while. We therefore abandon the above structure and move to the one that the team adopted.

When the technology architecture which connects both computers to the subordinates is used, transmission via the local link is indispensable, as all information received from lower hierarchy is directly duplicated within the team. The team chose to organize their work as depicted in Fig. 5.6. As there are fewer information-processing stages for each message, and as they can re-use the information contained in the received message, and as a consequence they do not have to manually co-ordinate as much, this organization processes information more quickly than the other team. In this interaction structure S1 and S2 mirror each other to a great extent; both print out messages and give them to C and A respectively (Fig. 5.6; stage 3). C transforms the information onto the map, but instead of forwarding the message to A, as in the serial team, he sticks it on a pin. A, who receives all incoming messages from S2, then consults the map and sometimes C, and evaluates and prioritizes between the messages. Then A tells S2 what to change in the incoming message and let him send it to the originator. Thus using this technology architecture A does not have to receive any paper strip from C. The interaction between A and C's information requirements is mainly managed via the map they have in front of them.

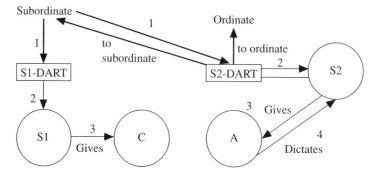

Figure 5.6. Shows the parallel interaction pattern when using the parallel technology architecture. The numbers denote the stages of information processing.

5.8. MANAGING BREAKDOWNS

These two forms of work organization, we believe, have implications concerning how the teams co-ordinate and manage breakdowns in their work. The task is naturally time-constrained and there is a trade-off between making decisions based on information which is as complete as possible and making a quick decision. And we have seen how the two teams cope with this in different ways. Team 1 is more debatively oriented while team 2 is more task-operatively oriented. The team members in team 1 furthermore talk more with each other, while those in team 2 steadily work with individually assigned tasks and they also chose the technology that supports such organization. Consider the following examples of breakdowns in the routine work (Tables 5.1 and 5.2). Both examples occur at the beginning of the training, and both are breakdowns arising after a period of low workload and when a new message asking for artillery fire arrives.

Table 5.1. Team 1

Who	Message	Other
C	Is that so, they are up here at 77, 88 [co-ordinates] and up here we have an enemy, that was at 2412. What is the time, 10? Could we say that to do it simply? We are starting to get a grip (pause)	Writes in new data on the map.
C	Will they try to get down there?	Point on the map.
A	Yes, they are moving. Now there is a platoon here. He [the enemy] will probably try to use the swamp and go around the hill on this side, maybe even like this. The enemy uses this way and . . . to find its way down here (a call on the radio closes the conversation)	

C and A are discussing equally about the future state of the system. Both ask questions and give answers. They make a hypothesis about what might happen and what the enemies will do next. They try collectively to assess the situation. Below we see the only breakdown in team 2 which includes a hypothesis. Instead of being debative, the dialogue between A and C is concerned with getting enough consensus or information in order to be able to do the job.

Table 5.2. Team 2

Who	Message	Other
	[C gives a message to A]	
A	No, what the hell should I say? WHAT THE HELL SHALL I SAY? It must be these (pointing at the map) who have moved or	
C	Hmm, yeah, it must be yes, they are dividing now yeah and trying it way up here	
A	What does that mean? It means like, like it looks like	
C	I think the enemy's simply trying a way where he does not meet resistance, huh	
A	And as here it is quite a big front here	
C	Yeah he has sent (inaudible) He goes here with different battalions and companies and tries to move forward and seek resistance. He should meet one hell of a lot of resistance because here is actually a battalion (hmm). So he will probably not get through here (hmm). There is a battalion [the same] and here there was a brigade or battalion or	
C	This 49 I think I can delete like (another person enters and closes the conversation)	

Team 2 also makes a hypothesis but this is taken as a statement of the system, and after a certain statement there is no arguing about its possible significance. Instead the thread is developed in a form of consensus. This is the only observed hypothesis about the future state of the system that this team makes. The observations and symbols on the map are most often taken for granted in order to be able to make the decision and perform the subtask as quickly as possible. Co-operation is oriented towards the concrete task, not the hypothesis of a future move by the enemy.

In team 1, which uses the serial work organization, the map is always updated before the decision about artillery is made. In the team 2 parallel organization it seems that A could easily receive and decide about a certain message before the map is updated, and thus make a decision on older information. Still they work as if C has got the latest information. In the above transcript from team 2 we can see that A does not know exactly what to do. A does not have, mentally, the information from which he could start to make a hypothesis. Nor does he contribute to the discussion by asking critical questions. The distribution of work is clearly assigned; C works with the map and A makes decisions about the artillery fire. In team 1 the work distribution is more blurred and both share the responsibility of the team task.

This sharp task distribution is even clearer in the next episode (Table 5.3), where A in team 2 recognizes a time error in the message. A does not then ask C, or consult the map to see, whether and at what time there have been reports about the enemy in the location where the company wants to shoot. Instead he calls the company over the radio to clarify this. He thus neglects the local resources, or does not see them as resources at all. After he has got the information he turns directly to S2 and completes the decision.

Taking these cases as illustrating different forms of co-operation after a prolonged period of using either of the technology architectures we can make the hypothesis that the interaction structures have different consequences for the outcome and process. First we might hypothesize that the serial work organization accepts that the participants possess more of the same information and as a consequence can co-operate in a more

Table 5.3. Team 2 (continued)

	Who	Message	Other
	A>S2	Did it just arrive?	
	S2>A	Yes	
	A>S2	Get it out, re-address it as before except NA, NB, then ZG	
	S2>A	OK	
Radio	A	RN, RN	
Radio	RN	RN COME	
	A	Have I got it right? That you want fire on the target 0932 hours – Shouldn't it be 0832? COME	
Radio	RN	That's right it is. . . . OVER COME	
Radio	A	Say again COME	
Radio	A	Confirmation from VN. We fire as soon as possible. OVER COME	
Radio	Rn	(??)	
	A>S2	ZG, VN, RN, ERO, ZG (yes) erase and put in 0835 2 rounds. end transmission.	

debative fashion. This is in contrast to the parallel work organization, where the team members are oriented more towards having each job done, and where they work less collaboratively. Secondly, we advance the hypothesis that the members of team 1 will develop more similar mental models or situation awareness than the team 2 members because they have co-operated in assessing the situation. In fact, in a case too long to be described here, the team 2 members almost destroyed one of their own units owing to a mismatch between different pieces of information and knowledge (thus mental models).

On the basis of this field study it is not possible to say that these hypotheses concerning the performances of the teams enable us to conclude that a shared situation awareness is preferable to having different perspectives in controlling a dynamic system.

5.9. CONCLUSIONS

When new technological systems are introduced into an existing environment, the full work system changes on several levels and structures. Requirements concerning work change, as do also the requirements and limits of prescriptive task allocation in particular practice, and the social organization of work has to fill the mismatch between new and old requirements which new technology has shaped in the organization. New technology also makes it possible to find ways of using the technology that differ from those originally intended by the designers. In this study we have shown that the work organization has to change as a consequence of a different use of the technology. The effect of the technology in this specific case is related to two conflicting goals: the speed of information flow and the situational awareness of the team and individuals.

As the electronic mail system makes the information flow more quickly between units, the difference between the time-scales gets smaller; the information-processing speed of the team becomes the bottleneck. But as a consequence of quicker processing, the team might develop individual mental models of the system instead of a shared one. There is so far no evidence to suggest one is better than the other. Rather it might be suggested that both are better in specific situations. Thus the serial work organization may be better when the information load is low, while the quicker parallel organization would be better under high information load and quicker decision requirements. But that would require the team to identify high/low information flow as well as change between the two organizations (as was the case at the start with team 2). This might not be the best idea, as changing the organization from time to time makes the routines and procedures less stable and makes the team less secure on how to process the information.

We cannot describe and show from this study which work organization best serves the objective, which is to delay the enemy in this case or generally to control a dynamic system.

Situational awareness seems to be a problem involving the interaction between, and the individual conceptions of, the officers. We can see from the required decision process that the artillery leader becomes less central in the local interaction in the parallel structure, which may suggest that the two officers will also build up different images of the system to be controlled as they do not attend to the same information and as neither of them knows what information the other is attending to for the moment. Of course, two individuals never have exactly the same conceptions or situational awareness, but if the two officers do not interact verbally at all they may build up very different situational awarenesses of the system and then have a problem when negotiating about the interpreted development of the system. Thus even if the individual images of the dynamic system do not have to be identical, they might have to be in phase with each other and be complementary, and not so different that negotiating and communicating each interpretation of the development of the situation and what to do next becomes a problem. This is a problem we will call "team-think". Questions that concern distributed cognition and situational awareness will be explicitly investigated in an experimental session in a micro world (called D^3FIRE by Brehmer & Svenmarck, 1994) which we have further developed with the different technology structures we have discussed in this chapter. From that study we will also be able to investigate whether the different technology structures have any consequences for the goal of controlling the dynamic system.

Introducing new technology is as much a social change as a technological one (Hutchins, 1990), and must also be related to the goal of the work. The goal can in turn give rise to sub-goals which may conflict. Then the trade-offs often rely on a situated social organization in order to repair the mismatch between different structures, goals and requirements. The role of the social organization is seldom recognized either at the management or at the practice level, but the consequences of ignoring it can be serious.

5.10. ACKNOWLEDGEMENTS

This study has been supported financially by the Swedish Work Environment Fund and The Swedish National Defence Establishment. I am grateful to Professor Yvonne Wærn for support in planning the study and help with analyzing the data and discussion. I would like to thank all the personnel of the military battalions that took part in the study.

5.11. REFERENCES

BREHMER, B. (1992). Dynamic decision making: human control of complex systems. *Acta Psychologica*, vol. 81, 211–241.

BREHMER, B. (1994). *Distributed decision making in dynamic environments*. Uppsala University, Sweden, Foa Report.

BREHMER, B. & ALLARD, R. (1991). Dynamic decision making: the effects of task complexity and feedback delay. In J. RASMUSSEN, B. BREHMER & J. LEPLAT (Eds), *Distributed Decision Making. Cognitive Models for Co-operative Work*. Chichester: John Wiley & Sons.

CONANT, R. & ASHBY, W. (1970). Every good regulator of a system must be a model of that system. *Int. J. Systems Sci.*, vol. 1, No. 2, 89–97.

DUFFY, L. (1993). Team decision-making biases: an information processing perspective. In G. KLEIN, J. ORASANU, R. CALDEWOOD & C.E. ZAMBOK (Eds), *Decision Making in Action: Models and Methods*. Norwood, NJ: Ablex.

HEATH, C. & LUFF, P. (1992). Collaboration and control. *Computer Supported Co-operative Work* (CSCW), No. 1, 69–94.

Human Factors (1995). Special Issue on Decision Making in Complex Environments, vol. 38, No. 2, June.

HUTCHINS, E. (1990). The technology of team navigation. In J. GALEGHER, R.E. KRAUT, & C. EGIDO (Eds), *Intellectual Teamwork: Social and Technical Bases of Collaborative Work*. Hillsdale, NJ: Erlbaum.

HUTCHINS, E. (1995). *Cognition in the Wild*. Cambridge, MA: MIT.

KLEIN, G. & THORDSEN, M. (1989). Cognitive processes of the team mind Ch2809–2/89/0000–0046. IEEE. Yellow Springs, OH: Klein Associates.

McGRATH, J. (1984). *Groups: Interaction and Performance*. Englewood Cliffs, NJ: Prentice-Hall.

ORASANU, J. & SALAS, E. (1993). Team decision making in complex environments. In G. KLEIN, J. ORASANU, R. CALDEWOOD & C.E. ZAMBOK (Eds), *Decision Making in Action: Models and Methods*. Norwood, NJ: Ablex.

SVENMARK, P. & BREHMER, B. (1991). D³FIRE: An experimental paradigm for the studies of distributed decision making. In B. BREHMER (Ed.) *Distributed decision making*, Proceedings of the third MOHAWC Workshop, Roskilde: Risö National Library.

CHAPTER SIX

Creation and loss of cognitive empathy at an emergency control centre

HENRIK ARTMAN AND YVONNE WÆRN

6.1. INTRODUCTION

We have analyzed some examples of communication and co-operation in an emergency control centre. The distribution of information and the distribution of tasks is a complex cognitive activity. In some cases this activity is regulated by institutional rules; in other cases the persons involved have to decide when to call on another person, how to transfer data and how to feed back data about the activities performed. For time-critical complex tasks like this, strict rule-based behaviour seems to be insufficient, as much of the success of managing this dynamic task seems to depend on flexibility and what we call "cognitive empathy".

6.2. PRESENTATION OF AN EMERGENCY CONTROL CENTRE

An emergency control centre in X-town was studied. The Swedish emergency services are organized so that anyone can call a specific telephone number and the telephone system connects the caller to the nearest emergency centre. At the emergency control centre all incoming emergency calls are handled and registered.

Usually, three persons (during the night two only) work together in shifts, taking the calls as they come in. As there might be several calls at the same time to the emergency centre, some work distribution is called for. As a rule one person is responsible for keeping track of the ambulances, while another is responsible for the fire brigades as well as for the use of helicopters. During office hours a third person is responsible for some more commercial tasks, such as different security alarms. However, everybody must be able to handle every kind of incoming call. This means that there is both a formal organization and some freedom for people to organize their work according to circumstances.

Each person sits in front of a computer, though the seating is arranged in a half-circle so that they can both see each other and have easy access to the computer (see Fig. 6.1). They each have a headset which covers one ear and allows the person to have his/her hands free while talking to the caller, at the same time as one ear is free to listen to conversations within the control room. The computer is used to register the call, so that any commission can be followed and read by anybody who chooses to look at the computer.

Figure 6.1. The control room setting. The third operator usually sits to the left of the second operator.

6.3. "TALKING TO THE ROOM" AND COGNITIVE EMPATHY

In several papers about co-operation where people are colocated it has been reported that people "talk to the room" (Heath & Luff, 1992; Heath *et al.*, 1996; Samurçay & Rogalski, 1993). By this we mean that people openly voice bits and pieces of information about what they are doing at the moment. These bits and pieces of information are not addressed to a specific recipient but rather to anyone who can make immediate use of the information or use it in a future task. In tasks where people act independently, "talking to the room" does not demand an overt response and is sometimes just dropped (Heath *et al.*, 1996). In other situations "talking to the room" might consist of an overt request for sharing a task (see Samurçay & Rogalski, 1993).

In the situations we have focused on, the institutional rules prescribe that the first person taking a call has to ask for assistance when the incident can be regarded as a "priority one" situation (i.e. life-threatening). However, the team members also use it as a way of confirming an informant's reliability when making a decision on how to act on the call. Often such decisions are stressful and demanding and it is advantageous to let the burden be divided between people. The persons working together must learn what we will call "cognitive empathy". Cognitive empathy not only implies knowing when and how to employ routine task distribution, but is also concerned with the ability to understand another person's need for help. In control rooms, such as those managing the underground transport (Heath & Luff, 1992), air traffic or industrial processes, the persons involved have a clear task assignment and much of the work is quite routine and familiar to all the personnel. However, in the emergency centre the presumptive supporting person has not always had the opportunity to understand the nature of the incident, what needs the caller has, and what needs the control companion has. *This puts the assisting person in a position where he or she has to figure this out without any explicit co-ordination mechanism except a signal.* Experienced operators in all the above situations have been observed to monitor the control room every time either they hear that another operator is overloaded with work or they themselves have less of a workload. In the emergency centre there are sometimes more acute "priority one" cases to be handled than there are personnel. At such times it is essential not only to monitor the workload and handle it co-operatively in a routine way, but also to monitor the information needs and emotional stress of fellow operators and to assess the incident in order to be of any help in managing the case. All this has to be carried out within a minimal time so that any rescue services can be deployed without delay.

6.4. CREATION OF COGNITIVE EMPATHY

If the case is judged to be a "priority one" incident, the interviewer is urged by institutionalized rules to call for "co-listening" from whoever is free at the moment. This enables the activities to be divided between the interviewer and the co-listener. Because of this division of labour the interviewer may be able to collect even more information from the accident reporter, which he or she can later transfer to the rescue service personnel so that they can prepare certain instruments or the like. At the same time the co-listener listens to the interview and can call the rescue services and give them the appropriate address and preliminary information which the co-listener have picked up during the interview etc.

In less straightforward cases the interviewer might ask for a co-listener because he or she is uncertain about the case or about the informant. In such cases the operators confer within the room in order to decide whether or not to send rescue services.

Often we can see how a presumptive co-listener monitors other operators and their voices, to prepare himself or herself to take over parts of the task. In serious or strange cases, both operators seek eye contact and so indicate whether or not there will be any transfer of activities. If operators notice that any operator is likely to transfer a case to them, they immediately turn to their computers and search for the case record. By doing so they can see how far the interviewing person has come. Consider the following quite straightforward case, where an asthma patient calls the emergency centre and can hardly talk (see Table 6.1).

Operator #1 receives the call. Operator #3 has just closed a conversation with operator #2, has no emergent task, and overhears #1's answer. At first he is just routinely attending this emergency call as there is nothing else to do, but by the sound of the operator #1's voice, as well as the hand gesture towards the "transfer button", he is able to predict the call for co-listening. Operator #1 then pushes the button (16), thereby indicating the need for support. Operator #2 is working independently and is not transcribed here. The text in italics refers to local co-ordination within the room.

All operators have several ways (on the computer screen, by the signal, and by a display) of noting that it is a call to the emergency number so it is no suprise that operators #2 and #3 end their conversation immediately when #2 has taken the call (5). When operator #1 asks the caller what she/he is saying, operator #3 starts to turn his chair attentively (7). This might be a way of showing that for the moment he is available, as Heath & Luff (1992) have suggested. When operator #1 says "asthma", #3 very clearly directs his full attention towards #1. #1 then moves her hand towards the button where they call for co-listening. #3 turns to the computer and starts co-listening to the call almost at the same time as #1 asks for assistance via the computer. #3 tells #1 that he

Table 6.1. Overhearing and co-listening in an asthma case

Time	Operator #1	Operator #3	Comment
1.	90000, emergency		#3 is free and is
2.	centre		checking if there is
3.			anything he can help
4.	What do you say?		with
5.	I don't hear		
6.	anything. Yes		
7.	Hello, have you got		#3 turns his
8.	asthma?		attention to #1 as
9.			soon as he hears the
10.			word "asthma", but
11.			then seems a bit
12.			relaxed until he sees
13.			#1 turn towards the
14.			"co-listening button"
15.			
16.	May I have your		#1 asks for co-
17.	telephone number?		listening, #3 takes it
18.			
19.	And the area code		
20.	is?		
21.	And where do you		
22.	live?		
23.		*I am with you*	
24.	Is it		
25.	x-street?		
26.	Yes	*Oh, this one is really*	
27.		*bad!*	
28.	And your name?	*I'll get an ambulance*	
29.			
30.	Can you open the		
31.	door when we		
32.	arrive?		
33.	It is open, OK		
34.	We are on our way		
35.			
36.	Thanks, bye		
37.	Oh . . .	*This one was really*	
38.		*bad*	
39. 6 seconds later		*She must have*	
40.		*waited a very long*	
41.		*time before she*	
42.	Uhmm, yes . . .	*called!*	
43. 3 seconds		*She had no air left*	
44.	No . . .		#3 calls ambulance

is with her (23) and thereby confirms that he will take care of the task. After being able to hear only a few "words" he is confirming through the headset phones to #1 that he also assesses the situation as serious, which indicates to #1 that she has assessed the situation correctly (26) and that he is about to call an ambulance (28). As the computer signal does not tell what kind of assistance #1 wants, #3 has to assess this by projecting his under-standing of the case. *The same goes for #1's interpretation when #3 says "This one is really bad" (26).* It is this illocutionary act that is used to create cognitive empathy, to assess another person's need for assistance without being told explicitly of the matter *or having been involved in the co-text.* We might also point out that #1 is flexible in her cross-checking of the authenticity of the call because of the obvious problems the caller has in speaking, and rephrases some questions so that the caller can only answer yes or no (24, 30).

Later in the case, while waiting for the ambulance to connect, #3 initiates a conversa-tion with #1 on his assessment of the mission (37). In this way each gives the other feedback on the situation and confirms that everything that ought to have been done actually has been done. This episode shows the importance of having some more personal debriefing of a stressful situation. Clearly, #3 assesses that #1 had a problem when interviewing the patient and possibly wants to initiate an discussion about that. This is a particular form of cognitive empathy, which is more than just the instrumental work of the team since it deals with the emotional situation as well.

6.5. LOSS OF COGNITIVE EMPATHY

In the following example (Table 6.2) a more complex case is illustrated, and here there is a higher workload, since two cases are going on at the same time. Operator #2, sitting in the middle, is working with a call concerned with a person lying in the street. He considers this call to be fake and tells this "to the room" several times, effectively to ask for assistance to make a decision. Operators #1 and #3, flanking operator #2, are collaborat-ing on a case concerning a bottle in someone's throat. There are several instances of turbulence and jumping between these two cases. We enter this case when operator #1 just called for assistance and #3 is about to give it. Operator #2 is about to end a case he thinks is a non-serious alarm.

When we enter the situation, #1 uses the computer to tell the other operators that she needs assistance (50). #3 takes it and tells her that he is with her on the phone; #1 turns towards #3 and tells him briefly and in an upset voice about the case (62). #3 understands at this moment that the assistance she needed was not to assess the situation, but rather to call an ambulance as fast as possible. #2 finishes his call and has promised that an ambulance will come (58), and #3 asks #2 (responsible for the ambulance) about the ambulance's whereabouts (68). #1 must overhear the question as she immediately answers it in a quite stressed and loud voice and says that she's got them in her computer (70, 76) ("on the shelf" means that you have got in touch with them). #2 has not noticed the turbulence about the case #1 is taking care of, and asks in a suprised voice about what is happening (86). #3 in turn has not noticed that #2 has got a job, but starts dividing the resources between them (88). #2 now tells them that he thinks this case is a fake (109), but does not get any empathic response at all. In fact #3 tries to redirect #2's attention from assessing the situation correctly to actually sending out an ambulance by saying "but you" (112), *indicating that he does not want any discussion.* #2 clearly has a prob-lem in deciding whether this case is serious or just a fake, but he does not get any response from the others while pointing this out. The situation continues in Table 6.3, with #2 agreeing to send an ambulance to the potentially fake alarm. Notice, especially, how insecure #2 is (in bold type).

Table 6.2. A fake call?

Time	Operator #1	Operator #2	Operator #3
48.			43 back at the
49.	I do not hear		station ready,
50. #1 calls for co-	Sure	He's lay – lying	end.
51. listening	[telephone number]	outside	[takes the co-
52.		[street] But what	listening]
53.	Yes	number?	
54.		[no.] OK	*[I am] with*
56.			*[you]*
57.	Do you know their	I'll send an	
58.	name or so	ambulance	
59.			
60.		They will be there	
61.	[towards 3]	in about ten . . .	
62.	*has got a bottle in*	fifteen minutes	
63.	*the throat (?)*	[ends this call]	
64. #1 talks to #3			
65.	[name]		
66. #3 asks #2	well, how old is he?		
67. about			*[towards 2]*
68. ambulances			*#2 which car is*
69.			*it, is it 142?*
70.	*No, they are not free*		
71.			*in Östhammar*
72.			
73.			*42 are free, or?*
74.			
75.	*42 are not free. I've*		
76.	*got them on the*		*Aha*
77.	*shelf here*		
78.	17 years. Yes,		
79.	they'll arrive		
80.	immediately		The water
81.			tower,
82.	Yes, bye.		Långegrund yes
83.			But then we'll
84.			have to take
85.			forty-
86.		*Have you got*	
87.		*something there too,*	
88.		*No,*	*Take 43 then*
89.		*you are not sane and*	
90.		*I have got one in*	
100.		*Öre-Schimo*	
101.			
102.			*Gimo?*
103.			*What are we*
104.			*going to do*
105.			*then?*
106. Ambulance	Hallo		*Is it urgent or?*
107. calling			
108. (Observe how		*This . . .*	
109. #2 tries to		*This I thought was*	
110. get attention)		*fake, you see,*	
111.	You are at home,		
112.	yes, OK	*Actually*	*But you . . .*

Table 6.2. Continued

Time	Operator #1	Operator #2	Operator #3
113.	[to the caller]	but – let's take	
114.	We have a (?)	ambulance, then	
115.			In Gimo yes
116.	on its way		
117.			
118.	yes		
119.	Mm		
120.			*Take Gimo*
121.			*Shall I check with 42 and hear*
122.			*what they are doing? Was it*
123.			*a*
124.		***Hm, I do not***	
125.		***know at all***	
126.		***I don't believe***	
127.		***this, you know***	
128.			*43 on the station, you know*
129.		*42 should be at*	
130.		*home, but they*	
131.		*should call for*	
132.		*information*	
133.	*They are at*		
134.	*home. I*	*Yes*	
135. New	*HAVE GOT*		
136. emergency	*THEM HERE*	*Yes, but take them*	
137. call		*then,*	
138.		*there, on your*	
139.	*Yes, but*		
140.	*shouldn't we*		
	call the doctor		
	out there		
141.			*Yes, we'll do this,*
142.			*but take each one a car first*
143.			*and they should have yes.*
144.			*And I'll take 90000 here then*
145.			
146.			
147.		*Yes, I'll take Gimo*	
148.		*on mine first*	
149.			90000
150.			
151.			ambulance
152.			
153.		***Very unclear***	Hello, yes
154.		***what this is all***	
155.		***about***	
156.			Yes, ambulance, fireguard
157.			Hello
158.			

This episode shows very clearly all the talking to the room (in italics). Much of it is related to overt local co-ordination, but #2 several times raises doubts about "his" mission (124–127, 153–154). We can see in this stressful situation that the operators clearly ignore all the emotional and more problematic questions about assessing #2's situation. The other two operators instead implicitly urge #2 to send an ambulance (112) and the local co-ordination is mainly concerned with getting all this right (124–138). #1 takes care of the ambulance for her case but asks someone to call the local doctor (139–140), which #3 takes care of after taking the third incoming call (148–157). Later, #2 even calls for a "big ambulance", which is an ambulance with a medical doctor (not shown here).

Despite the fact that #2 is uncertain about the seriousness of the case, he sends out an extra ambulance still later in the process. At first, #2 has taken this case rather calmly. Just at the end of this episode all operators are occupied, so even if #2 would like support in assessing the situation he couldn't get it. When he is talking to the ambulance drivers he is again telling them that he thinks the case is a fake. And afterwards he again tells the other operators within the room, but again with no response. The stress and the high pressure on the local co-ordination seem to make them forget empathy. It also seems as if #2 has been enticed by #3 to order two ambulances without having any good ground for considering the case *that* serious. This may be due to #3's heavy commitment (which #2 transfers to his own case) and to the long deprivation of any attention from #1 or #3.

6.6. CONCLUSION

These examples show that both the planning laid down in the organization and the situated collaboration affect the temporary co-ordination. A very important feature in collaboration seems to be people's preparedness to watch for each other's needs, which was shown in the first example. Another important feature is people's need for help from others. This was here shown in the second example, where a single person had to work alone on a difficult case, and tried in various ways to attract attention. Cases of mental or collaborative overload may then lead to nonoptimal decisions, as in the second case when two ambulances are sent to an accident one operator thinks is fake.

6.7. ACKNOWLEDGEMENT

This study has been supported by a grant from the Swedish Work Environment Fund.

6.8. REFERENCES

HEATH, C. & LUFF, P. (1992). Collaboration and control. *Computer Supported Co-operative Work* (CSCW), No. 1, 69–94.

HEATH, C., LUFF, P. & NICHOLS, G.M. (1996). The collaborative production of the document: context, genre and the borderline in design. In: Y. WÆRN (Ed.), *Co-ordination of Process Management*. Report to COST 14, June 1996.

SAMURÇAY, R. & ROGALSKI, J. (1993). Co-operative work and decision making in emergency management. *Le Travail Humain*, tome 56, No. 1/1993, 53–77.

CHAPTER SEVEN

Utilization of information technology in navigational decision-making

LEENA NORROS AND KRISTIINA HUKKI

7.1. INTRODUCTION

Navigators have traditionally been aware that safety in navigation is a result not only of technical features of the vessels but also, and foremost, of the navigator's skill. Due to the expansion of traffic and the fast pace of technological development of the vessels, the complexity of the navigation system has increased greatly. As a consequence, the requirements of proper operation of the system have become more delicate and the mechanisms of failure more difficult to understand.

In this chapter the safety of the navigation system is approached from the decision-making point of view. The focus of analysis is the navigators' on-line decision-making on the ship bridge. The navigation system as a whole is taken into account as boundary conditions for decision-making. We will discuss the navigators' decision-making from three different angles. After some methodological remarks concerning the analysis of decision-making in natural situations, we present results of two studies in which navigators' decision-making was analyzed with the aim of evaluating the appropriateness of new information technological tools for navigation. Finally, some central issues concerning the training of the ship bridge crews are raised.

7.2. DYNAMIC DECISION-MAKING ON BRIDGE

7.2.1. Analysis of human errors

Analysis of human activity in real-life situations is a complicated task. Human error analysis is one frequently used approach. The main idea of this is that through analysis of failures in the activity, insight is gained into the underlying error mechanisms, knowledge of which can be utilized for preventive actions.

The Finnish Maritime Administration has recently initiated a research project on human behaviour at the wheelhouse (Sorsa *et al.*, 1997). The aim of the work was to give simple guidelines in order to improve the wheelhouse procedures. A socio-technical model of the etiology of human error (Reason, 1990, 1995) is applied in the study. The methods and materials used are accident reports, observations of bridge team behaviour, evaluation of maritime educational and training systems and the regulations and guidelines of national and international authorities and organizations.

The analysis of the etiology of human errors and their role in accidental events has important practical significance. Through systematic analyses and classifications, databases are obtained which allow statistical analyses of causal factors. They provide possibilities for monitoring the development of the safety situation and control of risks. It should, however, be kept in mind that safety analyses are basically case studies in which certain methods are utilized for description of the causal chains of particular events leading to accidents. These analyses do not comprise the system functionalities and general boundary conditions of the activity. Neither do they take account of the purposive adaptation of the human actors in such real-life situations (Rasmussen, 1995). On the above basis it is easy to agree with Rasmussen's conclusion that "safety in the direct interaction with the work environment must be based on an identification of the boundary of safe performance by analysis of the work system, and the criteria that drive the continuous adaptive modification of behavior. Efforts for improvement must then be directed toward the control of performance in interaction with the boundary, not control of errors" (Rasmussen, 1995).

7.2.2. Analysis of decision-making in natural situations

Looking at human failures in aircraft cockpits and ship bridges, some systematic features can be recognized in their etiology. Various approaches have been applied for the categorization of accidents and incidents. Nevertheless, as Sorsa (1995) stated, those that can be called human performance accidents are, to a great extent, really are concerned with decision-making in a critical situation.

From the point of view of decision-making, error analyses always represent hindsight, because the method does not allow the situation as it was faced by the decision-maker to be taken into account. The course of events seems clear and self-evident for the analyst, who already knows the results of the activity. The situation is different for the operator in the loop, who faces the complexity and uncertainty of the step-by-step evolving course of events, on which he himself has an impact.

Consequently, it is characteristic of human behaviour in natural decision-making situations that the actors do not know what is going on and they try to make sense of the situation. This central task demand has recently been emphasized by the proponents of the "naturalistic decision-making" paradigm (e.g. Orasanu & Connolly, 1993, Cannon-Bowers et al., 1996). We agree with this view but will also add that, as Harré & Gillet (1994) have argued, the person's activity in a situation is constructed according to the significance it holds for him. Therefore, adoption of the actor's point of view as a starting point for the analysis of decision-making appears to be a necessary requirement for the adequacy of the analysis.

In the analysis of decision-making in natural situations it is necessary to pay attention to at least three major task demands. First, complex and changing environments include much uncertainty, which is a major constraint on the control of the system. As a consequence, then, the control of the system demands that an interpretation of the state of the system (a situation assessment) be formed. As we have indicated elsewhere (Klemola

& Norros, in press), the forming of an interpretation can be seen as a cumulative learning process, which interactively directs the observation of relevant information of the system. The control of the system can be viewed as the actor's accounts of the possibilities and constraints of the current situation. The subject's accounts can be identified through analysis of his ways of utilization of the available resources (Norros & Hukki, submitted a and b). Third, when analyzing decision-making in real-life situations it is also necessary to take account of the fact that decision-making is typically distributed among several actors. As coherent activity requires co-ordination between different actors' task performances, common awareness of the situation is needed. Different tools, e.g. information technical systems, used in the task performance provide representations of the object of control. Through this role the artifacts contribute to the co-ordination of actions. They also provide possibilities for common consciousness (Hutchins, 1990, 1995).

7.3. DIVISION OF WORK BETWEEN THE NAVIGATOR AND BRIDGE AUTOMATION

7.3.1. Ironies of automation

The utilization of ship bridge automation has increased considerably over the past ten years. This is due to the growth in the size of ships and the improvement in the accuracy of control through automation technology. It has been assumed that automation would enhance the reliability of the control of the system and diminish the navigators' workload. The extent of the utilization of automation is, however, a contradictory issue, as can be inferred from the words of an experienced pilot and human factors trainer who stated that he never met a pilot who wished to see more automation in the cockpit (Sorsa, 1995). The problem is that while automation increases the reliability of the system through standardization of routine operations, it simultaneously increases the complexity of the system and the probability of unpredictable novel situations. Moreover, automation systems are typically not working optimally in such situations.

While the benefits and potential negative effects of cockpit automation have been the topic of lively discussion within the aviation community, similar concerns have not yet been raised in the maritime circles. Recent accidents within the maritime industries have, however, indicated that both deficient design and unqualified operation of new navigation equipment may become important contributors to accidents. These experiences will certainly facilitate critical discussion about the role of automation in bridge decision-making.

We believe that in attempting to find a realistic distribution of tasks between human and machine it is necessary to treat automation in a wider perspective. The potential of automation does not lie primarily in its ability to amplify human cognitive abilities. Rather, automation changes the way practical tasks or problems in work are represented (Hutchins, 1990, 1995). Thus in navigation, for example, automation changes the composition and organization of the positioning and steering operations and the intellectual skills these operations call for. The challenge for advanced information technological tools in navigation would be to transform the task into such a form that the relevant features of the situation would be highlighted and the necessary actions made as apparent as possible, i.e. presentation of information would be *navigationally informative* (Norros *et al.*, 1995). Experience from various industrial processes indicates, however, that very often operators are loaded with an abundance of information which does not meet the requirements of the task. Therefore, especially in complicated or unexpected operating situations, expert users may be reluctant to use the new information tools.

The ability of an automation system to inform the users about its own functioning also greatly affects its usability. A recent example from navigation (Investigation report, 1997) has made clear that the operator's uncertainty about the system's current mode of operation may cause major misinterpretations and inadequate decisions. Thus, the system's interface should display relevant information on the system's design basis, which could be shared with the user in critical decision-making situations. This feature could be called *system informativeness* (Norros *et al.*, 1995).

A further major feature that affects the acceptability of the system is, of course, the *reliability* of the system. If the user has doubts about the accuracy or credibility of the presented information or he has known the system to break down frequently, his confidence in the system will be lost and he will not be willing to utilize it, especially in difficult or critical situations.

7.3.2. Appropriateness of bridge information systems

The possibilities of utilization of new technology on the bridge have been tackled at the Technical Research Centre of Finland, in a multidisciplinary research project including navigational, maritime engineering and human factors expertise. The above reflections on the role of automation in the control of complex systems have been the basis of the group's work. The particular aim of the project has been the evaluation of the appropriateness of information presentation on bridge.

7.3.2.1. Control of the ship's movements: the predictor display

In the first study (Heikkilä & Norros, 1993) the aim was to assess the usability of a predictor display. This is a display that provides the navigator with the history of the ship's movement and a prediction of its future sweep. Fig. 7.1 demonstrates the display. Based on navigational expertise, but without a detailed analysis of the information characteristics of this particular navigational aid, it was assumed that the display could facilitate observation of the ship's motion. In other words, this new development was supposed to provide navigationally informative information.

It was expected that the functional properties of the predictor display would aid conning through narrow fairways, which are typical in Finnish waters. Such a situation was simulated in a full-scale simulator. The critical navigational task was the control of the ship's movement when making turns in a very narrow S-shaped sound. The focus in the analysis of the total 106 simulated runs was the overall adequacy of conning. This was estimated with the help both of measuring the ship's deviation from the centre of the route at selected points and of expert evaluations of each performance. These were provided independently by two experts on the basis of a plotting of each run.

The main result of the study was that the use of the new display enhanced the overall adequacy of performance of the less experienced navigators. This result is demonstrated in Fig. 7.2, which depicts these runs in the two different display conditions, conventional (Fig. 7.2a) and predictor display (Fig. 7.2b). The benefits of the system manifested themselves particularly in the control of ship speed, which was considered critical in the approach into the sound. The more experienced navigators gained less in general from the new display. However, it was found that the actual passing through the sound was more successful when using the predictor display both in the inexperienced and in the experienced navigator groups.

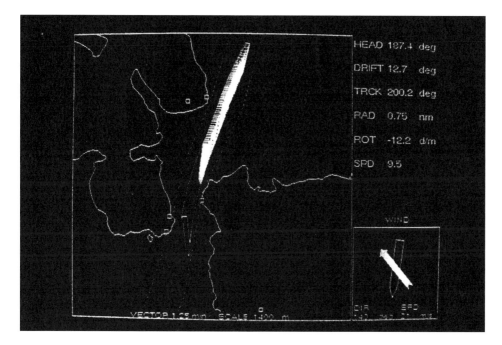

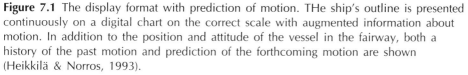

Figure 7.1 The display format with prediction of motion. THe ship's outline is presented continuously on a digital chart on the correct scale with augmented information about motion. In addition to the position and attitude of the vessel in the fairway, both a history of the past motion and prediction of the forthcoming motion are shown (Heikkilä & Norros, 1993).

The results indicated that the navigational usefulness of the predictor display was related both to the level of the navigator's skill and to the task demands. In the passing through the sound the navigators normally reduce the control mode of the autopilot in order to be able to make small manual adjustments according to the situational constraints, mainly wind. It seems that the utilization of the display contributes to adequacy of performance in this situation, which contains more uncertainty and therefore demands a more flexible performance. Feedback control of the ship's movement is facilitated by the predictor display system.

Thus, it can be concluded that the appropriateness of the predictor display was evident, and may be interpreted to be based on the navigational informativeness of the system. This characteristic of the system probably facilitated a situational way of navigating, which might be a typical way of coping with the task among the less experienced navigators. Probably this way of navigating was chosen by the experienced navigators according to the situational constraints of the task. Thus, the display provided help also to the more experienced navigators.

The study described above raises at least two important questions. First, could it be possible to develop deliberate criteria for the appropriateness of navigational information systems, and what would they be? Second, could it be possible to analyze in detail the performance of the navigators during the task performance in order to see more precisely what is the role of new tools in the bridge decision-making? Finding answers to these questions was the aim of the further study carried out by the research group.

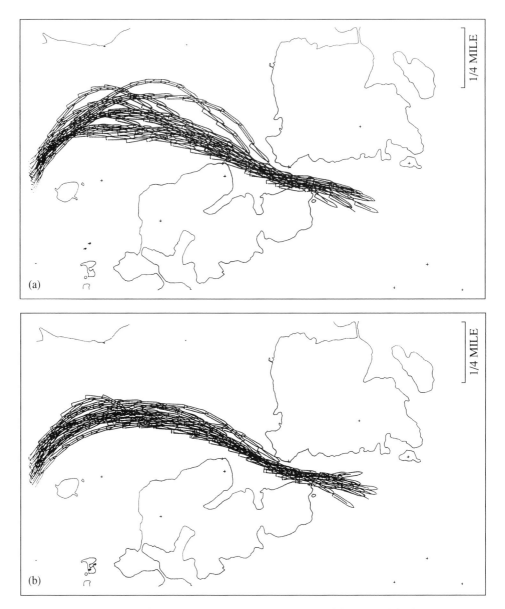

Figure 7.2. Predictor display validation experiment. Plotting of the runs of the less experienced navigators in two display conditions. (a) The results in the conventional conditions; (b) the results in predictor display conditions.

7.3.2.2. Aiding navigation and positioning: ECDIS

In a second simulator study (Norros *et al.*, 1995), which was carried out in co-operation with the Institute of Ship Operation, Maritime Transport and Simulation (ISSUS) in Hamburg, the information technological aid under investigation was different. In this case, as well as the standard equipment, the navigator was provided with an electrical sea chart and information system (ECDIS). This system is supposed to present navigationally relevant information regarding the hydrographic situation, the position and movement of the ship, and the traffic situation in an integrated way. Again, the situation in the simulation was designed according to the expected functional benefits of the system. Thus, in the simulation situation the navigator was asked to sail along a narrow passage towards the harbour with the demand to pick up the pilot at a certain point of the passage. The critical constraint of the task was heavy traffic.

Fig. 7.3 depicts the first part of the route the navigators were supposed to sail. Instead of focusing merely on the motion of the ship the navigator had to develop an overall conception of the situation and adapt his time plan accordingly. Vessel traffic service (VTS) information and the possibility to contact all relevant vessels and the pilot were provided for him. Twenty-two navigators, who were ordered in two experimental groups (with and without ECDIS), performed a one hour simulator run after which an interview regarding the task and the navigational properties of ECDIS was carried out. The specific aim of the study was to evaluate the appropriateness of this information tool. Inferences regarding the information system could be based both on the navigators' opinions of the system in a particular task and on the analysis of the navigators' on-line decision making on bridge during the performance of the same task.

Evaluation of the information presentation: A contextual evaluation framework was developed for a deliberate description of the appropriateness of information presentation. The framework was characterized as contextual because the evaluation of the system properties was connected with the functional purpose of the system (electric chart, predictor display, autopilot) and the navigational situation (the task and its boundary conditions). The framework has three successive phases: definition of the general requirements of information presentation; definition of context-dependent evaluation criteria according to the functional purpose; and evaluation of interface characteristics of a particular interface solution.

In the first phase, four general requirements for an information system were distinguished: *informativeness* (navigational and system informativeness), *flexibility*, *reliability*, and *ability to develop* (Norros *et al.*, 1995). All four requirements are relevant in the definition of the man–machine interaction on bridge, but informativeness can be considered most fundamental. Based on an analysis of the use of ECDIS in the navigational decision-making, the four requirements were operationalized into concrete evaluation criteria in phase 2. In the third phase these were utilized to evaluate the interface characteristic of the particular ECDIS version.

According to the navigators' conceptions of the properties of ECDIS, the system was regarded as appropriate for navigational task performance. The main contributor to its usefulness was the spatial continuity provided by the automatic change of chart. Navigational informativeness should, however, be improved through more advanced presentation of ship motion, and flexibility should be enhanced through independent chart operations. The future possibility to integrate the chart with radar information was considered to be the system's main developmental potential. On the contrary, the ability of the system to provide background information for the current navigational situation was not valued. The navigators had realistic opinions of the reliability of the ECDIS system. It was pointed out that an intelligent use of the system requires mastery of traditional positioning and navigation methods, and therefore knowledge of them should continuously be included in the basic training of navigators. Implementation of the system should include sufficient equipment training for the users.

In conclusion we can state that with the help of the evaluation framework described above it was possible to interpret the navigators' descriptive and situation-specific opinions about the system and integrate them into a more generalized evaluation of the system.

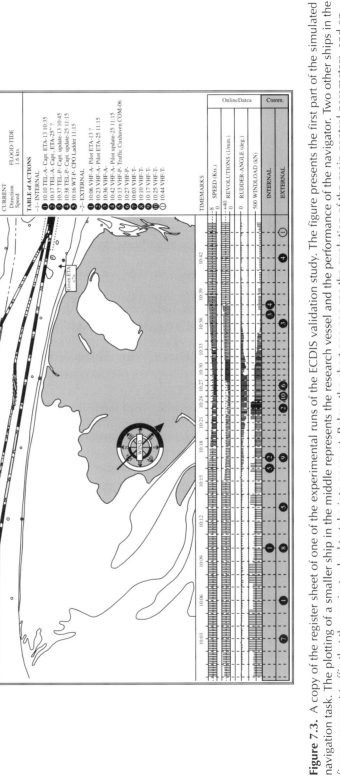

Figure 7.3. A copy of the register sheet of one of the experimental runs of the ECDIS validation study. The figure presents the first part of the simulated navigation task. The plotting of a smaller ship in the middle represents the research vessel and the performance of the navigator. Two other ships in the figure represent traffic that the navigator had to take into account. Below the chart one can see the evolution of the main control parameters, and on the right-hand side the navigator's critical actions are summarized.

Navigators' decision-making during the task performance: The navigators' performances in the simulated runs were analyzed from the decision-making point of view. A contextual method was used. Thus, the particular navigational demands of the task situation were first modelled with the help of maritime experts. The model provided a reference for the evaluation of the navigators' decision-making during the actual task performance.

The performance was first analyzed with regard to the adequacy of navigation (coping with time schedule, control of the ship movements, track keeping), and the utilization of information resources (utilization of communication, utilization of ECDIS information). The comparison between the navigators using ECDIS and those using traditional charts did not reveal differences in regard to the adequacy of task performance. Neither did the level of navigational experience have an impact on adequacy of performance. However, in the total sample, efficient utilization of external communication correlated significantly with adequacy of task performance. Moreover, in the ECDIS group an efficient use of chart information was weakly related to adequacy of task performance.

We may conclude that neither the type of information presentation nor the level of experience had a direct impact on the adequacy of task performance. Rather, it seemed that the adequacy of performance was modified through the efficiency of utilization of task-relevant resources, which possibly reflects qualitative differences in the ways of carrying out the navigational task.

The experimental data also provided some possibility to carry out more detailed analyses of the navigators' ways of utilizing co-operative and information resources during the task performance. Based on these analyses we were able to identify two different ways of navigating in this task. In the case of the first, situative way of navigating, the subjects claimed that due to the difficulty in predicting the navigational situation very precisely it was better to proceed without a tight time plan. This way of navigating was associated with preferences for cautiousness and safety. On the contrary, in the second, planning way of navigating, navigators attempted to work with a time plan which was updated several times during the passage. Subjects manifesting this way of navigating valued efficiency of performance, and risk-taking was not unusual among them. We could not find any clear relationship between way of navigating and the adequacy of task performance, but data suggested that the latter approach was more vulnerable to the increase of traffic. While the above results can only be considered tentative, we are currently carrying out research on the navigators' decision-making with the aim of defining characteristics related to approaches to navigation. The goal is to clarify the dynamics of navigational decision-making and the organization of performance on bridge.

7.4. TRAINING FOR PRESENT AND FUTURE NAVIGATION SYSTEMS

One of the problems in organizing co-operative decision-making in complex work is to create functional co-ordination between subactivities. The critical prerequisite then is the maintenance of a sufficient amount of redundancy between the functions. According to Hutchins (1990) this can be achieved through creation of a common awareness of the situation. There are several factors that can contribute to this.

A traditional way of creating a shared basis for decision-making is the apprenticeship system, where novices learn professional skills through participation in the activity with contributions that gradually increase in significance and complexity. The division of labour and the career development of personnel in industrial process control, and other work including complex experiential skills, follow this basic principle. It is also a typical learning method in the maritime field. Spatial proximity provides another evident possibility to create a shared understanding and consciousness of work situations. Process operators frequently report being aware of the other crew members' aims through observing their actions while simultaneously carrying out their own tasks.

Openness of communication, i.e. explicitness of the inference basis, is another factor that may serve as a means to achieve shared situation awareness. The significance of this factor has been identified in case studies of accidents and in experiments, whose results show that deficiencies in communication may be major contributors to problems in on-line decision-making in dynamic situations (Orasanu & Connolly, 1993, Orasanu & Salas, 1993, Norros & Hukki, submitted b). However, because professional practice is traditionally based on implicit or tacit knowledge, it might be necessary to pay deliberate attention to the development of openness of communication.

The currently increasing implementation of information technology may threaten the above mechanism of creating common awareness, for example, through implementing remote control, substituting VDU-oriented actions for spatially distinguishable actions in the control-room, or substituting electrical text for spoken communication. But new technology also provides possibilities for enhancement of communication. The realization of these possibilities requires openness of technology, for example, functional and system informativeness of the interface (Norros *et al.*, 1995).

The main methods that are available for the development of distributed decision-making are the design of procedures and deliberate training of teams in the utilization of the available co-operative resources. Both items have been defined as the major content in the so-called crew resource management (CRM) training, which has been widely utilized in aviation. Also, related training conceptions have been developed in other high-reliability surroundings. A representative example is simulator training in real-like situations. In aviation the so-called line-oriented flight training (LOFT) has been proposed. Moreover, research teams in different countries are currently working on scientifically based criteria for the evaluation of team performance and decision-making. The aim is to enable feedback regarding the nature of the performance process instead of merely its result (Norros & Hukki, submitted b). The former type of feedback has been proven effective in learning to cope with complex phenomena containing uncertainty (see, for example, Hammond, 1993).

In the past few years these new trends in training have created spin-offs in maritime industries. The typical example is the adaptation of crew resource management into bridge resource management (BRM). Also, concrete work has been carried out in this area in Finland. With the support of the Finnish Maritime Administration, experts from aviation and the maritime industry have together worked out and implemented a BRM training course.

7.5. CONCLUSIONS

Enhancement of safety in navigation is the ultimate aim of the research described in this chapter. The difficult question is how to proceed towards this goal. The problem is to identify the major risks and the right approach to controlling them. The approach adopted in this chapter focuses on decision-making on the bridge. With the help of the new contextual research methodology, the characteristics of particular decision-making situations were first modelled, and subsequently the models were used as reference in the analysis of the actors' decision-making during real task performances. This method acknowledges the principle that the subject's own accounts of the situation should form the bases of explaining his activity, without neglecting the constraints imposed by the situation and the task. We feel that the methodology utilized in our research corresponds to the position of Rasmussen (1995), who called for preventive control of performance in interaction with the boundary, instead of control of errors.

Our focus on bridge decision-making was based on the argument that the difficulties of mastering the maritime system become evident in the "sharp end". Other activities within the system, for example, design of bridges or activities of the shipping company, may, however, be equally important for overall safety. Therefore, the contextual approach adopted in the studies seems to be crucial. We feel that these other activities should also be studied from the decision-making point of view.

In the adopted approach the system functionalities are analyzed with regard to a certain navigational situation and for a specific task or, in the future, for classes of situations and tasks. The models also provide possibilities to define the navigationally relevant information that the navigator, according to his choice, may or may not utilize in the fulfilment of his goals. Thus, the methodology opens possibilities both to define task-oriented requirements for information presentation and also to analyze the navigators' decision-making from the point of view of utilization of available information. Consequently, it can serve as a tool in the design of bridge automation and as an evaluative training method for improvement of on-line decision-making.

Beyond methodological developments, the research carried out thus far has yielded some interesting concrete results. The research indicated that efficient utilization of available resources was a primary contributor to the adequacy of activity. The level of experience was not as influential. This means that expert performance is not a direct function of experience but is affected by the way resources are utilized in a situation, i.e. by the way of navigating. It was also found that the type of information presentation on the adequacy of task performance is probably affected by the subjects' ways of navigating. These results have important practical consequences, because utilization of resources is a factor that can be tackled in training. Enhancement of the utilization of resources is the central aim of the BRM training courses, and it can be promoted in other types of simulator training too. It should be emphasized, however, that effective training requires methods for the evaluation of performance. The method used in these studies has been adapted to meet the needs of nuclear power plant simulator training (Norros & Hukki, submitted b), and a similar application seems possible in maritime training.

According to the results, effective communication with other vessels, the pilot and the traffic control in a busy traffic situation contributed to adequacy of task performance. Communication and co-operation are aspects that traditionally have not been emphasized in navigator training. Increased effort should be devoted to this aspect of activity, which might become a decisive contributor to safe navigation as the density of traffic grows. Furthermore, it can be inferred from the result that VTS does not automatically enhance the control of traffic situation. Instead, the navigators should be advised to acquire a way of navigating that orients towards utilization of the additional information.

Communication within the navigator team on bridge must be an equally important factor. Our current research concerning the control of nuclear power plants has made it clear that openness of communication within a team, defined as explicitness of the inference bases, is a factor that differentiates crews' ways of acting (Norros & Hukki, submitted a). Research results from the aviation field indicate that explicitness of communication has implications for efficiency of performance (Orasanu & Connolly, 1993, Orasanu & Salas, 1993). Our research group has recently initiated a study on bridge decision-making in piloting situations, in which co-operation between the captain and the pilot is studied in real-life situations.

7.6. REFERENCES

CANNON-BOWERS, J.A., SALAS, E. & PRUITT, J. (1996). Establishing the boundaries of a paradigm for decision-making research. *Human Factors*, vol. 38, No. 2, 193–205.

HAMMOND, K.R. (1993). Naturalistic decision making from a Brunswikian viewpoint: its past, present, future. In KLEIN, G.A. ORASANU, J., CALDERWOOD, R. & ZSAMBOK, C.E. (Eds), *Decision Making in Action: Models and Methods*. Norwood, NJ: Ablex Publishing Corporation, 205–227.

HARRÉ, R. & GILLET, G. (1994). *The Discursive Mind*. Thousand Oaks, CA: Sage Publications.

HEIKKILÄ, M. & NORROS, L. (1993). A simulation study on the format of ship motion display to improve steering accuracy in restricted fairways. *Proceedings of the International Symposium for Marine Simulation and Ship Manoeuverability*, 26 Sept.–2 Oct., St John's, Newfoundland, Canada.

HUTCHINS, E. (1990). The technology of team navigation. In GALEGHER, J., KRAUT, R.E. & EGIDO, C. (Eds), *Intellectual Teamwork*. Hillsdale, NJ: Lawrence Erlbaum Associates, 191–220.

HUTCHINS, E. (1995). *Cognition in the Wild*. Cambridge, MA: MIT Press.

INVESTIGATION REPORT (1997). *The Grounding of the M/S Silja Europa at Furusund in the Stockholm Archipelago on 13 January 1995*, Final Report, Accident Investigation Board, Helsinki.

KLEMOLA, U.-M. & NORROS, L. (in press). Analysis of the anaesthetist's activity: recognition of uncertainty as a basis for new practice. *Medical Education*.

NORROS, L. & HUKKI, K. (submitted, a). Dynamics of process operators' decision making in a disturbance situation. A contextual analysis. *International Journal of Cognitive Ergonomics*.

NORROS, L. & HUKKI, K. (submitted, b). Analysis of operators' ways of acting (AWA). Development of a simulator training method for Nuclear Power Plants. *Le Travail Humain*.

NORROS, L., HUKKI, K. & HEIKKILÄ, M. (1995). *Informativeness of bridge information systems*. Unpublished research report prepared for the Finnish Maritime Administration.

ORASANU, J. & CONNOLLY, T. (1993). The reinvention of decision making. In KLEIN, G.A., ORASANU, J., CALDERWOOD, R. & ZSAMBOK, C.E. (Eds), *Decision making in action: models and methods*. Norwood, NJ: Ablex Publishing Corporation, 3–20.

ORASANU, J. & SALAS, E. (1993). Team decision making in complex environments. In: KLEIN, G.A., ORASANU, J., CALDERWOOD, R. & ZSAMBOK, C.E. (Eds), *Decision making in action: models and methods*. Norwood, NJ: Ablex Publishing Corporation, 327–345.

RASMUSSEN, J. (1995). *Converging paradigms of human sciences*. Unpublished paper, Swedish Center for Risk Research and Education.

REASON, J. (1990). *Human Error*. New York: Cambridge University Press.

REASON, J. (1995). A systems approach to organizational error, *Ergonomics*, vol. 38, No. 8, 1708–1721.

SORSA, M. (1995). Modern decision-making tools in the management of aircraft cockpit. Key-note address at the *5th Conference on Cognitive Science Approaches to Process Control*, Espoo, Finland, 30 Aug.–1 Sept.

SORSA, M., LARJO, K., LEPISTÖ, J. & RUUHILEHTO, K. (1997). *Human Errors at the Warehouse*. Finnish Maritime Administration, Helsinki.

PART THREE

Microworld Studies

CHAPTER EIGHT

The C³FIRE microworld

REGO GRANLUND

8.1. INTRODUCTION

C³FIRE is a command, control and communication, experimental simulation environment using a forest fire-fighting domain. The goal of the system is to create an environment that can be used for investigation and training experimentation of *distributed decision-making* and *situation awareness*. C³FIRE can be viewed as a *microworld* with some important properties selected from a real domain. C³FIRE should retain the important characteristics identified in a field study of an existing military training system used to train infantry battalion staffs. The goal is that it should be a small and well-controlled environment for investigation and training experimentation. C³FIRE generates sessions where a forest fire-fighting organization can experience the task of commanding and controlling fire-fighting units in a forest fire. The generated session can be viewed as a simplified version of the work task in the studied military system reflected in a forest-fire extinguishing domain.

In the C³FIRE simulation there exists a *forest fire*, an environment with *houses*, different kinds of *vegetation*, *reconnaissance persons*, *and fire-fighting units*. The people who run the system are a part of a fire-fighting organization and are divided into a staff and two fire-fighting unit chiefs (see Fig. 8.1).

8.2. MICROWORLD SYSTEMS

C³FIRE can be classified as a microworld system. A microworld means that we select the important characteristics of the real system and create a small and well-controlled simulation system with these characteristics. In the field of psychology the concept of microworld is used to describe simulations that help the researchers to set a proper complexity level in their research environment (Dörner & Brehmer, 1993). The advantage of using a microworld is that the complex, dynamic and opaque characteristics that can be generated by a proper microworld represent the cognitive tasks that people encounter in real-life systems. The goal of our microworld is to achieve a well-controlled experimentation platform for our research.

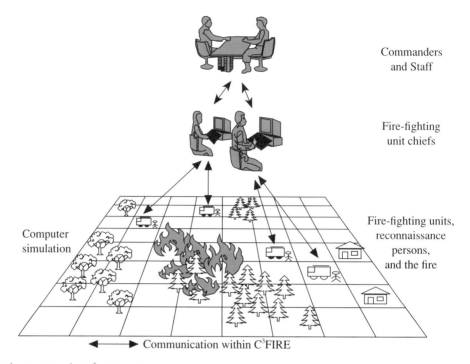

Commanders and Staff

Fire-fighting unit chiefs

Computer simulation

Fire-fighting units, reconnaissance persons, and the fire

Communication within C³FIRE

Figure 8.1. The C³FIRE environment.

As the base for our microworld we have chosen to use the D³FIRE microworld, which is an experimental system for studies of distributed decision-making in dynamic environments (Svenmarck & Brehmer, 1991, 1994). It generates a task environment in which people control fire-fighting units in a forest fire. The D³FIRE microworld is a good example of how a task environment can be generated. To adapt D³FIRE to our research, we have changed the roles of the people who run the system by introducing two explicit time-scales, and by changing the complexity of the task environment by introducing houses and different types of vegetation.

In the C³FIRE microworld we can study and train the subjects in:

- goal analysis – identifying priority among the goals, identifying sub-goals, resolving conflicting goals
- how the subjects collect and integrate information and how they form hypotheses about the hidden structure of the microworld
- how the subjects apply strategic and tactical thinking
- how the subjects make prognoses concerning the future developments in the system and define action alternatives
- avoiding common errors, for example, adopting *ad hoc* behaviour, thematic vagabonding or an encystment behaviour.

8.3. REQUIREMENTS TO BE MET BY C³FIRE

The requirements that are met by the C³FIRE experimentation environment are that it can be characterized by a dynamic context, distributed decision-making on different time scales, and that it can be used for investigation and training experimentation.

8.3.1. Dynamic context

The forest fire can be viewed as an ill-structured system which changes both auto-nomously and as a consequence of actions made on the system. This means that the forest fire is a complex dynamic autonomous system in the same sense as, for example, emer-gency target systems, air-traffic or military enemy force manouevres (Brehmer, 1994). The fire-fighting organization can also be viewed as a dynamic autonomous system, which in some degree can be controlled by the decision-makers in the organization. This view of the fire and the fire-fighting organization puts the decisions to be made in a dynamic context.

8.3.2. Distributed decision-making

The task of extinguishing the forest fire is distributed to a number of persons located as members of the staff or as fire-fighting unit chiefs. This means that these people need to co-operate to fulfil their task. The decision-making can be viewed as *team decision-making* where the members have different roles, tasks, and items of information in the decision-making process (Orasanu & Salas, 1993).

8.3.3 Time-scales

As in most hierarchical organizations, the decision-makers work on different time-scales (Brehmer, 1991). In C³FIRE the personnel work on two explicit time-scales. The fire-fighting unit chiefs are responsible for the low-level operation, such as concert fire-fighting, which is done on a short time-scale. The people in the staff work at a higher time level and are responsible for the co-ordination of the fire-fighting units and the strategic thinking.

8.3.4 Investigation and training experimentation

To be able to investigate the behaviour of the staff and the fire-fighting unit chiefs and create pedagogic and knowledge-adapted training situations for the staff, the environment and the behaviour of the computer simulation can be changed in a controllable manner. The simulations are controlled by configuration and scenario data. The configuration data include static information about positions of the houses, vegetation types, default fire speed and fire-fighting speed. The scenario data make it possible to create descriptions over time that describe the simulated actor's behaviour, and the weather changes. When a session is running, the C³FIRE system makes a complete log of the session, which makes it possible to make a replay of the whole session.

8.4. WORLD SIMULATION

The simulated world in C³FIRE is represented by a 20 * 20 matrix (Fig. 8.2). In the environment there can exist different kinds of vegetation, houses, fire, fire-fighting units, and reconnaissance persons. Nothing exists outside the 20 * 20 matrix and thus fire will not spread outside this area.

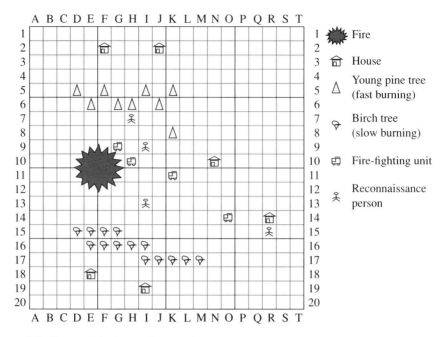

Figure 8.2. Concepts in the environment.

8.4.1. Vegetation and houses

The geographical environment in C³FIRE is built up of vegetation and houses. There exist three types of vegetation: normal tree, young pine tree (fast burning), and birch tree (slow burning). The role of the houses is to make some areas more important to save than others. This will create a complex goal situation, where the staff can decide to protect some houses or some large forest area. In a session the fire-extinguishing organization is supposed to use the environment information in its tactical reasoning to understand which important areas to save, and where critical fast-burning forest areas are.

8.4.2. Wind

The weather in C³FIRE is represented by wind direction and wind speed. The wind model represents the phenomena that wind changes the spreading direction and spreading speed of the fire. In the C³FIRE microworld the wind can analogously vary between strong and slow. Strong wind increases the fire spreading speed in the same direction as the wind blows. Slow wind makes the fire spread slowly in all directions. If there is the same type of vegetation and a wind of constant direction and speed, the wind will blow the fire into an ellipse; the greater the wind speed, the more eccentric the ellipse will be. The wind is the same over the whole geographical environment and it is controlled by the scenario for a session.

8.4.3. Fire

The fire simulation model is based on the fire model in D³FIRE, but it has been changed so that it can handle different types of vegetation. Each position in the geographical matrix can be in one of four states: not burning, burning, closed-out, or burned-out. A non-burning position can be ignited if a burning neighbour position has burned a certain length of time. When a fire has ignited, a fire-fighting unit can extinguish the fire or the fire can burn itself out due to lack of fuel. The fire intensity is low in the beginning and at the end of the burning time, and it has the highest intensity in the middle of the burning time. This means that the fire is easier to put out before it has gained in strength. A new fire cannot be ignited at a position which has been closed out or burned out. The spreading speed and the spreading direction of the forest fire are dependent on two factors – the vegetation and the wind. The decision-makers need to know the characteristic behaviour of the fire in different types of vegetation and weather conditions to be able to perform their task in a suitable way.

8.4.4. Fire-fighting unit

The fire-fighting units are controlled by the fire-fighting unit chiefs and can move around in the environment and extinguish fire. A unit can be in five main states: doing nothing, moving, mobilizing, fire-fighting, demobilizing. It can move all over the geographical environment and it has an unlimited tank of water.

8.4.5. Reconnaissance persons

Every fire-fighting unit has one reconnaissance person who can move around the fire-fighting unit and report what they see. The reconnaissance person is a computer-simulated autonomous agent that can react to questions and commands from the fire-fighting unit chief.

8.5. FIRE-FIGHTING ORGANIZATION

C³FIRE consists of four layers of organization and can be seen as a typical hierarchical emergency organization. The layers are the emergency alarm central, the command and control staff, the fire-fighting unit chiefs and the ground units (see Fig. 8.3). The persons who run the system are located in the staff and fire-fighting unit chief levels. Besides the actors inside the emergency organization there are also computer-simulated actors outside the organization.

8.5.1 Emergency alarm centre

The top layer is a computer-simulated actor that can be viewed as an emergency alarm centre. It can send textual messages to the staff. The goal of the alarm centre is to let the staff acquire information from a position higher up in the emergency hierarchy. The alarm centre can be viewed as a task assigner.

8.5.2. Staff

Staff work strategically on a higher-order time-scale by trying to understand the current situation and predict future critical situations. The staff's work is to command and control

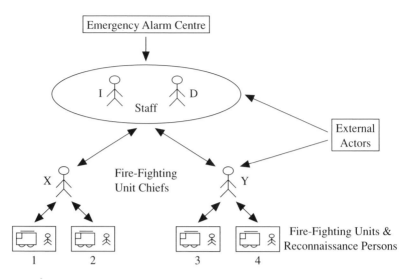

Figure 8.3. C³FIRE organization.

the fire-fighting organization. This means that they should collect information from the fire-fighting unit chiefs so that they acquire an awareness of the situation. On this basis they plan and transmit orders to the fire-fighting unit chiefs in order to direct and co-ordinate actions in the organization. The staff functions as decision-maker only and does not operate directly on the system.

The staff consists of two persons – one information handler (I) and one decision-maker (D). The *information handler* receives messages from the fire-fighting unit chiefs and is responsible for updating a map that describes the situation. He or she is also responsible for informing the decision-maker when important information arrives, and for contacting the fire-fighting unit chiefs when information is missing for building a mental picture of the situation. The *decision-maker* is responsible for strategic thinking, predicting the future, and giving orders to the fire-fighting unit chiefs, and for the organization of the whole fire-extinguishing process.

8.5.3. Fire-fighting unit chiefs

There are two fire-fighting unit chiefs, X and Y, in the system. Each chief co-ordinates two fire-fighting units and two reconnaissance persons. They use the fire-fighting unit vehicle to extinguish the fire and the reconnaissance person to acquire geographical information. The fire-fighting unit chiefs' main responsibility is to follow the commands from the staff and extinguish the fire. They are also responsible for informing the staff on what they see, do and plan to do.

8.5.4. Fire-fighting units

The *fire-fighting units* can move around in the environment and extinguish fire. The fire-fighting unit chiefs can command the fire-fighting unit to move towards some intended position. If it stands still at some position where there is a fire, it starts to extinguish the

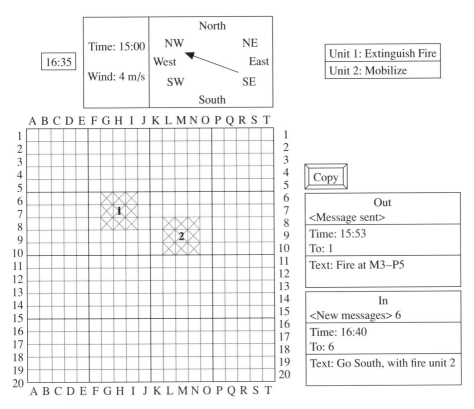

Figure 8.4. C³FIRE user interface.

fire. The fire-fighting unit position and the fire status around the unit are displayed on the fire-fighting unit chief's map (see Fig. 8.4). The fire-fighting units are controlled by mouse commands on the displayed map.

8.5.5. Reconnaissance person

The *reconnaissance person* is a computer-simulated agent that can react to questions and commands from the fire-fighting unit chief. Each reconnaissance person is connected to a fire-fighting unit and can only move in an area around the unit. The maximal distance from the unit is 5 squares. The task of the reconnaissance person is to inform the fire-fighting unit chiefs about the geographical environment. The behaviour of the reconnaissance person is controlled by a scenario that makes it possible to influence and create required training situations. The reconnaissance person can spontaneously or on command report information about the fire status, vegetation type, and house location. The fire-fighting unit chief can command the reconnaissance person to go to a certain location on the map.

The commands are:

- go to some certain position, "go to E5", "G E5"
- provide description of current position, "R info", "RI?"
- provide description of the position of the fire-fighting unit, "U info", "UI?".

Examples of messages:

- "Pos E5, fire in north"
- "Pos H6, fast-burning forest here"
- "Pos H2, house in south east".

8.5.6. External actors

The external actors are computer-simulated and scenario-controlled actors outside the hierarchical organization. They represent persons such as civilians or other organizations and can send textual messages to the staff or fire-fighting unit chiefs.

8.6. USER INTERFACE

The user interface in the C^{3}FIRE system can be separated in four parts: time and weather information, map, fire-fighting unit information, and communication interfaces (see Fig. 8.4). The fire-fighting unit information interface in the upper right square gives information on what the fire-fighting units are currently doing. The map describes the fire status around the fire-fighting units. In a session the people in the staff have the time and weather information and communication interface. The fire-fighting unit chiefs have all four information interfaces.

8.6.1. The map

The map of the C^{3}FIRE world is a 20 * 20 matrix and is used to give the fire-fighting unit chiefs a visual image of the fire in the world. One position in the matrix can be in one of four different states: notburning, burning, closed-out, or burned-out. A fire-fighting unit chief can see only the states of the squares around his or her fire-fighting units. This means that the fire-fighting unit chief sees only two 3 * 3 squares of the world.

The fire-fighting units are controlled by direct manipulation commands from the fire-fighting unit chiefs. The fire-fighting unit chiefs can command the fire-fighting unit by setting a pointer at an intended position by pointing to a position on the map with the mouse pointer. The fire-fighting unit position and the fire status around the fire-fighting unit are displayed on the fire-fighting unit chief's map.

8.6.2. The message system

The people and the computer-simulated actors use the message system to exchange textual information. The message interface consists of a send and a receive window and a copy button. The copy button is used to copy a message from the receive window to the send window.

The staff can communicate with the fire-fighting unit chiefs and receive messages from the emergency alarm centre simulation. How the staff handle the incoming messages depends on the sessions setting; it can be serial, parallel and changeable.

The *serial setting* means that the information-handling persons get all the information coming from the fire-fighting unit chiefs and that the decision-maker only gets the information from the emergency alarm centre.

The *parallel setting* means that all messages from the fire-fighting unit chiefs go to the information-handling person and to the decision-maker. Only the decision-maker gets the information from the emergency alarm centre.

In the *changeable setting* the decision-maker can decide when he or she wants to use the serial or the parallel setting.

The fire-fighting unit chiefs can communicate with the staff and the computer-simulated actors, the fire-fighting unit and the reconnaissance persons.

8.7. SESSION MANAGEMENT

When defining a C³FIRE session a large number of parameters can be used to control the settings. These parameters are contained in two separate text files – a configuration file and a scenario file. Besides the property of defining a session, the C³FIRE system creates log files that make it possible to do a replay of the sessions.

8.7.1. Configuration

The configuration file consists of the static parameters for a session and should be used to make a suitable setting for an experiment or training session. The configurations concern the properties of the geographical environment, fire, and the fire-fighting units. The following parameters can be specified.

Geographical environment: The geographical environment is defined by positions of the houses and positions of normal trees, young pine trees (fast burning), and birch trees (slow burning).

Fire: Forest fire behaviour is defined by the propagation velocity, the burn-out time, and the relation between wind and the fire propagation velocity.

Fire-fighting units: For each fire-fighting unit the configuration defines moving speed, fire-fighting time, mobilization time, demobilization time, start position, and communication facilities. The moving speed is defined in term of the number of squares moved at each time step, for example 0.5. The fire-fighting speed, mobilization and demobilization speed are defined by the number of time steps needed to perform the activity. The total time for a fire-fighting activity at a certain position is the sum of the mobilization, fire-fighting, and demobilization time.

A small change in some of the parameters that control the fire or the fire-fighting unit's behaviour can result in a large change in the dynamic behaviour of the whole system. It is important to verify the dynamic behaviour of the system with some complete game sessions after changes have been made to these critical parameters.

8.7.2. Scenario

The scenario describes the dynamic characteristics of the session settings. It consists of events that will affect the session at some specified time. The events can be separated into two categories: the events that affect the behaviour of the fire, and the events that affect the computer-simulated actors. The following events can be specified.

Fire: Start positions for new fires.

Wind: Wind speed and direction.

Static messages: Textual messages that will be sent from some reconnaissance person or some external actor outside the fire-fighting organization at some specified time.

Behaviour of reconnaissance person: The behaviour of each computer-simulated reconnaissance person can be manipulated by changing two parameters – the information-load parameter and the message-error parameter. The *information-load parameter* defines the number of spontaneous messages sent from the reconnaissance persons. With this parameter the system can change the information load for the fire-fighting unit chiefs. The *message-error parameter* defines the truth value of the messages. With this parameter the reconnaissance person can send a message with some special type of error to the fire-fighting unit chiefs. A message error can be specified for the vegetation, house or fire, and the error can be specified to change "exist" to "does not exist" or "does not exist" to "exist", for example "Time 23:45, reconnaissance person number one will see a non-existing fire" or "Time 14:52, reconnaissance person number three will not see the next visible house".

Scripts: In the current version of C³FIRE there are some hard-coded scripts that can be activated by a scenario event. The script is a procedural event description that works in combination with the simulation and reacts to the activity of the fire-fighting units and reconnaissance persons. The script activates canned text messages that will be sent from some simulated actor if some special event sequence occurs. Scripts can be used to activate a certain pedagogically-defined sequence of activities or instructions. An example of a hard-coded script is as follows: If no reconnaissance unit has been in a specific critical area, then we know that the staff has no knowledge about it. They should have asked for this information if they had responded appropriately to the situation. So we can now give the staff some hints that hopefully will attract their attention to this area. This can be done by a message from a farmer. If the staff after some time have still not asked for any information about the area, then we can help them by providing some help information. This script is an example of a script that contains two basic parts: one is a description of a certain correct way to work; two contains the proper instructions if this correct way to work is violated.

8.7.3. Replay

All important events during a session are stored in a log file. All communications, positions, activities, and intentions that can be registered are recorded. The stored information is detailed enough for a play-back of the whole session. This replay function should be used in the debriefing phase after a session. The information shown in a replay is time, map with fire status, weather, and the messages received by the staff members, fire-fighting units, and the reconnaissance persons. Fig. 8.5 shows a replay window from a session where the fire started at F10 with fast burning forest in the north. Fire-fighting units one to four are displayed on the map.

8.8. REFERENCES

BREHMER, B. (1991). Distributed decision making: some notes on the literature. In J. RASMUSSEN, B. BREHMER & J. LEPLAT (Eds), *Distributed Decision Making: Cognitive Models for Co-operative Work.* New York: John Wiley & Sons, 319–334.

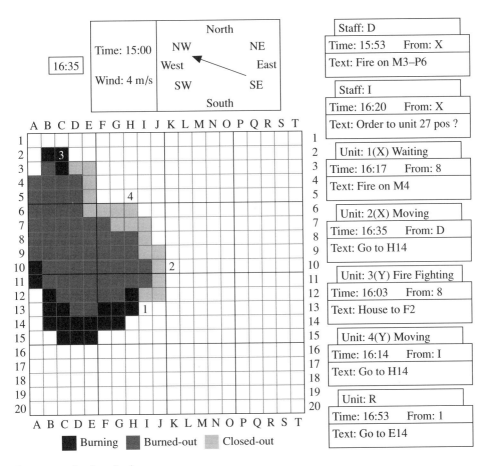

Figure 8.5. Replay display.

BREHMER, B. (1994). *Distributed decision making in dynamic environments.* Uppsala University, Sweden, Foa report.

DÖRNER, D., BREHMER, B. (1993). Experiments with computer-simulated microworlds: escaping both the narrow straits of the laboratory and the deep blue sea of the field study. *Computers in Human Behavior*, vol. 9. 171–184.

ORASANU, J. & SALAS, E. (1993). Team decision making in complex environments. In G. KLEIN, J. ORASANU, R. CALDEWOOD & C.E. ZAMBOK (Eds) *Decision Making in Action: Models and Methods.* Norwood, NJ: Ablex.

SVENMARCK, P. & BREHMER, B. (1991). D³FIRE: An experimental paradigm for the studies of distributed decision making. In B. BREHMER (Ed.) *Distributed Decision Making*, Proceedings of the third MOHAWC workshop. Roskilde: Risö National Library.

SVENMARCK, P. & BREHMER, B. (1994). *D³FIRE – an experimental paradigm for the study of distributed decision making.* Nutek-report, Uppsala University.

CHAPTER NINE

Visualized co-ordination support in distributed decision-making

PETER SVENMARCK

9.1. INTRODUCTION

This chapter is concerned with support of the communication of intentions, as this information is important for individuals co-ordinating locally. A visual communication of intentions was attempted by visualizing the behaviour of actors on a dynamic blackboard shown to all participants. The experiment was inspired by results in social perception, where subjects perceived intentions directly from body movement. The blackboard was implemented in D^3FIRE, a general paradigm for studying distributed decision-making where a group of four subjects are charged with the task of fighting a simulated forest fire and compared with individuals communicating only by electronic written messages. Contrary to expectations, performance decreased when the blackboard was used. There was, however, a significant decrease in the frequency of communicated intentions since this information was present on the blackboard. Some possible explanations are discussed. First, the design of the blackboard where the location of the units is always visible might explain the reduction in communication of important information about the progress of the fire-fighting and this could result in overconfidence in the control of the fire. Second, just presenting behaviour could be insufficient for visualizing the processing involved in fire-fighting. More factors, such as the wind direction and the location of the fire-fighting units in relation to the fire, could be required for an unambiguous perception of what the subjects are doing.

9.2. BACKGROUND

The issue of how to achieve successful co-ordination among individuals in a complex dynamic system is a pressing concern in many modern tasks, for example, process industries (Daele, 1993), military systems (Brehmer, 1988), and air traffic control. In these tasks the situation continually changes and it is impossible to make a complete prediction of all situations that might occur. Therefore, overall plans for how and when to act will be valid only at a general level. There are at least two different forms of uncertainties.

Proper co-ordination requires individuals to assess which type of situation they are facing, and even then the process evolution might not be completely known. Further, to cope with the complexity of the situation individuals must co-operate. Co-ordination and adaptation to the demands of the situation are required on the basis of only the individual and partial models of the task (Brehmer, 1988). Models can be focused on either special aspects of the task where information about the system is directly available, or more general, but less detailed, factors. A single model of all aspects of a situation can, however, never be formulated due partly to complexity and partly to unpredictability.

Traditionally, the problem of co-ordination is addressed with a hierarchical organiza-tion where the different levels are formally responsible for monitoring the relevant time scales (Brehmer, 1991). Consider for example the task of fighting a forest fire. Due to the time delay in moving fire-fighting units, it is necessary to consider both the rapid local development of fires and the development of the fire as a whole over larger areas where the size of the areas corresponds to the time delay in moving fire-fighting units over longer distances. Thus, in this task there are at least two time-scales, one slow overall time-scale where decisions are made regarding fire-fighting in large and general areas, and a rapid local time-scale where decisions are made regarding specific areas to attack. Without prediction of the slower overall development of the fire, the efforts spent on local fire-fighting may be directed to locations where it does not contribute to stopping the fire as a whole. Thus, there is a hierarchical relationship between time-scales, where decisions concerning the slower time-scale have precedence over decisions in the rapid time-scale. Further, it is important to consider how to obtain the necessary information for decisions in these time-scales. Information for the local fire-fighting is normally dir-ectly available to the fire chiefs, but fighting the fire at the appropriate location requires an overall assessment of how the fire develops, and in a hierarchical organization there is an increased possibility that this assessment is available in at least one decision-maker by centralizing the communication at one place. Without this information performance is hampered, since the overall assessment of the fire development is incomplete (Brehmer & Svenmarck, 1995).

However, in their experiment Brehmer & Svenmarck (1995) also noted that groups which co-ordinated only locally reached a reasonable performance level, despite there being no central collection of information. Instead, these groups used a form of co-ordination based on intentions. The rationale for intentions is that co-ordination of beha-viour takes time and it is therefore necessary to predict the behaviour of the other decision-makers using some information other than their current activities. If the co-ordination is based on information about their current activities, there is always a risk of being late since the activities might have changed by the time the co-ordination is completed. The time delay until the others' intentions become their current activities can only be handled with information about their intentions. For example, in fire-fighting the co-ordination of efforts takes time due to the time delay in moving fire-fighting units. Co-ordination based on information about the other unit's current area under attack will be of little use if the unit the fire chief attempts to co-ordinate with has moved to some other location when the co-ordination is completed. If the fire chief instead has informa-tion about the intention of the other fire chief, there are better possibilities for successful co-ordination, since the time delay to move the fire-fighting unit is compensated for by information for prediction of the expected future state when the units are in place.

Some means of communicating intentions is probably important for successful local co-ordination. In the experiment by Brehmer & Svenmarck (1995), intentions were com-municated verbally using electronic messages. This form of communication is, however, sensitive to time pressure (Serfaty *et al.*, 1994) and mental load, and it is therefore important to consider other non-verbal modes of communication. Results by Runeson & Frykholm (1983) indicate such an alternative where only a minimum amount of information about a person's movement was sufficient for *direct perception* of the person's intention. In their experiment, actors were video-taped while performing various activities, for example lifting a box with sufficient weight for a marked effort by the actor to lift the box. Strips of retro-reflectant tape were attached to the actor's knees, elbows etc., and with appropriate contrast and brightness settings during replay, the strips looked like bright patches against a dark background. When shown as snapshots these patches give very little information about what is being performed, but when moving as normal there is no ambiguity. The patch-lights give only direct information about the kinematics of the actor, and nothing about the dynamic characteristics such as facial expressions. The subjects' task in the experiment was to estimate the actual weight of the box by only watching the lead-in movement of the actor before the actual lifting of the box. This was sufficient for the subjects to give very accurate estimates of the actual weight of the box, despite nothing being shown about the effort to actually lift the box. The intention of the actor to lift the box produced distinct predispositions of the actor's knees and elbows that were perceivable in the movement of the patch-lights. And the joint behaviour of these patch-lights specified the intention to lift the box, sufficiently for the subjects to perceive different behaviours as different intentions that corresponded to the actual weight of the box. The kinematic pattern of the actor's preadjustment was sufficient for perceiving his intention.

These results can be explained with a general principle – kinematic specification of dynamics (KSD). *Dynamics* are the causal underlying factors that determine the kinematic pattern, and this principle explains how and when these factors are specified in the behaviour, *kinematics*, of any system, both linear and non-linear. When an individual is engaged in a sufficiently complex activity in a system with many degrees of freedom, the dynamic properties and characteristics of the individual (for example, activity, intention, and gender) will produce a distinct behaviour, and are thus in principle perceivable as invariants in the kinematic pattern. In the experiment by Runeson & Frykholm (1983), the intention to lift the box produced a distinct behaviour well-correlated to the actual weight of the box, and was thus perceivable. Similar results were obtained in linear collisions where the kinematics specify the weight of the objects relative to each other and the damping caused by material decomposition (Runeson, 1977). These higher order properties are cospecified, since they simultaneously influence the behaviour. However, generally an intention is a very complex mental state and is not specified entirely in behaviour only (Vedler, 1993). Further, there is no empirical evidence of the principle's validity for non-linear systems in general.

Finally, studies using animated film techniques have shown the importance of motion as a basis for social perception (Kassin, 1982). The classic study using this technique is the experiment by Heider & Simmel (1944). In their experiment subjects watched a short film where a small triangle, a large triangle, and a circle moved along various paths at various speeds. When asked about what they had seen, all except one of the subjects described the film in anthropomorphic terms. Commonly, the film was described as a scenario where a large male bully (the large triangle) had a fight with an other male (the small triangle) and then chased a woman (the circle) until the other male helped her to escape. The movement of the objects is the main information for perceiving the film as a scenario, rather than their structure (Berry *et al.*, 1992). When the resolution of the film was reduced to only blocks of information that completely disrupted the structure of the objects, three of four still described the film in anthropomorphic terms, but when the movement was disrupted in a film with snapshots, only one-third described what they had seen in anthropomorphic terms. To perceive self-generated movement and social characteristics in abstract information as these films is a basic ability, or one that is learned early. In a way similar to adults, children as young as four years old described the film in anthropomorphic terms, although the average proportion was less than for adults (Berry & Springer, 1993).

9.2.1. Objective

This experiment attempted to communicate intentions in distributed decision-making by visualizing information about movement in a non-linear system on a dynamic blackboard that was displayed simultaneously to all subjects. If this movement was vigorous enough to produce a distinct behaviour for all higher-order properties of the subjects, then, according to the principle of KSD, the higher order properties of the subjects could be perceived directly without any verbal formulation, for example of their intentions. The objective of the experiment was to test the hypothesis that intentions of subjects can be directly perceived in their movement, and this non-verbal mode of communicating intentions would be superior to a verbal mode. Since intentions are important for the co-ordination of groups which co-ordinate only locally, performance should increase for groups given this visualization of movement as compared to groups without this decision support.

9.3. METHOD

9.3.1. Subjects

Thirty-two undergraduate students participated in the experiment, and they received general instructions and opportunity for practice. The subjects were randomly assigned to subgroups, with four subjects in each group, and experimental condition. Thus, there was a total of eight quartets, with four in each condition. They came on two occasions and worked two hours each time. They were paid about 50 USD for their participation.

9.3.2. Experimental task

The subjects' task was to fight simulated forest fires in D³FIRE, a general experimental paradigm for the study of distributed decision-making in dynamic systems (Svenmarck & Brehmer, 1991). In this paradigm, distributed decision-making is defined as the co-operation of decision-makers towards a common goal, but where each decision-maker has only a limited view of the overall task (Brehmer, 1991). Fig. 9.1 provides an overview of the task. D³FIRE has many similarities with earlier paradigms for the study of individual dynamic decision-making (DESSY, Brehmer & Allard (1991), and NEWFIRE, Løvborg & Brehmer (1991)).

The definition of distributed decision-making influenced the task in two ways. First, each subject controlled only one unit and not all as in the individual paradigms of dynamic decision-making. Second, they received information on where the fire was only

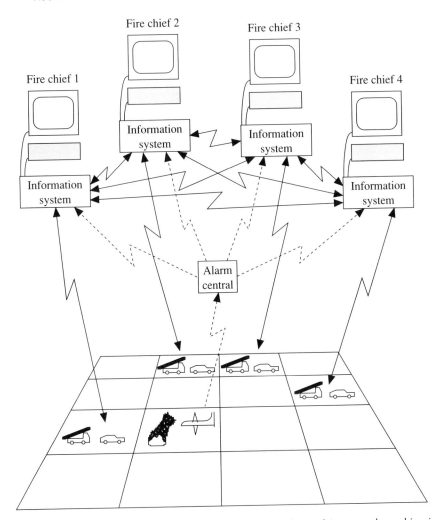

Figure 9.1. The general characteristics of D³FIRE. There are four subjects, each working in front of his or her own terminal. An alarm central informs the subjects where the fire starts, and to stop the fire, subjects communicate to co-ordinate their efforts and direct their fire-fighting to appropriate locations.

through a limited window on their terminal. Fig. 9.2 shows the layout of the subjects' computer screen. The area map was displayed on a grid of 20 × 20 cells where subjects could see a window of 3 × 3 cells. The cover story for this limitation was the restricted range of the transmission for the communication equipment utilized by the unit's fire scouts. The scouts were placed around the unit to report any fires, and since there were only eight scouts, the subjects could see only a 3 × 3 window of the fire where the subjects' unit was always located in the middle. This window offered only information on a local time-scale. The only command the subjects could issue to their unit was an order where to go, and they did this by clicking on the destination on the screen. The unit always took the shortest route and the scouts followed automatically. When the unit arrived at the destination it started to fight any fire automatically. The speed of the units was one cell step per time unit, in this case 30 seconds.

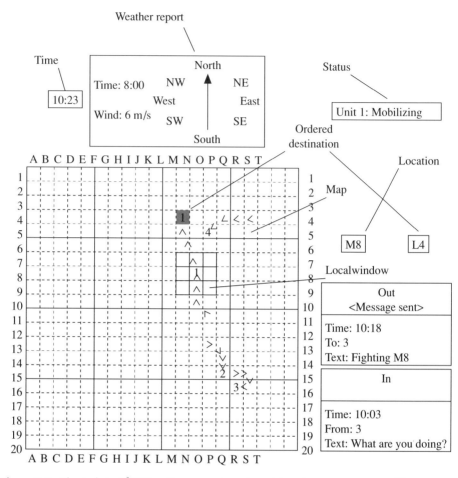

Figure 9.2. The task in D³FIRE as it appeared on the subjects' computer screen. The map was displayed on a grid of 20 × 20 cells. Subject could observe the fire only through a local window of 3 × 3 cells. The visualization of movement was displayed only in the blackboard condition. Subjects without a blackboard could only see the location of the others when they were within the nine cells covered by the local window.

To co-operate and co-ordinate their efforts, the subjects communicated by electronic mail using the two boxes to the right. To send a message, the subjects simply clicked on the "Out" box and typed the number of the receiver and the message on the two rows available. When a message arrived, the subject was notified with a beep and a blinking text in the reception box. Messages were stored in the order of their arrival, and to see the next message the subjects just clicked on the "In" box. The communication with electronic mail was independent of the updating of the map. In both conditions in this experiment subjects communicated freely with one another in a fully-connected architecture.

There were two experimental conditions, one where all subjects in the groups utilized visualized information about movement of fire-fighting units in the forest on a common dynamic blackboard, and one where subjects did not receive any special support for co-ordination. In the blackboard condition information about movements was visualized by small trains of arrows moving at 1 cm/s at a 15 Hz refresh rate along a B-Spline path with 3 control points over the four latest positions and the ordered destination (Pärletun *et al.*, 1989). The spline function was adapted to calculate the tangent direction and a constant three-quarters of a cell-width distance between arrows. This visualized information of the movement of all units was displayed simultaneously to all subjects on their terminals. The cover story for the movement of arrows over positions and destinations was that the units were connected to the satellite navigation system GPS (General Positioning System). This system stored all information about destinations and positions, and the subjects were informed directly about changes in locations and orders to units. No special explanation was given for the movement of arrows, other than that they moved over positions and destinations.

The quartet's goal was to fight the fire with a minimum loss of squares. An experimental trial ended when the fire had been put out or when the maximum time of 50 minutes was reached. The fire scenarios were selected to be difficult enough to require co-ordination of all units. Thus, there was always one fire centre starting at the middle of a map border around any of the four areas A10, J1, T10 and J20, with a rather strong wind, in this case 6 m/s towards the centre of the map. The units always started in separate corners of the map. After 8 minutes there was a 90° wind change, and after 16 minutes it started to rain, which slowed down the fire considerably, and there was no wind. When a fire initially started the subjects were informed about the fire location from an alarm centre. This was necessary since it would have taken too long to find the fire by unplanned search. It took four updates to fight a fire and the fighting could not be interrupted after it had started. Finally, it took five updates for the fire to spread from one cell to the next in the wind direction.

9.3.3. Design

As mentioned above, the experiment was designed to compare quartets utilizing decision support for local co-ordination with quartets without any special support. In both conditions, the quartets received three trials. Thus the design of the experiment was a 2 (blackboard versus no blackboard) by 3 (trials) design with repeated measures of the second factor.

9.3.4. Procedure

All quartets were informed about the general nature of the task, how to fight fires and communicate, and which type of fires they would face (possible fire centres and wind changes). They were instructed to fight the fire with a minimum loss of cells, but the details of how to perform this was left to the subjects to decide. They received two training fires of about 30 minutes each and then the three trials. They performed one of these trials the first day and two the second day.

9.4. RESULTS

Several dependent variables were derived from the data that D³FIRE registers on a trial. In this experiment three of these were analyzed: the number of cells lost to fire (as it was the subjects' main goal to save forest), the frequency of messages, and the different types of messages the subjects sent to each other.

9.4.1. Number of cells lost to fire

Table 9.1 gives the result of an analysis of variance (ANOVA) for the number of cells lost to fire. Although the probability of a significant main effect is above the conventional .05 significance level, performance is in fact most likely reduced for groups using a blackboard. As can be seen in Fig. 9.3 groups using a blackboard performed worse on all trials, especially their first trial, than groups without. Since there are only four groups in each condition, the difference is too large to be ignored. In both conditions the groups improved over time as shown by a trials effect ($F\ 2/12 = 14.7$, $p < .01$).

Table 9.1. The results of an ANOVA for the number of cells lost to fire

	df effect	MS effect	df error	MS error	F	p-level
Support	1	1232.67	6	241.42	5.11	.067
Trials	2	4138.04	12	281.54	14.7	.001
Support and trials	2	460.04	12	281.54	1.63	.236

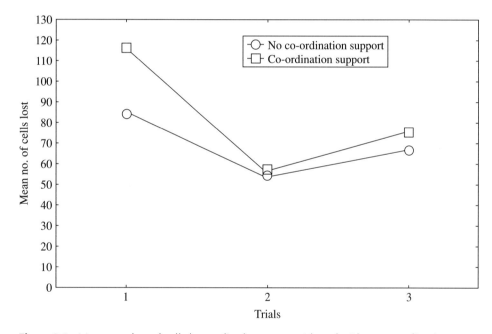

Figure 9.3. Mean number of cells lost to fire for groups with and without co-ordination support over trials.

9.4.2. Frequency of messages

Since the time to fight a fire varied from trial to trial depending on the group's performance, the number of messages sent was normalized by computing the frequency of messages sent per minute in each trial. Table 9.2 gives the result of an ANOVA for the frequency of messages. Groups with a blackboard sent about 1 message fewer per minute than groups without a blackboard, 4.9 messages per minute compared to 6.2, but the difference was not significant. This is surprising since the information on the blackboard, about the others' current location and destination, normally comprises about 40% of the communication. Neither was there any significant change in the frequency of messages over time.

Table 9.2. Results of an ANOVA for the frequency of messages

	df effect	MS effect	df error	MS error	F	p-level
Support	1	9.733	6	5.155	1.888	.219
Trials	2	1.877	12	.487	3.859	.051
Support and trials	2	.141	12	.487	.290	.753

9.4.3. Message types

To analyze the communication in more detail, the messages sent by each subject were classified into 15 categories. The categories were the same as in previous experiments with D^3FIRE, and were selected since they were theoretically relevant and covered most of the messages sent. No difficulties were encountered in categorizing the messages since they were mostly short and to the point. The following categories were used.

Communication concerning strategy (S)
Questions

- questions about some other subject's intentions (QI)
- questions about the location of the fire (QE)
- questions about some other subject's activity (QA)
- questions about some other subject's location (QL)

Information

- information about intentions (II)
- information about fire (IE)
- information about one's own activity (IA)
- information about one's own location (IL)

Commands (C)
Requests for clear command (RC)
Offers of help (OH)
Requests for help (RH)
Acknowledgements (A)
Miscellaneous (M)

Messages concerning strategy involved the implementation of some strategy or suggestions concerning some possible strategy. The "Miscellaneous" category comprised mainly social chit-chat. The "Commands" category contained all cases when the subject told or suggested to the recipient to move to some specified location and extinguish any fire in that location. Questions about intentions concerned what the recipient planned to do, or where he/she planned to go. Questions about location involved the current location of the recipient, and questions about activity addressed the current activity of the recipient. The information items were either responses to these questions or spontaneous information, usually concerning intentions.

In this experiment the most interesting of these categories were QI, QE, QL, QA, II, IE, IL, IA, and C, since they dealt with the fire-fighting activity and they comprised most of the messages. The analyses below of frequency per minute, and the percentage of categories, were therefore limited to these. When computing the percentages, the "Miscellaneous" category was excluded since it did not deal with fire-fighting activity. It comprised about 6% of the communication in both conditions.

9.4.3.1. Frequency of categories

Table 9.3 gives the mean frequency of message categories sent per minute and subject. As in previous experiments, groups which co-ordinated locally sent many messages with information about intentions (II). Subjects using a blackboard sent significantly fewer messages with information about intentions (II) and locations (IL), since this information was present on the blackboard. The difference was significant for both II (F 1/6 = 35.8, $p < .001$), and IL (F 1/6 = 37.6, $p < .001$). The remaining information about intentions (II) for subjects using a blackboard mainly concerned general directions such as upwards, downwards, etc. There was a significantly higher frequency of QE (F 1/6 = 7.65, $p < .05$) for subjects using a blackboard since they seemed to be more concerned with where the fire was heading than groups without support. Finally, subjects using a blackboard sent significantly fewer QL (F 1/6 = 6.18, $p < .05$) and IA (F 1/6 = 9.43, $p < .05$).

Table 9.3. Mean number of messages sent per minute in the respective categories by the average subject in groups with and without co-ordination support

Category	Frequency per minute	
	Without co-ordination support	With co-ordination support
Commands (C)	.103	.117
Questions about activity (QA)	.003	.008
Questions about fire (QE)[*]	.154	.264
Questions about intention (QI)	.022	.023
Questions about location (QL)[*]	.063	.001
Information about activity (IA)[*]	.201	.041
Information about fire (IE)	.423	.503
Information about intention (II)[†]	.666	.131
Information about location (IL)[†]	.096	.002

[*] Significant at $p < .05$.
[†] Significant at $p < .001$.

9.4.3.2. Percentage of categories

The differences in assessment of the fire's behaviour are clearer in the percentage of messages sent with questions and information about fire location. Subjects using a black-board spent a larger part of their messages on the assessment of where the fire was head-ing than groups without. The differences in percentage of both QE (22% compared to 9% for subjects without a blackboard) (F 1/6 = 38.7, $p < .005$) and IE (41% compared to 22% for subjects without a blackboard) (F 1/6 = 16.5, $p < .01$) are significant. However, the frequencies are too small for an overall awareness of where the fire was heading.

Correlations between categories and the number of cells lost to fire. To investigate any direct relationship between the frequency of message categories and the number of cells lost to fire, the correlations were analyzed. No correlations were significant, either with or without a blackboard.

9.5. DISCUSSION

Contrary to expectations, the information on the blackboard did not improve perform-ance. There is a reduction in frequency of information about intentions and locations in groups using a blackboard, since this information is directly available to these groups. But the reduced demand on communication resources was not used for a better awareness of where the fire was heading, or a better local prediction of the spread of the fire.

One possible explanation for the reduced performance is that groups with a blackboard were led into a false sense of control of the fire propagation and neglected to commun-icate important information. Although they were more concerned with where the fire was heading than groups without a blackboard, they actually communicated much less about which cell they were fighting at the moment and the progress of the fire-fighting. In groups without a blackboard there was a message concerned with current activity (IA) about once a minute, but in groups using a blackboard only once every fifth minute. This reduced frequency can be explained by the design of the blackboard. Since they always saw the other units' current location, it was possible to derive when a fire had been put out by observing the delay for a unit to move from one cell to the next. But this implicit form of communicating current activity could result in overconfidence about the control of the fire. With the high demands on attention it is probably difficult to remember exactly how long each unit has stayed at the current location, and this could result in the assumption that the fire is under control in that area. A reduced awareness of the current progress of the fire-fighting could result in overly optimistic decisions about which cell to fight next. Instead of supporting each other, subjects might continue with the local fire-fighting and this would reduce performance. After the first trial, the awareness of the progress of the fire fighting seems to improve. Since the performance is worse in all trials with the blackboard, the awareness of the progress of the fire fighting might never have been the same as for groups without co-ordination support, however.

Further, the subjects' confidence in the co-ordination was the same in both conditions since the frequency for questions about intentions (QI) was nearly the same both with and without a blackboard: they both sent a message about once every ten minutes. If the blackboard had been considered useful, questions about intentions would have been reduced. There are several possible explanations for why the blackboard was not useful. First, the lack of specific instructions about the movement could have increased the confusion about the actual usefulness of the information on the blackboard. The constant loss of control of the fire during the first trial for groups using a blackboard may have caused distrust in the usefulness of the information provided. As discussed below, it is quite difficult to perceive what the other subjects are actually doing from the information on the blackboard about their behaviour. Second, the visualization with arrows could be too complicated to be useful to the subjects. Third, the movement on the blackboard might not be vigorous enough to reveal the underlying information. This is related to both the resolution of the map in D³FIRE (20 × 20 cells) and the time period between updates (30 seconds). The visualized motion in a system with these degrees of freedom could be too slow and indistinct for accurate perception of intentions.

A more interesting question is whether the factors in the visualization, earlier locations and current destination are sufficient for generalizing the principle of KSD to D³FIRE. In the case of social perception, the intention to lift the box sets off a complex interaction of motion centres to compensate for the dynamics of the body and maintain the balance when the weight of the box is applied to the actor. This is very active behaviour where the properties of the actor, length, strength, and so on are combined with the weight of the box to produce a controlled response. During our evolutionary history we have been equipped with a highly skilled perception mechanism to integrate and perceive the meaning of this complex movement of other actors, since it has a functional value to us. To directly perceive whether the other is a friend or a foe is crucial to survival. In the present visualization in D³FIRE, however, there is not much visual information that shows how the other subjects are trying to fight a forest fire. There is a confused pattern as the subjects try to cope with the time constants of the fire, and an even more confused pattern if the subjects have totally lost track of where the fire is heading. How the subject tries to handle the time constants in relation to the wind, the current location of the fire, and the location and intentions of the other subjects is not integrated in the visualization. The factors currently included could simply be insufficient to show that there is fire-fighting going on and nothing else. A better integration of the cues in the simulation and their relationships could be necessary for a visualization to give enough information about the intentions subjects formulate to cope with the fire. Further, separate visualizations in the relevant time-scales could be required for a perception of how the fire will develop. At present only local information is visualized, and nothing in the longer time-scale that could be similar to what the central subject in a hierarchical architecture perceives of the fire's behaviour.

Finally, perception of higher-order invariants in general non-linear systems where we cannot rely on our evolutionary history could require inferences concerning intentions based on more information about the causes of the behaviour. This is the idea behind implicit co-ordination. When time pressure is high, co-ordination is more implicit and based on prediction of the others' behaviour from knowledge about their situation (Serfaty et al., 1994). There are some serious difficulties with this form of co-ordination. To succeed in predicting behaviour, the subject must know the others' model of the task and the situation they currently face, and this is normally very difficult in a dynamic task with limited communication resources. In some situations this is the only alternative, however. In the case of D³FIRE more direct information about the movement of the fire subject's face could be required to reduce ambiguities about intentions.

However, the possibility that higher-order properties, such as intentions, could be perceived directly with appropriate visualization of changes in system variables is an interesting approach to support control of dynamic systems which should be investigated further.

Currently, our methods of analysis are too general to verify the explanation proposed above that the reduced performance for groups with a blackboard is caused by differences in communication about the current activity, while the co-ordination of the units is the same in both conditions. Co-ordination can only be evaluated on a moment-to-moment basis and there are other factors that contribute to the number of cells lost to fire. First, the efficiency of the subjects in stopping the fire locally varies between individuals. Anything from a careful model of the time constants to constantly being too late is possible. Second, the amount of communication varies. In this experiment, the frequency of information about fire (IE) varied from one to three messages per minute for groups with a blackboard. Third, even if two groups have the same information about where the fire is heading, there might be different solutions to the problem of co-ordination. New methods are needed to measure these factors separately. This problem could probably be solved if there were some model available for how the fire propagates over larger areas when subjects are trying to fight the fire. The simulation models the lowest level of how an individual cell is put out, but no higher level, not even an area that corresponds to what the subjects see in their local window. Such a model would, of course, require a different form of representation of the fire than in the simulation where the spread from individual cells is modelled as known ignition times (Svenmarck & Brehmer, 1991). With a more general classification that measures different tactical configurations, and where the hierarchical relationships between areas of different sizes and the corresponding time-scales are modelled, then both the local fire-fighting and the co-ordination of units in the overall time-scale could be measured as the delay in the spread of the fire compared to an uncontrolled fire. Which form of representation is most suitable is an open question at the moment, but the concepts from hierarchically iterated function systems could provide a framework (Haeseler *et al.*, 1995). With such a model, the explanation above could be verified by comparing the average local and overall delay in the fire propagation for groups with and without a blackboard. A possible model for the assumed reduction in awareness about the progress of the fire-fighting is to consider a fire in a cell to be under control if there is a fire-fighting unit there. The overall delay of the fire should then be similar for both conditions. By comparing the delays of the fire propagation in the different time-scales it would also be possible to examine whether the improvement over time is due to improved local efficiency or better co-ordination.

9.6. ACKNOWLEDGEMENTS

This research was supported by a grant from the Swedish Council for Research in the Humanities and Social Science. The author is grateful to Yvonne Wærn, Berndt Brehmer, Martin Helander, and Norman Geddes for insightful comments on a previous version of this work. The experiment was based on Berndt's ideas and would never have been done without his supervision and strong interest in distributed decision-making.

9.7. REFERENCES

BERRY, D.S., MISOVISCH, S.J., KEAN, K.J. and BARON, R.M. (1992). Effects of disruption of structure and motion on perceptions of social causality. *Personality and Social Psychology Bulletin*, vol. 18, No. 2, 237–244.

BERRY, D.S. and SPRINGER, K. (1993). Structure, motion and preschoolers' perceptions of social causality. *Ecological Psychology*, vol. 5, No. 4, 273–283.

BREHMER, B. (1988). Organization for decision making in complex systems. In L.P. GOODSTEIN, H.B. ANDERSEN & S.E. OLSEN (Eds), *Tasks, Errors, and Mental Models*. London: Taylor & Francis.

BREHMER, B. (1991). Modern information technology, time scales and distributed decision making. In J. RASMUSSEN, B. BREHMER & J. LEPLAT (Eds), *Distributed Decision Making: Cognitive Models for Co-operative Work*. Chichester: Wiley.

BREHMER, B. & ALLARD, R. (1991). Dynamic decision making: the effects of task complexity and feedback delay. In J. RASMUSSEN, B. BREHMER & J. LEPLAT (Eds), *Distributed Decision Making: Cognitive Models for Co-operative Work*. Chichester: Wiley.

BREHMER, B. & SVENMARCK P. (1995). Distributed decision making in dynamic environments: time scales and architecture of decision making. In J.-P. CAVERNI, M. BAR-HILLEL, F.H. BARRON & H. JUNGERMANN (Eds), *Contributions to Decision Making*. Amsterdam: Elsevier Science.

DAELE, A. (1993). Coping with complexity in process control: the effects of co-operation. In *Proceedings IEEE Systems, Man, and Cybernetics 1993*.

HAESELER, F., PEITIGEN, H.-O. & SKORDEV, G. (1995). Global analysis of cellular automata: selected examples. *Physica D*, vol. 86, 64–80.

HEIDER, F. & SIMMEL, M. (1944). An experimental study of apparent behavior. *American Journal of Psychology*, vol. 57, 243–259.

KASSIN, S.M. (1981). Heider and Simmel revisited: causal attribution and the animated film technique. *Review of Personality and Social Psychology*, vol. 3, 145–170.

LØVBORG, L. & BREHMER, B. (1991). *NEWFIRE. A flexible system for running simulated fire fighting experiments*. Roskilde: Risö National Laboratory Report M-2953.

PÄRLETUN, L.G., HANSSON, P. & KARLSSON, G. (1989). *Datorgrafik och CAD-teknik*, Lund, Sweden: Stundentlitteratur.

RUNESON, S. (1977). *On visual perception of dynamic events*, Doctoral dissertation. (Uppsala, Sweden: Department of Psychology).

RUNESON, S. & FRYKHOLM, G. (1983). Kinematic specification of dynamics as an informal basis for person and action perception: expectation, gender recognition, and deceptive intention. *Journal of Experimental Psychology: General*, vol. 112, No. 4, 585–615.

SERFATY, D., ENTIN, E.E. & DECKERT, J.C. (1994). Implicit co-ordination in command teams. In A.H. LEVIS and I.S. LEVIS (Eds), *Science of Command and Control: Part II/Coping with Change*. Fairfax, VA: AFCEA International Press.

SVENMARCK, P., & BREHMER, B., 1991, D³FIRE, an experimental paradigm for the study of distributed decision making. In B. BREHMER (Ed.), *Distributed Decision Making*, Proceedings of the Third MOHAWC Workshop, Belgirate, Italy, 15–17 May 1991. Roskilde: Risö National Laboratory.

VEDLER, D. (1993). Intentionality as a basis for the emergence of intersubjectivity in infancy. Acta Univ. Ups., *Comprehensive Summaries of Uppsala Dissertations from the Faculty of Social Sciences*, vol. 37. Uppsala, Sweden: Department of Psychology.

CHAPTER TEN

Co-operation and situation awareness within and between time-scales in dynamic decision-making

HENRIK ARTMAN

10.1. BACKGROUND

Modern organizations which are handling dynamic complex situations are typically distributed geographically and knowledge-wise. It is very important for researchers and organizations to understand how different communication architectures affect the process and outcome of controlling dynamic systems. On the one hand different communication structures and organizational arrangements can affect the process of co-operation between different distributed units; on the other hand co-operation and situation awareness within a command team may be affected.

In their investigation of different ways of handling large dynamic environments, Brehmer & Svenmarck (1995) have shown that a hierarchical organizational arrangement leads to better performance than in all-connected organizations, where all participants can talk to all. One reason for this is that much information is centralized in the hierarchical organization, and the central person who has this pool of information is able to produce an image of the global environment, a so-called second time-scale, rather than just having the limited local view. In their experiments the higher ranking subject has the task of organizing his own units at an operative level as well as co-ordinating other units with a common goal, which requires the co-ordinator to work on two time-scales at the same time. Such double work, of course, poses greater attentional demand than a single time-scale as it requires both an understanding of how the event develops locally and the ability to hypothesize about the global development. In real situations such as emergency co-ordination centres, military command and control (see chapter 5 of this volume) and underground control (Heath & Luff, 1992), the co-ordinating team often works exclusively on one time-scale, and distributes goals and information to higher or lower levels in the hierarchical web, who are then able to consider other time-scales. The present experiment uses a microworld set-up, based on Brehmer's microworld but where the organization is clearly separated between time-scales. We wanted this experiment to illustrate co-operation between different time-scales and to illustrate the effects of different communication support within a command team.

10.1.1. Co-operation between and within time-scales

Organizations that try to control complex dynamic systems often are organized in some hierarchy so as to be able to consider different time-scales (Brehmer, 1991). One example is the typical handling of large fires where there are firemen who work to extinguish an actual fire. They in turn give information from their point of view to a fire chief at the base, who then gives information to his chief, etc. Each higher level in the hierarchy is then able to consider a new time-scale of the process. Depending on our starting point we can talk about degrees of time-scales. Often a higher time-scale has the authority to command a lower one. By this organization it is possible for those with more general, widespread information on the higher (and slower) time-scale to command attacks on areas which might not be known to the majority who, because of their limited "window" of the situation, work on a lower (and quicker) time-scale. Furthermore, people on a higher time-scale can set goals for the lower time-scales so that they can work co-operatively within their time-scale to process something which is appropriate from the higher time-scale(s) point of view, for example saving a town from catching fire. This also means that each time-scale might have to compromise between goals (e.g. goals that are locally relevant and goals that are globally relevant). This is a conflict evident in most organizations, and it becomes critical in organizations with complex, unpredictable, problems and where actions are time-critical, or real-time, decisions.

There are in principle three ways of co-ordinating action to control a dynamic environment – via centralized execution, a prescribing plan, or individual action execution – but in actual practice co-ordination is typically achieved by a combination of the three (Brehmer, 1994). Successful co-ordination requires a shared situation awareness of the vital parts of system, sharing of resoures and co-ordination of action. All these depend on some information-sharing. Here we want to look at what information successful organizations share between teams, and how it is dealt with and interpreted within teams. Brehmer & Svenmarck (1995) have shown that hierarchical and fully-connected organizations differ in their information sharing. Fully-connected organizations exchange more information about intention and location because information is not centralized. In our cases the communication between teams is not varied, but we want to study the effect of different information-sharing within the higher time-scale, as well as how successful and less successful teams differ in their information-sharing between units.

Co-operation between and within time-scales can be crucial for handling a complex system. On the one hand the different time-scales have to work independently of each other, and on the other hand different time-scales can compensate for each others' "faulty decisions": if for example, the lower hierarchies have a goal and find new and more important information on the way they can redirect their effort. What the higher hierarchies lose in details they can compensate for in breadth, and vice versa for lower hierarchies. In both cases, of course, accurate and appropriate information is essential for best results. Co-operation between time-scales must acknowledge the time it takes for teams to process the information. Within time-scales this means that the teams or individuals must work proactively. To work proactively the team must have some awareness of how the situation in the area looks and form a hypothesis about how it might evolve.

10.1.2. Situation awareness and situation assessment within local teams

In order to control a dynamic environment successfully one has to understand how the system evolves and know its specific state from time to time. This means having situation awareness. Endsley (1995, p. 36) has defined situation awareness as "the perception of the elements in the environment within a volume of time and space, the comprehension of their meaning, and the projection of their status in the near future". Controlling large dynamic systems such as a conflagration, emergency co-ordination or, for that matter, large organizations such as a military battalion, is beyond the competence of one individual. Instead a team works co-operatively, and often synchronously, to co-ordinate and control the environment. Just adding the situation awareness of individuals is not enough, as they at all times share information with each other via different represention media and verbal communication. The situation model, shared or individual, is in constant development, as is also the system to be controlled. There has been a debate over the terms "situation awareness" and "situation assessment", which points to a need for a distinction between process and product (see *Human Factors*, 1995). Situation awareness is regarded as the product, and situation assessment as the process. In teams this constructed distinction is naturally blurred. Individual situation awareness becomes an interaction process when articulated, and may start a process of situation assessment that in turn alters the collective and individual situation awareness. We use the terms "situation awareness" and "situation assessment" interchangeably, and usually to emphasize the different stages in the process of achieving control of the dynamic system. We must also remember that most situation awareness research deals with perceptual problems in, for example, aircraft cockpits, while this chapter deals with teams who try to assess the situation through linguistic means. Linguistic information may force mental simulation, or reflection, more than direct visual perception does.

Klein & Thordsen (1989) find that more effective teams deliberately simulate mentally difficult aspects of the tasks during planning to enable the team members to understand challenges and intentions, while less effective teams ignore or give little attention to such matters. Samurcay & Rogalski (1993) point out the importance of a clear distribution of tasks and confirmation of the execution. Almost all researchers in the area of team situation awareness point to the importance of verbalization and note that incomplete or interrupted communication is an indicator of decreased situation awareness (Bolman, 1979; Schwartz, 1990; Orasanu, 1995; Salas *et al.*, 1995). We thus suspect that teams that communicate a lot and where the communication is distributed, permitted and uninterrupted will do better than other teams.

10.1.3. Objectives

The study presented here builds on a field study of military staff training aimed at enhancing "team work" capacity. In the field the training was performed with the support of a full-scale simulated command-and-control environment (see chapter 8 of this volume). The technology architecture could be configured to support different kinds of work organizations. The two teams studied used different work organization without being told to do so. One team let the information within the team flow in a serial way, where every next person within the team got fewer and more specific pieces of information about the process on the lower level. Team members constituted a filtering mechanism for each other. The other team at first chose a moderated version of this serial organization, then after a while they used a parallel organization, where the persons or subgroups within the team received the same information. Since they were interested in different information or a different part of the process they had to filter the information themselves. These different uses of the technology were also related to different interaction and communication patterns which we hypothesized would make a difference in the situation awareness displayed by each team (see chapter 5 of this volume).

It is impossible from this particular field study to tell which of the communication structures is the more efficient. There are too many other factors working to affect the outcome. Furthermore, the workprocess is not directly coupled to a specific outcome as there are several ways to compensate for a "faulty" decision (see Woods *et al.*, 1994). Still, we suspected that the teams assessed the situation and attacked the task differently as a consequence of the use of technology and accompanying interaction patterns. Therefore, a microworld study was planned in order to look more closely at the effects of the different organization of communication. In this experiment our aim was to ascertain if the different communication structures within the commander team would change the process and the result.

We are interested in co-operation and situation awareness and how they change as a consequence of the information filtering processes. We suspected from the field study that teams which have serial communication and where relevant information is passed on to the next person would produce fewer hypotheses and make equal contributions. On the other hand, we thought that they might be caught by the trap of group-think or, in Doerner's (1980) terminology, encapsulate one problem, as only one person is filtering the information. We hypothesized that parallel processing on the other hand would make the team members develop different situation models which in the end might lead the team members to talk about different situations. Furthermore, we hypothesized that these different models would also let the team produce many hypotheses about the process, and possibly "vagabond" between them.

As co-ordination centres typically are verbally very dense, we want to investigate the role of technological architecture where situation awareness is concerned. As we observed in the military, staff people working in the serial organization worked more calmly and methodologically, and at the same time seemed to share more information (their contributions were more equally distributed) than those working under a parallel organization. This may have simple explanations since in the parallel organization each individual had to filter (read but not deal with) more information than in the serial organization (where every person who is earlier in the sequence filters and takes care of information for the next person). Which condition then is the most appropriate for the control of dynamic environments: is it when people in the team have received the same information and have to filter it themselves or when they filter it for each other? Is it when the team develops a shared model of the system or when people in the team have different models of the system? The former might result in group-think and in the encapsulating of goals, where opinions different from the dominant ones are ignored, while the latter might result in the opposite, in what we call team-think, where the team members have such disparate models of the system that they hardly speak of the same object. But at the same time, because situation awareness within the team differs we think they avoid encapsulating a single goal, and might instead start to vagabond between several different goals and hypotheses. In order for the team to be able to work debatively (Schmidt, 1991) they must have different information since otherwise there would be nothing to share, but they must also share something because if they did not they might not direct themselves towards a common object, plan or goal.

10.2.1. General description of the C³FIRE microworld

The questions are approached by an experiment, performed in a microworld, which is a development of the D³FIRE microworld paradigm by Svenmarck & Brehmer (1994). D³FIRE simulates a fire. The task is to extinguish this fire with four fire units. The problem is that each fire unit subject can see only a limited window, 3×3 squares, around his/her two units. The whole area is 20×20 squares. This calls for co-operation and co-ordination. D³FIRE has been developed to investigate the co-ordination of dynamic distributed decision-making (Brehmer, 1994), and investigates how people with individual tasks within a common goal co-ordinate their actions. The development of D³FIRE which we call C³FIRE (communication, command and control) is more explicitly made to investigate how a team assesses the situation and how the team distributes information within different information conditions as well as how and if a second time-scale constituted by a team affects the outcome.

To be concrete, C³FIRE has put a second time-scale above the individual unit chiefs. This consists of a team of two persons who are allowed to command the unit chiefs on the lower time-scale. The task for the team is to follow the development of the fire and the activities of the unit chiefs on the lower time-scale, as well as issuing commands in order to make concerted work possible. By using the second time-scale the team can attack the problem from a different angle to that available to the lower time-scale unit chiefs who are constrained by their narrow window on the actual process. The decision-making team is of course also constrained by the lower decision-makers as well as by the information these provide, but in turn the participants in the team can obtain information from several decision-makers, and so gain access to information from a larger geographical area, as a consequence of accumulation (see also chapter 8 of this volume).

The distributed organization that we have planned for implies that each subject controls only his own units. This means that a commander team can command their "own" unit chiefs below, and they in turn can command their fire-fighting units. Thus each decision level functions in part as a centralized control unit, but is must be remembered that each specific level can exercise control successfully only on its own time-scale, as no information on the other time-scales is available because of time-delay, restricted windows and limited information flow. Thus, the commander at the higher time-scale must set goals and issue commands from his/her perspective and the decision-makers on a lower time-scale must then take action from their point of view in accordance with these goals or commands.

As a larger fire cannot be extinguished by one unit alone, there is a need for co-operation. Each unit chief has a limited window on the process, and if the lower decision-makers do not forward information to the commander team they have no information at all and therefore cannot appropriately co-ordinate units. On the other hand, if the commander team does not forward information, the lower decision-makers will not know what the others are doing and might therefore have problems co-ordinating actions within their time-scale.

The general idea is the following. A commander has subordinates who carry out orders at company/platoon level and a control staff which co-ordinates more general actions between superiors and subordinates and between different subordinates. In this way the staff obtains an overall view of the whole situation while the subordinates have a local view. So, those in the control team deal above all with information, while those at the action level all deal with the concrete actions.

10.2.2. Details of the C³FIRE set-up

Of the four persons in C³FIRE, one is assigned to be the information handler and one a commander with corresponding duties as liaison adjutant and commanding officer in the field study (chapter 5 of this volume). These are regarded as superior in rank to the other two persons, called unit chiefs, in C³FIRE who are to control all four fire engines as ordered by their superiors. All are to be able to communicate by electronic mail, but the communication structures are to be varied as conditions vary. The information handler and the commander sit together in the same room and can thus talk to each other.

The following general responsibility and work structure was proposed by instructions to the subjects: the information handler is to collect and file general information relevant to the general state of affairs in the system (corresponding to the liaison adjutant in the field study), the commander is to give orders to his two subordinates concerning how they are to carry out directions (corresponding to the commander in the field study), two persons are to function as unit chiefs and control two fire engines each. They are to report to the information handler and supply possible proposals or findings from the operative level (the playing field). Neither the information handler nor the commander will have any operative information about the field status other than that supplied via electronic mail, and information regarding wind and weather that is received from the game, as well as a map which corresponds approximately to the actual area. They are given no other direct information concerning where the fire is or how it is spreading etc.

Reconnaissance troops are also added to the game, and these tell E and F what is happening outside their field of vision. These troops are designed as autonomous artificial agents and are there to enable the players (on the one hand, the fire chiefs; on the other hand, their superiors) to obtain information about the course of the fire and to engender a richer flow of information. These autonomous agents simulate hierarchically lower agents and are considered to correspond to someone who phones a co-ordination centre or who tells the operative chiefs about their findings with regard to an area out of sight of the units. The fire chiefs can communicate with these agents via a simple command language.

Each subject has a PC. The interface is inherited from the D³FIRE (see Svenmarck & Brehmer, 1994). The change we have made at the interface is a "Copy button", which makes it possible to copy a message from the inbox to the outbox. For the commander team the map is omitted, and under one condition one person has a button where he or she can choose which information flow he or she wants.

The goal is to fight the fire(s) with a minimum loss of squares. A trial ends when the fire(s) have been put out, or after a maximum trial duration of one hour. When the fire has started the commander team is informed via electronic mail from the co-ordination centre, and must in turn inform the lower decision-makers and command them to a chosen position. After 15 minutes there is a false alarm about a new fire and at 45 minutes the team is told that a specific area includes explosives. We included these in order to have multiple goals and as a check to see if the team would notice those messages and would send out a specific unit to confirm, or preferably reject, this information. We have also included three sorts of forests, one slow burning, one fast burning, and one which is regarded as normal (thus mixed). Furthermore, we included houses and told the subjects that these were to be prioritized. These extra conditions were added as we wanted the commander team to be able to choose between interconnected goals (e.g. minimize forest fire and save houses) and induce them to set strategic goals.

10.2.3. Independent variables and design

This experiment was designed to investigate whether there was a difference between conditions where the commander team got information through one channel, through two channels, or they could choose. In the first condition only one person in the commander team got information from the lower decision-maker. When two channels were used both subjects in the commander team got exactly the same information from the unit chiefs. In the last condition the commander in the commander team could choose which condition he or she would like. We call these conditions serial, parallel and optional respectively.

In all conditions the subjects received three trials, one pilot and two experimental ones, which were recorded. In this chapter we discuss only the first experimental session. All computer-mediated communication and actions were recorded by a computer log. The actions and communication in the commander team were also recorded on video. All subjects had exactly the same maps, though this map was not an exact copy of the area they were facing. Some houses were placed slightly differently in the microworld in respect to the map.

10.2.4. Subjects

Sixty undergraduate students were paid 300 SEK each to serve as subjects. There were a total of 15 quartets, five within each condition. The subjects were randomly assigned to each condition. All subjects had good to very good experience of using computers. They participated in response to a call for participation.

10.2.5. Procedure

All quartets were informed about the general nature of the task, their respective individual roles, how the communication network was configured (the conditions), the manual map and its relation to the area, about the fire, wind, the different types of forests, and were instructed that they should try to save the houses as well as extinguish the fire. They were given thorough training in how to use the interface and were then allowed to familiarize themselves with the display and the electronic mail.

Each quartet performed two trials. One experimenter observed and took notes of the commander team during the trials; another experimenter monitored the two other team members at the lower time-scale. Between the trials they were interviewed. The two persons in the commander team were interviewed individually and the other two were interviewed together. They also answered a small questionnaire which included questions about the information they valued the most, where they thought the fire (fires, in case they detected several fires) started, and how these developed.

10.3. RESULTS

In the system it is possible to register all computer-mediated actions that occur during a trial. From all this data it is possible to construct a number of dependent variables. We have here chosen four such, which are presented in Table 10.1.

Table 10.1. Statistics ordered after sucess in the first column

Condition	Saved green squares	Check out False alarms	Left unburnt houses	Saved Burnt house
Serial				
1	241	yes/no	4	0
2	151	no/no	3	1
3	130	yes/yes	2	2
4	32	yes/yes	0	4
5	2	yes/yes	0	3
Parallel				
1	254	no/no	5	1
2	71	no/yes	2	4
3	15	yes/yes	1	2
4	8	yes/yes	0	3
5	2	yes/yes	0	2
Optional				
1	148	yes/yes	2	1
2	9	yes/yes	0	2
3	6	no/yes	0	3
4	3	yes/yes	0	2
5	1	no/yes	0	1

10.3.1. Overall effectiveness of the teams

Effectiveness was calculated in two different ways: firstly in terms of absolute numbers of lost squares, and secondly in a relative score where the number of houses saved and the checking of the (false) alarm were also incorporated.

Let us first look at the absolute success in extinguishing the fires, i.e. minimizing the number of lost squares in the area. At first glance it seems that the teams having the serial condition have a higher overall success rate. However, the variance within experimental conditions is so great that the difference is not significant, using an ANOVA calculation. By using a nonparametric calculation, a sign test, ranking the groups and assigning those above the median to one group and those below to another group, and by using the chi-square test we found that the serial and the optional condition differed on a 10% level ($\chi^2 = 3.6$, $P = 0.06$). This result indicates that the serial condition is slightly better suited than the optional condition in terms of taking care of a single overall goal.

The relative success score is calculated by giving 1 point for checking out each false alarm, 2 points for saving a house and 1 point for putting out the fire in a house on fire. By a Kruskal-Wallis test we found that the difference between the conditions in terms of this score was significant on a 10% level ($H = 4.94$, 10%, 2 df). Once, again, it was the optional condition that had less success in terms of this weighted score.

This result suggests that the people in the optional condition found it difficult to gain control over the dynamic system, in respect of both simple criteria and multi-goal criteria. But we cannot, in any way, attribute the difference in success to the particular conditions.

10.3.2. Communication and co-operation between time-scales

All communications between the commander team and the fire chiefs were categorized according to the schemata of Brehmer & Svenmarck (1995). As we also have houses and different forests in the area, we had to extend the categories with factors regarding these problems. The categories were strategies (S), commands (C), offers of help (OH), request for help (RH), request for clear command (RC), acknowledgement (A), six types of information (intention (II), fire (IE), location/position (IL), activity (IA), forests (IA), houses (IH)), and six types of question (location/position (QL), fire (QE), activity (QA), forests (QF) houses (QH)), and miscellaneous (M). We calculated statistics on the commander team and the fire units singly as well as together. It seems that the teams have not differed very much *between time-scales* with respect to co-operative behaviour between conditions. Using ANOVA statistics we found that the optional conditions commander teams sent four times as many messages categorized as strategies as the other two conditions ($F = 4.04$, $P = .05$). This is interesting, as the optional seems to be less well-suited for controlling a dynamic system. It might be that when one cannot think of a good idea one simply sends out the first strategic idea that comes to mind. We have not counted relevance – this could have been purely local – and in any case the number of strategic messages does not say anything about their quality.

Furthermore, we found that the commander teams in the parallel conditions asked their unit chiefs about their unit positions twice as often as the other two commander teams ($F = 4.24$, $P = .04$). This indicates that the parallel commander team had difficulty assessing and creating an image of the progress of the units, as discussed further below.

Since the experimental variation gave few significant results we divided all the results into two according to their success in terms of forest saved, and we found that the better commander teams did not send as many messages as the poorer ones (ANOVA $F = 4.03$, $P = .07$). Considering that relevance is not counted the result is not very surprising, as the subjects can easily get overloaded with information and then might direct all their efforts to reading rather than thinking and acting. What is surprising is that unit chiefs who were in a less successful organization tended to acknowledge an order or other information more often than those in successful teams ($F = 3.30$, $P = .09$). This may be connected with the overall information overload, but it may very well interact with the time delay. When the unit chiefs acknowledge something some time has already passed, and then it takes more time for the commander team to read it.

Since we have seen that communication and co-operation between the time-scale units do not differ in any obvious manner, we can now look for differences within the commander team and their situation awareness and co-operation.

10.3.3. Situation awareness and co-operation within the commander team

It was hypothesized that agreement in situation awareness might differ between groups with different communication organizations (and technological architectures), as a result of the information distribution and the possibility to assess the situation. Here we have asked the subjects to note on a blank map where they regarded the fire as having started (and if they experienced that there were many fires, to note where they started and number them). We then compared the maximum difference between the team members' assessments of where they thought the first fire started by counting the number of squares distance (see Table 10.2). The difference between the teams was significant on a 10%

level ($H = 4.64$, 10%, df 2). We then also made a chi-square test between the parallel and serial groups and found that they also differed on a 10% level. The difference between the fires recorded by the parallel team was greater than that recorded by the serial teams. This is in agreement with our hypothesis. In both conditions one team member was given the duty of updating a map, but in the serial condition all information from the lower decision-maker is received by this member and thus the other team member depends on his map and knowledge. In the parallel condition the decision-maker in the team can look at the coordinator's map, but at the same time he must also look at his own messages, and thus may create an independent model of the fire.

Table 10.2. Statistics of the maximum difference between the two commander team members in their assessment of the first fire

Condition	Serial	Parallel	Optional
Max. difference	3	5	1
between first fire	2	2	2
	1	9	3
	1	3	2
	1	3	1

As mentioned above, the parallel team had even more difficulty in assessing the position of the units, which is reflected in that they asked the units chiefs more about the actual positions of the units (ANOVA $F = 4.24$, $P = .04$; Kruskal-Wallis $H = 7.02$, 5%). This shows that the parallel teams had much more difficulty in assessing the two dynamic factors in the system, the fire units and the fire itself.

We also looked at three teams which in order represent a successful, an average and a less successful team in terms of forests saved. As the serial condition seems to have the most shared situational awareness and the parallel condition the most disparate, we randomly chose the most successful team from the serial condition and the least successful one from the parallel condition. We did this in order to find out what information each team had processed during the session, since it might indicate what kind of information processing is best. These three sessions have been fully transcribed. We have also categorized each speaker's turn, i.e. coherent uninterrupted speech, in respect of the messages the team members shared. One turn might for instance contain several messages. The categories were initially informed by Bolman's (1979) four suggestions for good SA, i.e. monitoring position-specific information, confirming and cross-checking information, communicating relevant situation to others and co-ordinating activities, but these had to be extended. All the categories, their distribution over three variously successful teams and examples are shown in Table 10.3.

This table suggests that the more the team talks, the better they are able to control the environment, something which John Hughes (at a seminar in Aarhus, Denmark) also said about air-traffic control: "their work is to talk". Thus it seems that the more you talk about the tasks within a time-scale around the room, the better you manage to organize successful team work: within limits, of course. This emerges clearly in the fourth category, where the more successful team cross-check each other more often. This is not very surprising as the successful team also works under the serial condition and then the commander can get information only by asking the information handler who receives all information. The optional condition is mainly using the parallel technology architecture

Table 10.3. Count of categories in three groups with different success rates in controlling the dynamic environment (percentages in parantheses)

	Successful team (serial)	Averages (optional)	Less successful (parallel)	Example of message
Monitoring communication (MC)	157 (24.6)	163 (36.2)	182 (42.6)	Unit 1 at C3, fire at D4
Monitoring question (MQ)	60 (9.4)	42 (9.3)	32 (7.5)	Where is Unit 1?
Confirmation of information	80 (12.5)	65 (14.4)	61 (14.3)	Unit 1 at C3 (I got it)
Cross-checking information	63 (9.9)	28 (6.2)	13 (3)	Did you say C3?
Hypothesis of future process	28 (4.4)	37 (8.2)	55 (12.9)	The fire should be at when . . .
Evaluating actual process	27 (4.2)	11 (2.4)	13 (3)	We are doing fine at D4
Planning	21 (3.3)	5 (1.1)	5 (1.2)	We should attack the fire with Unit 1 and 2 from . . .
Intention	25 (3.9)	9 (2)	7 (1.6)	I send unit 1 to D4 because . . .
Suggestion for action	13 (2)	10 (2.2)	11 (2.6)	Couldn't you send unit 1 . . .
Task distribution	8 (1.3)	8 (1.8)	3 (1)	Could you ask unit 1 to . . .
Task confirm	56 (8.8)	15 (3.3)	7 (1.6)	I ask unit 1 . . .
Task confirm (late)	5 (0.8)	2 (0.8)	9 (2)	I have asked unit 1
Task question	13 (2)	6 (1.3)	1 (0.2)	Have you asked unit 1?
Meta-organization	21 (3.3)	15 (3.3)	10 (2.3)	We should both use the map
Plain question	14 (2.2)	5 (1.1)	5 (1.2)	Pardon, sorry, what
Other	47 (7.4)	29 (6.4)	13 (3)	Jokes and things we did not understand
Summary:	638	450	427	

(overall up to 70%) and so both the other conditions provide both parties in the commander team with information, and both team members can check the information themselves. But we suspect that it is very important to talk aloud to the room in order to update and maintain the team's collective situation awareness and then be able to work co-operatively in a coherent manner. Furthermore, when one person talks out loud, the other team member is able to monitor this person's line of reasoning, as well as reflect upon his own. This seems important for hypothesis-making and planning.

Hypotheses and planning are closely related, and hypothesizing is obviously a requirement for effectively planning how to attack a problem. However, hypothesizing about the future state of the dynamic system does not include how to stop this development. Without planning, too many hypotheses might make the team start to vagabond between different goals. In the Table 10.3 we can see that the successful team had a ratio of 28 hypotheses to 21 planning, while the less successful one had a ratio of 55 to 5. It seems that the less successful team had trouble in making something out of their hypotheses, and thus could not co-ordinate their information in a coherent co-operative way.

Both planning and intention seem to be vital for controlling a dynamic environment. While planning includes several units working co-operatively to attack a problem, intention concerns only one unit. Again, communicating one's intention of commanding (or anything else) a unit to a certain place affords the other team member an opportunity of monitoring this line of reasoning, and enables him/her to prepare himself/herself for such a development. Evaluating the process aloud in the same way is also important. Both planning and intention enable proactive action rather than just reactive action to present states. Proactive action is definitely crucial, as there always is some time delay between the moment something is decided at the commander team level and the actions of the units on the lower time-scales. Late action implies useless action in controlling a dynamic environment.

Secondly we might confirm the finding of Samurçay & Rogalski (1993) that it is very important to distribute work explicitly within the team, or even better to tell the others that you are going to take care of a certain task. This, of course, strengthens the shared model of the team work (Orasanu & Salas, 1993). Members of the less successful team seldom confirmed that they were going to take care of a certain task, and when they did so they did it after the fact. They may have believed that the task distribution was given by their actual roles within the experiment, which in a way may have been the case, but if they did not tell the other team member he or she could not know what task was to be performed and when.

10.3.4. Information value

Between the two sessions (only one is examined here), we gave the subjects a survey asking them to rate which information they regarded as the most or least important. Over all conditions and all team member roles the location of fires was regarded as the most important information together with unit position. It is quite interesting to note that even the lower time-scales regarded unit position as the most important information. They considered it important to know about the other fire chiefs' unit positions in order to do a good job. In the optional condition commands were also regarded as important information, which may reflect that participants in this condition have received less of this information than in the other experimental conditions.

The least important information was more diversified. At the command team the information handlers regarded unit activity and commands as the two items of information they could do without, and the commanders thought they could do without information about the vegetation (fast, normal or slow burning forest). At the lower time-scale the fire chiefs also felt that vegetation information was of less value, as well as information about the wind.

That both the commander and the fire chiefs regarded vegetation information as useless is quite surprising, as this is vital information if one wants to plan ahead of the progress of the fire and plan how to extinguish it in the most efficient way.

10.4. DISCUSSION

Although the differences between conditions are barely significant, they have a consistent direction, and this makes them interpretable.

The results indicate, first, that it is better to have a fixed information flow than having to decide it on one's own. In order to be able to save houses and take care of the false alarm one has to keep track of the positions of fast and slow burning forest to save time. Both the serial and the parallel conditions have been able to collect, organize and keep track of the fire. Secondly, we think that commander teams should work in a way that enables as much interaction as possible. All subjects should be trained to talk about their reasoning and show it to others who then can monitor it.

By observing the commander teams, we could see that the teams that had a fixed information flow configuration were better at getting ahead of the fire and thus preventing the fire from reaching a house. The teams that could choose between information flow configurations could not decide which structure they preferred, and thus switched between the two structures (even though 70% of the time the parallel condition was chosen). This switching between structures may have made the optional condition less reliable and made the people less confident in their roles. Furthermore, the commander who also decided which structure to use seldom told the other person in the team about his choice of organization. This made it impossible for the information handler to know when to organize his work so that the commander would also get the information. This may be regarded as a perfect example of failing to pass on vital information, but such negligence may be due to the fact that the information in this case concerns the organization of work (a metalevel) rather than the task, which is the focused information. From observations we could see that groups that faced the parallel and optional condition more often came up with a creative use of the technology. For example, one group used one of the two mail boxes as a reservoir and saved all mail, in order to be able to retrieve a specific item (mail). Unfortunately this also meant that they did not observe the (false) alarm.

That the optional condition chose the parallel condition for approximately 70% of the time might have to do with a feeling of control. By choosing the parallel condition both team members have the possibility to monitor and be involved in the process of controlling all aspects of the system. And this, it seems, was a false feeling.

Concerning situation awareness, it may be suggested that the team members had different ideas about where the fire started, according to whether the information flow configuration was parallel or serial. Furthermore, the commander teams in the parallel conditions had more difficulty in assessing where the units were.

What is more surprising is that these different models of the fire in the team did not seem to make any difference to either the absolute or the relative success in managing the fire. It might be equally advantageous to have different models of the system as to have similar models of the situation, for the following reasons:

1. approximate information databases are good

2. there might be a trade-off between communication and action

3. participants compensate for differences in models.

It is also noticeable that the optional condition did not differ significantly from the other conditions as regards differences in situation awareness within the team. This might be due to the participants' need for discussion and thus their dependence on each other in all situations, because they lacked a fixed information flow organization. The other groups had an organization which offered mediating structures that were shared between the participants and that they could use without having others guide them.

This experiment might inform system developers that verbally mediated communication is very important. Instead of trying to cut down on verbal communication within teams they should encourage it. It not only makes information-sharing easier, it also gives team members the opportunity to monitor and reflect upon their line of reasoning and their work routines. Technologically naive persons might not think that a new form of technology or, as in this case, of technology achitecture might change the propagation of information, the practices within the team and the results of their performance as long as the right information gets to the commander team. But the processing and the opportunity to process information might have a greater effect than initially expected.

10.5. REFERENCES

BREHMER, B. (1991). Organization for decision making in complex systems. In J. RASMUSSEN, B. BREHMER & J. LEPLAT (Eds), *Distributed Decision Making. Cognitive Models for Co-operative Work*. Chichester: John Wiley & Sons, 335–348.

BREHMER, B. (1994). *Distributed Decision Making in Dynamic Environments*. Uppsala University, Sweden, Foa Report.

BREHMER, B. & SVENMARCK, P. (1995). Distributed decision making in dynamic environments: time scales and architectures of decision making. In J.-P. CAVERNI, M. BAR-HILLEL, F.H. BARRON & H. JUNGERMANN (Eds), *Contributions to Decision Making – I*. Amsterdam: Elsevier Science, 155–174.

BOLMAN, L. (1979). Aviation accidents and the "theory of the situation". In G.E. COOPER, M.D. WHITE & J.K. LAUBER (Eds), *Resource Management on the Flight Deck: Proceedings of a NASA/Industry Workshop*. Moffett Field, CA: NASA Ames Research Center, 31–58.

DOERNER, D. (1980). On the difficulties people have in dealing with complexity. *Simulation and Games*, vol. 11, No. 1, March, 87–106.

ENDSLEY, M.R. (1995). Toward a theory of situation awareness in dynamic systems. *Human Factors*, vol. 37, No. 1, March, 32–65.

HEATH, C. & LUFF, P. (1992). Collaboration and control. *Computer Supported Cooperative Work* (CSCW), No. 1, 69–94.

Human Factors (1995), vol. 37, No. 1, March.

KLEIN, G.A. & THORDSEN, M.L. (1989). A cognitive model of team decision making. Yellow Springs, OH: Klein Associates.

ORASANU, J. (1995). Situation awareness: its role in flight crew decision making. *8th International Symposium on Aviation Psychology*.

ORASANU, J. & SALAS, E. (1993). Team decision making in complex environments. In G.A. KLEIN, J. ORASANU, R. CALDERWOOD & C.E. ZSAMBOK (Eds), *Decision Making in Action: Models and Methods*. Norwood, NJ: Ablex Publishing Corporation, 327–345.

SALAS, E., PRINCE, C., BAKER, D.P. & SHRESTHA, L. (1995). Situation awareness in team performance: implications for measurement and training. *Human Factors*, vol. 37, No. 1, March, 123–136.

SAMURÇAY, R. & ROGALSKI, J. (1993). Cooperative work and decision making in emergency management. I. *Le Travail Humain*, vol. 56, No. 1, 53–77.

SCHMIDT, K. (1991). Cooperative work: a conceptual framework. In J. RASMUSSEN, B. BREHMER & J. LEPLAT (Eds), *Distributed Decision Making. Cognitive Models for Cooperative Work*. Chichester: John Wiley & Sons, 75–110.

SCHWARTZ, D. (1990). *Training for Situation Awareness*. Houston, TX: Flight Safety International.

SVENMARCK, P. & BREHMER, B. (1994). *D³FIRE – an experimental paradigm for the study of distributed decision making*. Nutek report, Uppsala University, Sweden.

WOODS, D.D., JOHANNESEN, L.J., COOK, R.I. & SARTER, N.B. (1994). *Behind human error: cognitive systems, computers, and hindsight*. CSERIAC report.

CHAPTER ELEVEN

Effects of time pressure in fully connected and hierarchical architectures of distributed decision-making

BERNDT BREHMER

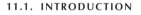

11.1. INTRODUCTION

Many tasks facing human decision-makers are simply too large to be handled by individuals, and require that many individuals co-operate. When fighting a forest fire, for example, a number of fire-fighting units must co-operate in a coordinated way to cover the burning area. Fighting forest fires is thus an example of a task requiring *distributed decision-making*.

As defined by Brehmer (1991) a distributed decision problem requires a number of decision-makers to co-operate to achieve a common goal. Each decision maker owns part of the resources required to achieve this goal, but nobody has full control over all resources. The decision makers must therefore share resources, as well as co-ordinate their activities to achieve their common goal. This co-ordination is difficult, however, because each decision-maker has only a limited "window" on the task, and no one has the overall view required for the co-ordination that is required. Hence the decision makers must communicate to achieve the common understanding (or "situational awareness", to use a popular term; see Wellens (1993) for a discussion of it in distributed decision-making) that is necessary for their co-ordination.

Co-ordination is possible only if there is information about the state of the task as a whole in at least one place in the system. Because of their limited windows, no decision-maker has this overall view. It must be constructed on the basis of their communication. A fundamental problem in distributed decision-making, therefore, is how the communication among the decision-makers should be organized. In so far as they do not achieve the overall picture that is needed, their co-ordination will suffer. This does not mean that they will not achieve their goal. It may be achieved also on the basis of local co-ordination (see Brehmer & Svenmarck, 1994), but their performance will be less than optimal. For example, a fire may be extinguished also when each fire-fighter does not have a perfect picture of the fire, but the extinction process will take longer, and require more resources, than if the fire-fighters have a good shared picture of the fire.

The requisite method for co-ordinating the efforts of the decision makers in a distributed task depends on the nature of the task. In the present context, we are interested in distributed decision-making in dynamic problems, rather than static problems.

Brehmer & Allard (1991) point to three defining characteristics of a dynamic decision problem:

- it requires a series of interdependent decisions
- the state of the task changes, both autonomously and as a consequence of the decision-maker's actions
- the decisions must be made in real time.

Fighting a forest fire is obviously a dynamic task in this sense. Thus, the fire fighting units must move from location to location (a series of decisions is required). When they are in one location it is impossible to use them in a different location (the decisions are interdependent, i.e. current decisions constrain future decisions). The state of the fire changes, both as a result of the strength and direction of the wind (i.e. autonomously) and as a consequence of how the fire is being fought (i.e. as a consequence of the decision-maker's actions). Finally, the decisions must be made when changes in the fire require them, rather then when the fire chief feels good and ready to make them (i.e. the decisions have to be made in real time).

Under these circumstances, the forms of co-ordination that can be used in a static problem will not work. For example, it is not possible to rely on a general plan for the co-ordination of the efforts of the fire-fighting units, for the situation is not stable, and the fire may behave in ways that have not been foreseen in the plan. Nor is it possible to pre-assign tasks to the individual fire-fighting units, for the dynamic character of the problem makes it impossible to predict exactly what their tasks will be, or where these tasks will materialize. Instead, the co-ordination will have to be made on-line and on the basis of feedback information, to adapt to the changing nature of the problem.

Because communication takes time, the overall picture that is constructed on the basis of the information will always be old. In fire-fighting, for example, the commanders of the individual FFUs will always have more accurate and up-to-date information about the state of the fire in their local windows than that represented in the overall picture which is constructed on the basis of their communication. Therefore, it is not possible to exercise control only on the basis of the overall picture; the local commanders must have some control over his resources, especially in situations where there is potential for danger. In a dynamic task, a central commander cannot have the information required to exercise "micromanagement" of the local task, to use Kleinman's (1990) term, unless the state of the system changes very slowly compared to the time required for communication. As a consequence, total centralized control is often not feasible in these tasks. On the other hand, control cannot be completely distributed either since co-ordination is required and this cannot be done on the basis of the information in the local windows only.

To achieve co-ordination is thus a central problem in distributed decision-making. The dynamic character of the task makes it impossible to base this co-ordination on a pre-existing plan. It must be adapted to the changing circumstances based on communication. The important question, therefore, is who should communicate with whom and about what so that the appropriate "situational awareness" can be constructed.

This is the problem of the requisite *architecture of distributed decision-making*, to use a term introduced by Rasmussen (1991). There are, of course, many possible architectures (see Rasmussen, 1991), but here we will consider only two of them: a *fully connected architecture* (FC architecture) in which every decision-maker can communicate directly with every other decision-maker, and a *hierarchical architecture* where all communication has to pass through a centrally placed decision-maker.

In the present context, the important difference between these two architectures is that because all communication has to pass through one central decision-maker in the hierarchical architecture, there is a better chance that at least one decision-maker in the network will have an adequate picture of the state of the task as a whole in this architecture. He or she may then use this picture to co-ordinate the efforts of the network members. In an FC this may not happen, because each decision-maker may receive only part of the information that is needed. Assuming that the central decision-maker is also able to translate this information into appropriate commands, we would therefore expect that a hierarchical architecture would be more effective than an FC architecture in distributed dynamic decision-making.

Results from a study by Brehmer and Svenmarck (1994) lend support to this hypothesis. They compared an FC architecture with a hierarchical architecture in an experiment using D³FIRE. D³FIRE is a simulation based on the concept of distributed decision-making proposed by Brehmer (1991) where groups of four subjects must co-operate to extinguish forest fires (the simulation is described in detail below). Brehmer and Svenmarck (1994) found that performance was better with the hierarchical architecture than with the FC architecture. Although the central subjects in the hierarchical architecture had not been given the status of formal leaders, they nevertheless assumed responsibility for co-ordination and issued commands to their fellow subjects. Moreover, they were apparently able to translate the information that they received from the other subjects into effective commands that led to better co-ordination since they were more efficient than the subjects in the FC condition.

However, even though performance was better in the hierarchical architecture than in the FC architecture, the difference between the two conditions was rather small. This was not because informal leaders emerged in the FC architecture: there was no indication that any of the subjects in the FC groups took on the task of co-ordination. Instead, the subjects in the FC networks co-ordinated on the basis of local communication between pairs of subjects. This communication involved mainly intentions; the subjects informed one another about what they were going to do. This is, of course, exactly what is needed. Co-ordination takes time, and the subjects will have the time needed only if they know what the person with whom they have to co-ordinate is planning to do. If they only know what the person is doing, they will not be able to co-ordinate because the other person may have gone on to do something else before they are in place. These results show, then, that it may be possible to perform a distributed task in different ways.

The subjects' task in D³FIRE is not only a distributed task, it is also a dynamic one where they must make decisions in real time. That is, the decisions have to be made when developments in the task require them, rather than when the decision-maker feels ready to make the decisions. As a consequence, the decision-makers will often be subject to time pressure. The effects of time pressure should be stronger in a hierarchical architecture than in an FC architecture. In the former architecture, all messages have to pass through one central decision-maker, and the time available to process this information should be critical. In the FC architecture with local co-ordination, messages are spread more evenly over the four subjects, and each subject has less information to process than

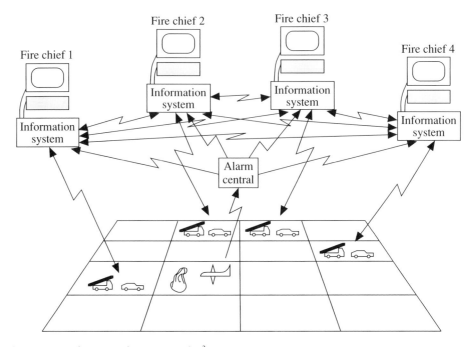

Figure 11.1. The general structure of D³FIRE.

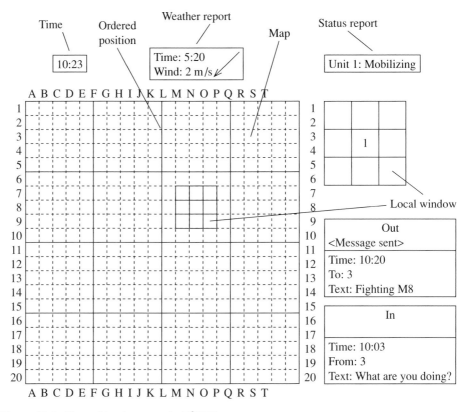

Figure 11.2. The subject's screen in D³FIRE.

the central decision-maker in the hierarchical architecture. When there is time pressure, attempts at central co-ordination may therefore break down. The more local forms of co-ordination in the FC architecture, on the other hand, may be more resistant to time pressure.

The present study was designed to test the hypothesis that time pressure will have a stronger effect in a hierarchical architecture than in an FC architecture in an experiment using D³FIRE.

11.2. METHOD

11.2.1. Subjects

Sixty-four undergraduate students from the University of Uppsala were paid about USD35 to serve as subjects. They were divided into four conditions with four groups of four subjects each on the basis of the order in which they signed up for the experiment.

11.2.2. Simulation

The experiment used D³FIRE, a simulation that requires the subjects to assume the role of fire chiefs charged with the task of fighting forest fires (see Svenmarck & Brehmer, 1991). It is a so-called microworld, i.e. a simulation developed for experimental purposes (see Brehmer & Dörner (1993) for a description of the microworld methodology in psychological research). A microworld is not designed to be a high-fidelity simulation of some real system. It is designed to incorporate those aspects of a system that are relevant for the purposes of the experimenter. D³FIRE is thus not an attempt to create a simulation that incorporates all the features of fire-fighting, but a simulation that embodies the definition of distributed decision-making proposed by Brehmer (1991). That is, it presents a situation in which four decision-makers must co-operate to solve a problem of mutual concern, but where their co-operation is made difficult because each decision-maker has only a limited window on the task. Since no subject has the overall view required for co-operation, they must achieve their co-ordination by means of communication. D³FIRE is thus based on a definition of distributed decision making as a problem of co-ordination.

The general structure of the simulation is shown in Fig. 11.1. Each subject sits in front of a computer terminal. The subjects are asked to act as fire chiefs in command of fire-fighting units and scouting units. Their task is to extinguish forest fires. On their screen (see Fig. 11.2), they have a map of the forest represented as a square divided into 19 × 19 cells. Each subject is in command of a fire-fighting unit and eight scouting units, each of which covers one square, so that he or she can "see" only 3 × 3 cells as indicated in Fig. 11.2. The position of the fire-fighting unit is always in the middle, and it is surrounded by the eight spotter units which can report about the presence of fire, but cannot fight it. Fire can be fought only by placing the middle square over the cell where the fire-fighting should take place. In order to fight new fires that might occur in the neighbouring cells after the fire in the cell where the fire-fighting unit is has been extinguished, the subjects must move the unit to that square. The unit has no intelligence of its own but relies on the subject. This is as it should be, since the subject is actually in command of the unit, and should make the decisions required.

As shown in Fig. 11.1, a spotter plane flies over the forest and it reports the location of a fire as it starts. Thus, the subjects do not have to search for a fire (which might take too much time). The subjects can move their 3×3 windows by clicking on a cell in the map with the mouse; the square then starts to move towards that location at the speed predetermined by the experimenter, and it will stop when the middle cell has reached the position selected by the subject. If there is fire in that location, the fire-fighting unit will start fighting that fire. No specific command is required for the fire-fighting process to start; fire fighting starts if there is fire in the location to which the fire-fighting unit has been ordered to go, or when fire reaches this location. Thus, the subject does not have to issue any special command to start the actual fire fighting process. It is sufficient that his or her fire fighting unit is a location where there is fire. The subject's task, therefore, is to decide where the fire should be fought and to move his or her unit to that location.

The subjects are able to communicate via electronic mail. Each message must consist of information about the addressee and a string of words. The messages are limited to twenty positions. Each message can be sent to only one other subject; it is not possible to send a message to all other subjects at once. Subjects can type and receive messages also between updates on the screen. In an earlier experiment in this series, Svenmarck and Brehmer (1992) found that subjects communicating via electronic mail did not differ from those communicating orally and face-to-face with respect to performance or with respect to what was communicated. Therefore, the more convenient (from the experimenter's point of view) electronic form of communication is used in this experiment, as it has been in all previous experiments, with the exception of the Svenmarck and Brehmer study just mentioned.

The screen is updated at predetermined intervals. In the present experiment, variation of the interval between updates was used to manipulate the time pressure and the update intervals were 15 seconds and 60 seconds. Subjects can type in and receive messages also between screen updates.

11.2.3. Design

Two factors were varied in the experiment: *time pressure* and *architecture*. Time pressure was manipulated by a variation in the interval between screen updates, and there were two levels here: 15 seconds and 60 seconds. Architecture was manipulated by means of variation in the communication possibilities. In the fully connected (FC) architecture, every subject could communicate with every other subject; in the hierarchical architecture, all communications had to pass through one central subject. In all four conditions, the subjects performed three trials, extinguishing one fire in every trial.

11.2.4. Procedure

The subjects came to the experiment on two different days and worked for about 2 hours each day. On the first day, they received the instructions and practised with the simulation for about 20 minutes until they felt confident that they could handle the message system and the simulation. They then performed the first trial. On the second day, they performed two additional trials.

The instructions emphasized that the subjects' goal was to extinguish the fires as quickly as possible, but gave no hint about how the subjects should proceed to achieve this goal.

11.3. RESULTS

D³FIRE stores everything that happens on a trial, and a variety of measures can be derived from this information. In the present experiment, we analyze time per trial, which gives a basic measure of efficiency; the number of cells lost to fire, which is a measure of performance; and the number and the content of the messages sent among subjects, which give information about how they co-ordinated their activity.

11.3.1. Time per trial

In terms of the rate of screen updates, the difference between the two time pressure conditions is 4:1. If the subjects had extinguished their fires with equal effectiveness in both conditions, the difference in time per trial should be 4:1 also. The results of the analysis of variance on time per trial shows that fires were indeed extinguished faster in the high time pressure condition than in the low time pressure condition (20.3 min vs. 59.8 min, F 1/12 = 370.88, $p <$ .01), but the difference was smaller than that expected if the subjects had been equally effective in both conditions in terms of screen updates. Thus, while the difference in updates in 4:1, the difference in terms of time per trial is about 3:1.

11.3.2. Performance

The primary task of the subjects is to extinguish the fire as quickly as possible. The number of cells lost to fire at the end of a trial gives a measure of the extent to which they were able to accomplish this goal. The analysis of variance performed on these scores yielded a significant main effect of time pressure (F 1/12 = 18.17, $p <$ .01). This effect is illustrated in Fig. 11.3. The figure shows the expected effect: subjects generally performed much better in the low time pressure condition than in the high time pressure condition.

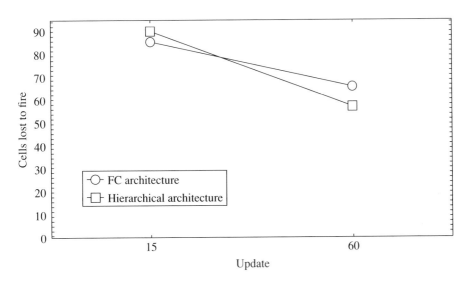

Figure 11.3. Performance in terms of cells lost to fire for the two time pressure conditions in the FC architecture and the hierarchical architecture.

To test the hypothesis that time pressure would have a greater effect in the hierarchical architecture than the FC architecture, Tukey HSD tests were performed on all pairs of means shown in Fig. 11.3. The results showed that while the performance was significantly better in the low time pressure condition than in the high time pressure condition in the hierarchical architecture, the difference between the two time pressure conditions did not reach significance in the FC architecture. This supports the hypothesis for the study. The effect must, however, be considered rather weak, and the difference between the two architectures is not significant for either of the two time pressure conditions, nor was the overall interaction between time pressure and architecture in the analysis of variance (F $1/12 = 1.20$, $p < .30$).

11.4. COMMUNICATION

11.4.1. Number of messages

Subjects sent many more messages in the low time pressure condition than in the high time pressure condition (F $1/12 = 21.43$, $p < .01$). As in the earlier Brehmer and Svenmarck study, subjects sent more messages in the FC architecture than in the hierarchical architecture (F $1/12 = 3.18$, $p < .10$). When this measure was normalized by dividing the number of messages by the number of minutes to yield the number of messages per minute, there was, however, no significant difference between the two time pressure conditions (4.4 vs. 4.8 messages/minute, F $1/12 < 1$). The difference between the two architectures was more pronounced, however (5.6 messages/minute vs. 3.6 for the FC and hierarchical architecture, respectively, F $1/12 = 4.26$, $p = .06$). This difference is less than the number of possible message paths, which is 12 in the FC architecture and 6 in the hierarchical architecture.

There was no interaction between architecture and time pressure for either measure. This suggests that the subjects sent a constant number of messages per minute in each architecture. This means that they sent about four messages per update in the low time pressure condition while they sent only one message per update in the high time pressure condition.

11.4.2. Message content

The messages sent by the subjects in the four conditions were categorized using the same 18 categories that were used in the earlier experiment (Brehmer & Svenmarck, 1994). Here we concentrate on *nine* of these categories, which comprise the majority of the messages sent. Four of these contain questions that the subjects have asked: questions about the location of some other subject (QL), about the activity of another subject (QA), about whether another subject sees fire and where the fire is (QF), and, finally, questions about some other subject's intentions (QI). Corresponding to these four categories of questions, there are four categories of answers, or information, that the subjects may transmit; information about one's location (IL), information about one's activity (IA), information about fire (IF) and information about one's intentions (II). The ninth category, C, comprises commands, i.e. messages in which one subject has either told another subject to do something (i.e. to go to a given location) or asked him or her to do something. Before looking at the results with respect to these nine categories, however, we turn to the category of "miscellaneous", a category that mainly comprises social chit-chat, to ascertain whether the subjects' increased frequency of communication in the low time pressure condition just consisted of more conversation or was aimed at exchanging task-relevant information.

The results of this analysis show that there was indeed more social chit-chat in the low time pressure condition. The frequency of messages per minute in this category was .27 for the low time pressure condition and 0.04 in the high time pressure condition (F 1/28 = 14.04, $p < .01$). There was a higher frequency of social chit-chat in the FC architecture than in the hierarchical architecture (0.23 vs. 0.08, F 1/28 = 5.60, $p < .05$). Thus, only a very small part of the communication was not task-relevant even in the FC architecture with low time pressure where it reached 0.4, i.e. less than 10% of the total frequency of messages. The fact that there is some social chit-chat in both time pressure conditions suggests that the subjects were not totally overwhelmed by the demands of the task in either condition.

There was no difference between the two time pressure conditions with respect to the frequency of messages sent for any of the nine message categories considered here. Fig. 11.4 shows how the frequency of different message categories varied for the three kinds of subjects: subjects in the FC architecture and central and non-central subjects in the hierarchical architecture.

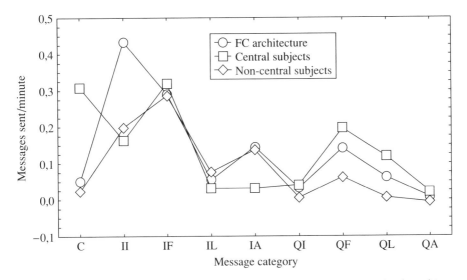

Figure 11.4. Messages sent per minute for each of the nine message categories for subjects in the FC architecture and the central and non-central subjects in the hierarchical architectures. For explanation of the message categories, see text.

As can be seen from Fig. 11.4, central subjects in the hierarchical conditions sent more commands than the non-central subjects and the subjects in the FC architecture (F 2/18 = 24.02, $p < .001$). *Post hoc* tests, using Tukey's HSD procedure, confirmed this interpretation of the effect. Subjects in the FC-architecture send more messages with information about intentions than subjects in the hierarchical conditions (F 2/18 = 5.58, $p < .05$), and the *post hoc* tests confirmed that the effect was due to a higher frequency for the FC architecture than for the two hierarchical conditions. For the messages with information about the fire (IF) and about one's own position (IL), there were no differences among conditions. Central subjects sent significantly fewer messages about own activity than the non-central subjects and the subjects in the FC conditions (F 2/18 = 5.50, $p < .05$, interpretation confirmed by Tukey HSD *post hoc* tests). The three kinds of subjects did not differ with respect to the frequency of questions about intentions and activities, but non-central subjects sent fewer questions about others' location (F 2/18 = 7.60, $p < .01$) and about the fire (F 2/18 = 12.77, $p < .001$).

The messages received (Fig. 11.5) are, of course, related to the messages sent. Looking first at the central subjects, we find that they receive more information about the fire (F 2/18 = 19.66, $p < .001$), more information about the location of other units (F 2/18 = 8.56, $p < .01$), and more information about the activity of other units (F 2/18 = 16.57, $p < .01$). The non-central subjects receive less information about the intentions of other subjects (F 2/18 = 18.28, $p < .001$) and fewer questions about the fire (F 2/18 = 13.55, $p < .01$). There were no differences with respect to the number of commands received (remember that the frequency of commands from the central subjects have to be distributed over three subjects) and no differences among subjects with respect to questions about intentions, activity and locations. The mean frequency of commands was significantly lower in the high time pressure condition than the low time pressure condition (F 1/18 = 5.70, $p < .05$). This was due to the fact that one of the central subjects in the high time pressure condition issued no commands at all. This effect was visible also in the analysis of the commands sent above, but did not reach significance in that analysis.

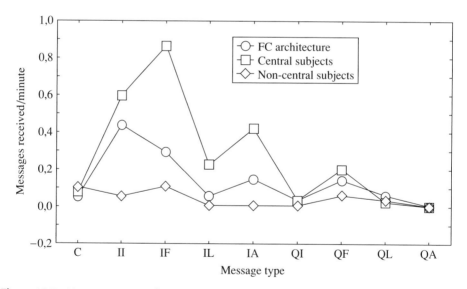

Figure 11.5. Messages received per minute for each of the nine message categories for subjects in the FC architecture and the central and non-central subjects in the hierarchical architectures. For explanation of the message categories, see text.

11.4.2.1. Why is the difference between the two architectures so small?

If the subjects in the hierarchical architecture received information that they obviously thought good enough to be translated in commands, why did this not lead to better performance in this condition compared to the FC architecture? To answer this question, we must look at the quality of the commands that were issued. A command will be useful if the subject arrives at his or her destination before the fire or at least before the fire starts to spread. Examination of the commands and their consequences showed that the commands did not meet this condition. About 53% of all commands that were obeyed put the obeying subject in a cell where there was not only fire, but also fire that had started to spread or was ready to do so. There were no differences between the two time pressure conditions here, and very little (nonsignificant) improvement from the first to the last trial (from 63% to 45%). This means that rather than being ordered either to a cell where the subject would be in a position to stop approaching fire or to a cell where he or she could extinguish fire before it would start spreading to the next cell(s), the subjects were often ordered to cells where their activity could not actually contribute to the extinction of the fire.

11.5. DISCUSSION

The results of this experiment support the hypothesis that time pressure will have a greater effect on performance in a hierarchical architecture than in an FC architecture. Thus, while subjects in both architectures performed worse when time pressure increased, the effect was significant only for the hierarchical architecture. According to the hypothesis for the study, this is because the central subjects in this architecture do not have the time to process the information they must process to be effective. Indeed, one of the quartets in the high time pressure condition simply did not develop the hierarchical control structure that is characteristic of this architecture in this and other experiments (Brehmer & Svenmarck, 1994).

In the FC condition, subjects in the high time pressure condition also tended to perform at a lower level than the subjects in the hierarchical condition, but the difference between the two time pressure conditions was smaller than in the hierarchical condition, and it was not significant.

The co-ordination processes were clearly different in the two architectures. In the hierarchical architecture, the central subjects assumed the responsibility for the co-ordination. They received more information about the fire, and they transformed this information into commands to the non-central subjects. In the FC-architecture, co-ordination was effected by the communication of intentions. As a consequence, no subject in the FC-condition had to process as much information as the central subjects in the hierarchical condition, who became something of a bottleneck. The subjects in the FC-condition are therefore not so much affected by having less time to process the information, and their co-ordination suffers less from the time pressure.

In the present experiment, the subjects required about 15 seconds to send a message in all four conditions. As a consequence, they could send four times as many messages per update in the low time pressure condition as in the high time pressure condition. This means that the subjects had much less information for their co-ordination in the former condition than in the latter condition. The fact that the performance was lower in the high time pressure condition presumably means that co-ordination is dependent on the number of messages.

However, even if time pressure affected the number of messages that the subjects sent, it did not affect the kinds of messages that they sent. That is, time pressure did not affect *how* the subjects co-ordinated their activity. They achieved their co-ordination in the same way in both conditions, but with fewer messages per update. As noted above, the difference in messages in the number of messages does not express social chit-chat. This shows that there is no simple and direct relation between the number of messages and performance even when only the number of relevant messages is taken into consideration.

The difference in performance measured as time per trial or number of cells lost to fire was lower than would have ben expected on the basis of the differences in updates. Thus, while the difference in updates was 1:4, the difference in time per trial was 1:3 and in cells lost 88 vs. 62, or 1.42:1. That is, the subjects were not four times worse in the high time pressure condition, although they could only send one fourth of the messages per update in this condition compared to the low time pressure condition. It is not altogether clear how these results should be interpreted. The low ratio may be due to efficient fire fighting in the high time pressure condition as well as to inefficient fire fighting in the low time pressure condition.

A theoretical analysis of the demands in this situation suggests that a hierarchical architecture should be more effective than an FC architecture (Brehmer, 1991). This is because efficient co-ordination requires an overall view of the fire. No subject has such an overall view; each subject has only a limited view on the task. The overall view must therefore emerge on the basis of what the subjects communicate among themselves. As noted in the introduction, there is an important difference between the two architectures in this respect. In the hierarchical architecture, where all communication passes through one subject, there is a much greater chance that at least one subject will have an adequate picture of the current state of the fire than in the FC architecture, where each subject is free to communicate with whomever he or she chooses. Provided that the central subject in the hierarchical architecture is able to integrate the information that he or she receives from the other subjects, and then derive the appropriate commands to the other subjects, conditions for co-ordination should exist to a greater extent in a hierarchical architecture than in the FC architecture. We would therefore expect that performance would be better in the former architecture than in the latter.

This is also what Brehmer and Svenmarck (1994) found in an earlier experiment with D³FIRE. The difference was small, however. In the present experiment, we could not replicate this result.

In this experiment, as in the earlier Brehmer and Svenmarck experiment, the central subjects in the hierarchical condition assumed the role of leaders and translated the information they had received into commands to the rest of the subjects in their groups. Despite this, the performance was not better with the hierarchical architecture. The explanation for this seems to be the quality of the commands that were issued by the central subjects in the hierarchical conditions. In about half the cases, these commands put the subject obeying the command in a situation where he or she could not contribute to the extinction of the fire. This suggests that the problem facing the subjects in D³FIRE is not only the co-ordination as such, but a lack of understanding of the dynamic characteristics of the fire on the part of the subjects who issue the commands. Because they do not have a precise understanding of how the fire spreads, they cannot issue the correct commands, even if they have a good picture of the state of the fire. This means that giving the subjects in D³FIRE co-ordination aids will not be sufficient to improve their performance. They also need aids to understand the dynamic nature of the fire.

An important consequence of these results is that the findings obtained with D³FIRE cannot be interpreted as a result of the subjects' ability (or their lack thereof) to co-ordinate their efforts. It is a complex result of their ability to handle a complex task and co-ordinate their efforts at the same time. In this respect, the conditions of a D³FIRE experiment are likely to mirror the circumstances in real world distributed decision tasks.

11.6. ACKNOWLEDGEMENTS

This study was supported by a grant from the Swedish Council for Research in the Humanities and Social Sciences. The author is indebted to Peter Svenmarck for assistance in collecting and analyzing the data.

11.7. REFERENCES

BREHMER, B. (1991). Time scales, distributed decision making and modern information technology. In J. RASMUSSEN, B. BREHMER & J. LEPLAT (Eds), *Distributed Decision Making: Cognitive Models of Cooperative Work*. Chichester: Wiley.

BREHMER, B. & ALLARD, R. (1991). Dynamic decision making: The effects of complexity and feedback delay. In J. RASMUSSEN, B. BREHMER & J. LEPLAT (Eds), *Distributed Decision Making: Cognitive Models of Cooperative Work*. Chichester: Wiley.

BREHMER, B. & DÖRNER, D. (1993). Experiments with computer-simulated microworlds: escaping both the narrow straits of the laboratory and the deep blue sea of the field study. *Computers in Human Behavior*, vol. 9, 171–184.

BREHMER, B. & SVENMARCK, P. (1994). Distributed decision making in dynamic environments: Time scales and architectures of decision making. In J.-P. CAVERNI, M. BAR-HILLEL, F.H. BARRON & H. JUNGERMANN (Eds), *Contributions to Decision Making*. Amsterdam: Elsevier Science.

KLEINMAN, D.L. (1990). Coordination in human teams. *Proceedings of IFAC conference, Tallinn*.

RASMUSSEN, J. (1991). Modelling distributed decision making. In J. RASMUSSEN, B. BREHMER & J. LEPLAT (Eds), *Distributed Decision Making: Cognitive Models of Cooperative Work*. Chichester: Wiley.

RASMUSSEN, J., BREHMER, B. & LEPLAT, J. (Eds) (1991). *Distributed Decision Making: Cognitive Models of Cooperative Work*. Chichester: Wiley.

SVENMARCK, P. & BREHMER, B. (1991). D³FIRE – An experimental paradigm for the study of distributed decision making. In *Distributed Decision Making. Proceedings of the Third Mohawc Workshop, Belgirate, Italy, 13–15 May 1991*, B. BREHMER (Ed.). Roskilde: Risø National Laboratory.

SVENMARCK, P. & BREHMER, B. (1992). Face-to-face communication versus communication by means of electronic mail in distributed decision making. In B. BREHMER (Ed.), *MOHAWC: Separate Papers*, Roskilde: Risø National Laboratory.

WELLENS, A.R. (1993). Group situation awareness. In N.J. CASTELLAN, Jr (Ed.), *Individual and Group Decision Making. Current Issues*. Hillsdale, N.J.: Lawrence Earlbaum Associates.

PART FOUR

Training

CHAPTER TWELVE

Co-ordination training in Emergency Management

JOHN DOWELL AND WALTER SMITH

12.1. THE ISSUE OF CO-ORDINATION IN EMERGENCY MANAGEMENT WORKSYSTEMS

Catastrophic accidents and natural disasters require many professionals to work together if the emergency rescue operation is to be effective. Co-ordination between different agencies is especially difficult when, as is often the case, those agencies are faced with severe uncertainties, hazards and time limitations.

Consider the example of the fire at the King's Cross underground station in London, UK. Without a reliable assessment of the hazards, and with poor communications, the Fire Service was under pressure to decide on an evacuation route. A tactical level decision on the best evacuation route would have required co-ordination with the underground railway company, to establish the available exits and to control the movement of trains. In the event, some people were evacuated by the trains which, oblivious to the fire, continued to run as normal. Other people were led towards station exits through the booking hall. However the movement of the trains fanned the fire, and contributed to the fatal "flashover" into the booking hall. The public inquiry (Fennell, 1988) was later to comment on the lack of co-ordination between agencies.

Co-ordination is now a well-recognized training need in Europe and the USA (Auf der Heide, 1989). In the UK, the emergency services have established a regime of training practices including seminars and "live" simulation exercises. Increasingly, tabletop simulation exercises are being used with the principal aim of providing training in co-ordination. Tabletop exercises use a physical model of a catastrophe (displayed on the top of a large table) to promote discussion about the organization and implementation of the emergency operation. The trainees may include agents from each of the agencies that would be involved in the real emergency operation.

Tabletop exercises are an evolutionary development in training technology. They were developed within the emergency management community through the appropriation and modification of techniques used by military trainers. An alternative approach, which might be described as technology-led, is now making its appearance in the form of

147

computer-based simulations of emergency management tasks. This new technology is accompanied by promises of benefits for co-ordination training. Yet neither the evolutionary nor the technology-led developments seek to specify a training agenda for the cognitive behaviours of the worksystem. As a consequence, they are an insufficient basis for the design of effective co-ordination training. By contrast, a cognitive engineering approach would specify solutions to the cognitive design problem of co-ordination training for emergency management; it would then implement those specifications in an appropriate form of technology and practice (Long & Dowell, 1996).

This chapter aims to contribute to such a cognitive engineering approach. It first summarizes an agenda of co-ordination training needs for emergency management. An account is then given of how the agenda can be used to evaluate the physical simulation provided by a tabletop exercise for training tactical level personnel from the emergency services. Finally, the same agenda is used in the comparative evaluation of two computer-based training systems. The comparison indicates desirable cognitive properties of both the physical and computer-based systems (see Table 12.1 for a summary) as a contribution to formulating the cognitive design problem of co-ordination training.

12.2. AN AGENDA OF TRAINING NEEDS FOR CO-ORDINATION

An agenda of training needs has been identified (Dowell, 1995) through a cognitive analysis of co-ordination failures in emergency management. The agenda identifies specific issues related to the co-ordination of planning, action, communications and knowledge, each of which must be addressed by training.

12.2.1. Training needs for co-ordinated plans

The contingency plans of each agency participating in an emergency operation can only be high level and conditional, and must be interpreted for the particularities of each emergency. If this plan interpretation is conducted implicitly, co-ordination will suffer, leading to actions which are duplicated, are in conflict, or neglect important concerns. Because plan interpretation is conducted under "high temporal constraints" (Samurçay & Rogalski, 1993) and must be "reactive" to domain events (the "metronome" of co-ordinated behaviour, Hutchins (1990)), monolithic, decompositional planning must give way to a more opportunistic but fragmented form of planning.

Co-ordination requires that the contingency plans of each agency be explicitly interpreted, and that conflicts can be recognized and resolved. It requires that the priorities of all agents should conform with a unitary goal structure for the emergency operation. It also requires opportunistic planning to be made explicit.

12.2.2. Training needs for co-ordinated action

Rather than deriving from a "master plan", the sequencing of actions across agencies is determined by mutual constraints or "behavioural dependencies" (Hutchins, 1990). Action then becomes reactive to the effects of other agents' actions. Co-ordination relies on the recognition and negotiation of behavioural dependencies between agents, and it requires that the actions of each agent, and their effects, are visible to those who will need to act on them.

12.2.3. Training needs for co-ordinated communications

Emergency agencies commonly report that they are "only as good as our information". Co-ordination requires authoritative, validated and accurate information to be transmitted as rapidly as possible in an emergency operation. It requires an understanding of how others will respond to messages and actions. Co-ordination also requires the use of a common language for the communications between agencies.

12.2.4. Training needs for co-ordinated role and task knowledge

Co-ordination requires agencies and their agents to have redundant knowledge and skills. This redundancy enables differences in the division of labour to be negotiated. Furthermore, the cognitive horizon (Hutchins, 1994) which delimits the uniqueness and redundancy of an agent's knowledge allows recognition of which agents need extra support: if co-ordination means giving extra support where it is needed, then cognitive horizons must be sufficiently broad.

These issues for co-ordination might be considered as an agenda of training needs for emergency management. It is an agenda which might be used to assess both the effectiveness of current training practices and the design of future training practices. The following section uses the agenda to evaluate the effectiveness of co-ordination training provided by the tabletop exercise.

12.3. EVALUATION OF TABLETOP TRAINING

Tabletop exercises are an established form of co-ordination training, using a physical model and a disaster scenario to promote discussion about the emergency operation. The trainees represent the agencies that would be involved in the real emergency operation. The following is an account of a tabletop exercise concerning a railway accident scenario and observed by the authors.

Participating in the tabletop exercise were tactical level officers from the emergency services and managers of equivalent level from associated organizations including hospitals, the railway company, and the local municipal authorities. In all, some thirty trainees were attending the training exercise which was orchestrated by a "moderator" and his assistant. The exercise was directed towards a model of a section of urban railway line. To begin, the moderator summarized key features of the scenario, such as schools and roads, and answered questions from the trainees.

The moderator then delivered a narration of events to begin the exercise. The narration described how the police receive a report from a member of the public of a "loud bang" on the railway. The moderator then asked trainees, grouped into syndicates, to provide answers to the *first question*, concerning what would be the initial response of each agency, who would be notified, and how long it would take to arrive at the scene. A debriefing session allowed discussion of responses to the first question.

The emergency scenario was now extended and miniatures were added to the model representing a collision between a passenger train and a tanker train. Trainees from the emergency services were then invited to place on the scenario models of their respective units representing their current status. The *second question* then asked trainees to consider what would be the priorities of the first persons on the scene from each agency. The trainees again withdrew into syndicates to discuss their answers, and then re-convened for a debriefing of the second question. The tabletop exercise continued in this way; the scenario was extended (the tanker train begins leaking a toxic and volatile liquid), and further questions were posed by the moderator. The exercise was closed after the debriefing of the final question.

This example of a tabletop exercise can be evaluated in terms of its support for the agenda of co-ordination training needs identified above. The evaluation addresses each of the areas of co-ordination concerning planning, action, communication and knowledge.

12.3.1. Training co-ordinated planning

The basis of the individual training that preceded the tabletop exercise was the contingency plans of the respective agencies. Those contingency plans were implicitly referenced during the exercise, for example, in the response of a police officer to the second question:

> Our first priority is to scale the incident, and to identify the residual hazards and the casualties. We would contact Scotland Yard and declare it a major incident. We would likely then evacuate those two schools (and) set up a rendezvous point for emergency vehicles. . . .

The tabletop exercise disclosed the varying interpretation of implicitly referenced plans. For example, while the first police officer appears not to interpret the primary residual hazard to be other train traffic, a second police officer does make this interpretation correctly, although the apparent absence of procedure gives cause for concern:

> Hopefully the staff at the station. . . . should already be aware of what's happened and have stopped the trains to prevent any further disaster.

Conflicting views about priorities were disclosed in the interpretation of contingency plans. In contrast to the responses of the police officers, a fire services officer correctly identifies the priority of obtaining electrical isolation of the crash as necessary for the safety of the victims and rescuers.

> Our first priority is to get the line shut down, to protect people coming off the train and the services going in. By this time, you'd probably have shocked and confused people streaming all over the track.

So, through discussion, the tabletop exercise helped all the trainees to recognize common priorities in managing the emergency operation. Tabletop exercises, it would seem, provide training in resolving conflicts between different agents' and agencies' priorities that may often produce co-ordination difficulties. The tabletop exercise followed a "storyboard" sequence of events; however, it did not have a temporal dimension, merely a direction. Events and their responses were not constrained by any time-scale, and it seems implausible that explicit opportunistic planning could be learnt from the tabletop exercise.

12.3.2. Training co-ordinated action

The tabletop exercise disclosed the dependencies between agents that may dictate the sequences of their planned actions. For example, a fire services officer and railway official identify a mutual dependency for confirmation of the electrical isolation of the track before they can proceed with the rescue operation:

> *Fire services officer:* "But how will we know if the electricity is off? We'll be frazzled if we're not told!"
> *Railway official:* "Well it's our duty to get the lines switched off – to block other trains."
> *Moderator:* "So the priority has to be to stop the trains, then get the power off? Is this the overriding priority?"
> *Railway official:* "Yes – but in a crash like this, the current would almost certainly be off already . . . because of short circuits caused by the wreckage."

In this way, tabletop exercises appear to train recognition and negotiation of the dependencies between agents dictating sequences of actions, as necessary for co-ordination. Yet the process of discussion did not, and could not, simulate the visible execution of plans. Consider the later reaction of two other participants to the decision of the first police officer to establish a traffic exclusion zone around St Michael's church without considering access to the accident:

> *Fire services officer:* "We're all round the wrong side of the train at the moment. We need to be on the other side – 'cause access will be easier up the grassy bank. . . ."
> *Ambulance officer:* "There could be 750 injured people in those 8 carriages so I'd have called a major incident by now. We would also get up a rendezvous and a control point on the other side [of the train]."

Although it is now apparent that access to the accident should be from the other side of the embankment, by this time the rescue operation would already have attempted to scale the wrong side of the embankment. It would appear that tabletop exercises are unable to train the reactivity of actions that supports co-ordination.

12.3.3. Training co-ordinated communication

The tabletop exercise exposed all trainees to the same information at the same time; it did not simulate the progressive dissemination of information that occurs during emergency operations. That information was generally authoritative, since it was provided by the moderator, and it was generally validated, since it was apparent in the model. The information was also accurate, indeed, at one point a railway official is able to obtain an immediate clarification of facts:

> *Railway official:* "Well our first person on the scene is of course the driver; and assuming he's OK . . . ?"
> *Moderator:* "He's dead . . . and there's no guard."
> *Railway official:* "Ah . . . he's dead . . . and there's no guard, . . . right, so it's not a dangerous goods train, then. So it's down to the driver, then, of the tanker train, to inform the signal box and then to put detonators on the track. Mmh."

Although the initial report of a "loud bang" better simulates the uncertainty of communications, it would appear that tabletop exercises are unable to recreate the conditions of information dissemination required for co-ordination training. Because the tabletop exercise did not simulate the "channels of information" and their contents that occur during a real emergency operation, neither could it re-create the asynchrony of communications; all trainees could address all others directly and immediately. More generally, then, tabletop exercises appear unable to train the rapid and timely dissemination needed for co-ordination, and it is highly questionable whether they provide understanding of how others will respond to the information.

12.3.4. Training co-ordinated knowledge

There was no evidence in the tabletop exercise of differences between the nominal and real divisions of labour, for two apparent reasons. First, the scenario did not present the exigencies of a catastrophe which might force a difference between the nominal and real divisions of labour. Second, each trainee was playing the role of their entire agency, rather than the role of a single agent. Without evidence of the division of labour being negotiated, it may only be concluded that the tabletop exercise did not provide training in its configuration, as is necessary for co-ordination.

However, if the real division of labour requires a partial redundancy in knowledge and skills, that redundancy could be learnt through the discussion of individual responses. For example, all the trainees are exposed to the conceptual distinction between "stopping the trains" (i.e. via signalling) and "getting the power turned off" (i.e. protecting the victims of the crash and their rescuers from electrocution). This distinction was not apparent in the responses of the fire service and police officers. Those other agencies also appear to learn about the issues confronting the railway personnel in obtaining track isolation – and they learn that the wreckage will almost certainly have already short-circuited the current. Equally, the discussion would extend the cognitive horizon of each trainee. More generally, then, tabletop exercises appear to provide the redundant knowledge needed for co-ordinating the configuration of roles, for example in recognizing which agents need extra support.

12.3.5. Summary of evaluation

In summary, the tabletop exercise provides valuable but incomplete training in co-ordination. Trainees learn collectively to interpret contingency plans, to resolve conflicts between different priorities, and to recognize and negotiate mutual constraints. They may also extend their cognitive horizons, as is necessary for mutual support and configuring the real division of labour. However, the exercise does not provide training in the reactivity of planning to events, or in the reactivity of actions to the actions of others. It can provide no training in planning and decision-making under temporal constraints. Neither does the tabletop exercise appear to provide training in the dissemination of information, nor in handling the asynchrony of communications.

12.4. COMPUTER-BASED TRAINING SIMULATORS FOR EMERGENCY MANAGEMENT

Advances in computer-based simulation technology, in particular in agent-based intelligent systems and in dynamic rendering techniques, are supporting the development of training systems for emergency management. Those systems simulate physical and conceptual features of the emergency management domain and worksystem which were previously impossible. Two very different examples are the Iccarus and the Vistrain systems. An account of these systems is given below together with an assessment against the training needs agenda (see Table 12.1).

Table 12.1. Comparative evaluation of three alternative worksystems for co-ordination training in emergency management

Co-ordination training needs	Tabletop Multiple trainees with scripted physical simulation of domain scenario	Iccarus Single trainee with interactive computer-based simulation of domain scenario and co-ordinating agents	Vistrain Multiple trainees with scripted computer-based simulation of domain scenario
Planning			
Explicit interpretation of plans	✓	✓	✓
Recognition of conflict	✓	✗	✓
Resolution of conflict	✓	✗	✓
Unitary goal structure	✓	✗	✓
Explicit opportunistic planning	✗	✓	✗
Action			
Recognition of behavioural dependencies	✓	✗	✓
Negotiation of behavioural dependencies	✓	✗	✓
Making actions and effects visible	✗	✗	✗
Communication			
Authoritative and accurate dissemination	✗	✗	✓
Timely transmission	✗	✗	✓
Understanding others' responses	✗	✗	✓
Role and task knowledge			
Negotiation of division of labour	✗	✗	✓
Extended cognitive horizons	✓	✗	✗

12.4.1. Iccarus

Iccarus is a simulator for training fire service officers in managing large-scale fires (Workhouse, 1992). It consists of a set of modules for creating and running an event-based scenario (typically, a fire at a cinema). The simulator trains fire officers individually, and a training session runs as follows.

To begin, the simulator provides the trainee with a spoken introduction to the catastrophe scenario, explaining that they are currently driving towards a fire. The simulator video monitor presents a sequence of photographic images of a route through an urban area, during which can be heard various recorded radio messages concerning the incident and simulating the radio traffic being relayed to the fire control centre.

The scenario soon describes the trainee as entering the mobile Forward Command Post at the scene of the emergency operation. The trainee must now take over as officer-in-charge of the operation. They are briefed by the officer standing down using the standard protocol: "What have I got? What messages have you sent? What have you done?" The part of the officer standing down is played by the simulator; the dialogue is conducted by the trainee interrogating the officer through the simulator's graphical user interface, textual responses being displayed on the computer monitor. The monitor provides a strategist's representation of the emergency operation: a plan of the building and the current state of the fire; the current deployment of "resources" and those available for deployment. This representation re-creates paper-based planning aids typically used in managing emergency operations. It is a view of the computational domain model of the emergency operation as that model is executed by the simulator's transputer.

The domain model is an event-driven, dynamic model simulating the progress of the fire through the building and the location and properties of objects such as hazardous materials; in addition, it simulates the location and behaviour of firemen and agents of other emergency agencies and of members of the public trapped in the building, and it models the location and behaviour of equipment such as pumps. In his or her role as officer-in-charge, the trainee is able to manage the emergency operation by intervening in the state of the domain model, for example by requesting more pumps and officers, moving pumps and directing specialist teams, etc. These actions are taken by issuing commands: for example, to deploy a breathing apparatus team, the trainee uses the mouse to select the icon "BA Deploy" and an entrance to the building. The domain model responds to these instructions: for example, the breathing apparatus team are able to act with semi-intelligence to enter the building, locate trapped people or fight the fire. So, the effects of the trainee's instructions, the progress of the fire, and the behaviours of up to 200 "automaton" firemen and other agents are each visible to the trainee.

Photographic stills and video film are stored on videodisc within the simulator. The simulator also provides an acoustic environment of voices and noises typically heard at "firegrounds". As events unfold within the executing domain model, the simulator selects appropriate visual images and sounds, for example distraught people stating that someone is trapped in the building, or other agencies demanding information. The intended effect is to bombard the trainee and induce them to "suspend disbelief" (Hennessey & O'Shea, 1993). The training session finishes when the fire is controlled, or the building lost. All the scenario events and the trainee's actions are recorded and the record used to debrief the trainee. The debrief addresses at each point, whether the trainee has an overview, whether they are deploying resources effectively, whether communications are effective, and whether the trainee is being reactive to events.

As apparent from its debriefing structure, Iccarus is intended to provide comprehensive training in emergency management, including training in co-ordination issues. With reference to the agenda of co-ordination training needs, it is apparent that Iccarus might in principle enable the trainee to learn how to plan by experience. It is able to do this because its domain model is dynamic, it represents the time course of events of the emergency operation, and it is responsive to the decisions taken by the trainee. Further, the trainee might learn to plan opportunistically and reactively to domain events. However, because all the individuals with whom the trainee interacts are reduced to automatons, the trainee cannot learn to recognize or negotiate plan conflicts, nor to co-ordinate actions, communications and role and task knowledge.

12.4.2. Vistrain

Vistrain (video-based integrated system for training applications) is a multi-user training simulator intended for general application to management training (LTU, 1992) which has also been applied to training police officers in the management of emergencies. For example, one fictitious scenario relates to a collision between a heavy truck and a train. The system provides team-based training to support tactical level decision-making through the negotiation of plans. Teams are separated, their separations being task and role deter-mined. For example, Vistrain is intended to simulate the activities of a forward control point and the strategic-level command centre at a major incident. Within their different roles and locations, teams have access to different information. For example, the forward control point team might have access to the current status of trapped individuals in an emergency scenario, while the command centre would have access to information on spare capacities in the regional hospitals. That information is represented in different media, including simulated news broadcasts and video clips. The different teams are exposed to cues to which they are expected to respond. The cues include video images and radio and telephone messages. The teams must decide on their responses to these cues and communicate their decisions to other teams. Scenarios are run from a central workstation by a moderator who is able to call different events and responses to the trainees' actions. However, the scenarios are pre-authored and stored on multiplexed videodisc, so the variety of responses and scenario developments is limited.

The moderator monitors the activity of the different teams through shadowing the communications between teams and the information displays to which the teams are responding. The moderator's workstation provides a storyboard representation of the appropriate activities of each of the teams in response to specific events. This storyboard can be used to record and mark the behaviours of the team for later debriefing. Trainees using Vistrain reported through questionnaires that the system provides a more demand-ing and realistic training experience than the tabletop exercise (LTU, 1992). However, to assess the training value of Vistrain with respect to co-ordination, we can refer to the agenda of training needs.

For the training needs of co-ordinated planning, Vistrain can, in principle, support learning to plan by experience. It appears to support the explicit sharing of plans, and of the planning process, including the interpretation of contingency plans. However while the system possesses a dynamic domain model, that model has only a limited repertoire of responses. Trainees therefore have a limited learning experience of the need for plan-ning to be reactive and opportunistic. Nevertheless, co-ordination of priorities between the plans of different agencies can be learnt with the system which enables the negoti-ation of those priorities within a unitary goal structure. With respect to the training needs of co-ordinated action, the communication between distributed agents and agencies supported by Vistrain allows recognition of behavioural dependencies, and it allows rehearsal of the process of negotiation. With respect to the training needs of co-ordinated communications, Vistrain appears to support rehearsal of the dissemination of authorit-ative, validated and accurate information. It is able to do this because it simulates the properties and contents of different communication channels, making evident the diffi-culties that occur when information is not authoritative, valid or accurate. Finally, with respect to the co-ordination issues of roles and task knowledge, Vistrain may allow recognition of the negotiation of divisions of labour between agents. However the form of rehearsal-based training provided by Vistrain is less likely to promote redundant know-ledge of the tasks of other agencies, since that knowledge will only be implicit in the activities of those other agencies. As a consequence, Vistrain is unlikely to extend sig-nificantly the cognitive horizons of the trainees.

12.5. CONTRIBUTIONS TO COGNITIVE ENGINEERING AND THE SPECIFICATION OF CO-ORDINATION TRAINING

The tabletop exercise and the computer-based simulators evaluated in this chapter can be seen, respectively, as exemplars of evolutionary and technology-led approaches to the training of co-ordination in emergency management. The evolutionary approach has the advantages of carrying over the wisdom implicit in current emergency management practice. Computer-based solutions, in comparison, offer formal properties thought to be desirable on logical grounds; for example, interaction with a "real-time" event-driven domain, flexible scenario generation, behaviour recording and evaluation tools.

Cognitive engineering provides an alternative to both the evolutionary and technology-led approaches. In this view, the starting point must be an explicit agenda of training needs specified as those cognitive behaviours which underlie effective co-ordination in emergency management. Training technology is then designed with the goal of establishing these behaviours in the trainees. Such an agenda has been presented in this chapter and used to evaluate existing training technologies (see Table 12.1).

When compared with the training needs agenda, the Iccarus and Vistrain systems can be recognized as significantly different solutions to the co-ordination training problem. Iccarus, the individual user system, appears to provide an enhanced learning of co-ordinated planning because of the reactive domain model on which the system is constructed. However, the learning of coordinated action and communication is negligible, since other agents and agencies are reduced to automatons. By contrast, Vistrain, the multi-user system, appears to provide an enhanced learning of co-ordinated plan implementation and communication, since it constructs the real-time decision-making and communications channels and dynamics of multi-agency co-ordination. However, Vistrain's non-computational model ensures that planning cannot be reactive to domain events, and so, the opportunity for learning to co-ordinate planning is compromised.

A contrast can also be made between the two computer-based systems and the tabletop exercise. Neither Iccarus nor Vistrain appeared to train the vital co-ordination of roles and knowledge apparent in the tabletop exercise. Indeed, they appear to support a qualitatively different training experience to the one provided by the tabletop exercise: a difference often characterized rhetorically as a move away from "learning by talking" towards a form of "learning by doing".

To conclude, we have used an agenda of needs for co-ordination training to assess current practices which use the tabletop exercise. We used the same agenda to assess two different forms of computer-based training system. Qualitative and important differences between those training systems and practices are evident. It is similarly evident that evolutionary and technology-led developments will not ensure the most effective training system. We advocate a cognitive engineering approach to specify the training needs and the training system to meet those needs. The agenda of training needs, and the assessment of the tabletop exercise, are intended to contribute to that process.

12.6. ACKNOWLEDGEMENT

Work described in this chapter was supported by a grant from the Economic and Social Research Council under the Cognitive Engineering Programme.

12.7. REFERENCES

AUF DER HEIDE, E. (1989). *Disaster Response: Principles of Preparation and Co-ordination*. St Louis: Mosby.

DOWELL, J. (1995). Co-ordination in the management of emergencies and the tabletop training exercise. *Le Travail Humain*, vol. 58, 85–102.

FENNELL, D. (1988). *Investigation into the King's Cross Underground Fire*. London: Department of Transport (HMSO).

HENNESSEY, S. & O'SHEA, T. (1993). Learner perceptions of realism and magic in computer simulations. *British Journal of Education Technology*, vol. 24, 125–138.

HUTCHINS, E. (1990). The technology of team navigation. In J. GALEGHER, R. KRAUT and C. EGIDO (Eds) *Intellectual Teamwork*. Hillsdale, NJ: Lawrence Erlbaum.

HUTCHINS, E. (1994). *Cognition in the Wild*. Cambridge, MA: MIT Press.

LONG, J. and DOWELL, J. (1996). Cognitive engineering human computer interactions. *The Psychologist*, vol. 9, 313–317.

LTU (Learning Technologies Unit) (1992). *Report of the development of the control of crowds at major spectator events*. Sheffield: Department for Education and Employment.

SAMURÇAY, R. & ROGALSKI, J. (1993). Co-operative work and decision-making in emergency management. *Le Travail Humain*, vol. 56, 53–77.

WORKHOUSE, 1992. *Iccarus*. Sheffield: Department for Education and Employment.

CHAPTER THIRTEEN

Microworld systems for emergency management training

REGO GRANLUND

13.1. INTRODUCTION

This chapter describes a research project that deals with the design and construction of computer simulation in decision training systems, in particular with the development of simulation systems for training of commanders and staff in emergency decision-making and crisis management. This description focuses on the emergency management characteristics that influence the design and construction of a proper emergency management training system. The underlying assumption in this work is this: decision training systems, for emergency management, can be more effective if pedagogical strategies are integrated into the computer simulations. To examine how emergency management training can be generated, we have developed C³FIRE – a *microworld* simulation system. The microworld generates a task environment for a forest fire-fighting staff, where we can train a staff in commanding and controlling the fire-fighting units. The goal of the microworld is to have an experimental platform where we can study *distributed decision-making* and *situation awareness*, and at the same time experiment with different control strategies in order to obtain certain specified pedagogical goals. This work is based on empirical studies of an existing military training system used to train infantry battalion staffs.

13.2. BACKGROUND

Social systems, such as emergency management systems (for example forest fire-fighting, traffic accidents, earthquakes, pollution accidents) and military systems, can be characterized by their *dynamic behaviour* created *by co-operating actors*. To achieve good performance in these systems, it is important that the people who command and control the systems have a good understanding of the system and their role in the system. This requires the commanders and staff to be trained in real-world situations, so that they can experience the dynamic behaviour of the system. In these kinds of system it is often too expensive or humanly impossible to practise in real-life situations. In these cases we need training systems where we can train commanders and staff in commanding and controlling complex systems. The goal of a training system for commanders and staff is usually that they should experience the work situation that they will meet in a real situation.

13.3. EMERGENCY MANAGEMENT TRAINING

13.3.1. Emergency management

Emergency management systems (such as forest fire-fighting, traffic accidents, earthquakes, pollution accidents) and military systems have been classified by Brehmer (1991) and Hutchins (1990) as *social dynamic systems*, containing co-operating actors. One characteristic of these dynamic systems is that they are often so complex that the systems need some type of hierarchical organization (Brehmer, 1991). An abstract view of the world can in its simplest form be a world model consisting of a target system and a controlling system, based on the staff and their subordinates. Examples of a target system are fire in a forest-fire extinguishing operation or the enemy in a military operation. An example of the staff's subordinates is a fire-fighting unit (see Fig. 13.1).

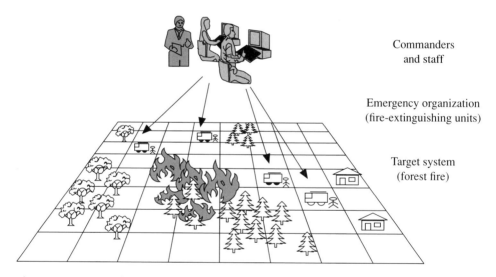

Commanders
and staff

Emergency organization
(fire-extinguishing units)

Target system
(forest fire)

Figure 13.1. A complex dynamic system containing a target system and a controlling system based on the staff and their subordinate units. Example: a forest fire-fighting domain.

The *target system* is the system that is the target of the emergency organization's operations. Examples of target systems include the fire in forest-fire extinguishing operations or the enemy forces in military operations. When civilians are in danger or when they can influence the target system, they can also be classified as a part of the target system. The target system can be classified as a *complex dynamic system*, which changes both autonomously and as a consequence of actions performed on the system (Brehmer, 1995).

The *controlling system* in an emergency organization comprises the staff's subordinates and can be seen as the staff's tool in their task of controlling the target system. Examples of a subordinate unit include fire-fighting units, ambulance units, and military units. In large hierarchical organizations, such as a military brigade, the emergency organization can consist of several levels – companies, platoons, and so forth. The controlling system is only *semi-controlled* by the staff and can, as the target system, be viewed as a *complex dynamic system* (Brehmer, 1995). It changes both as a consequence of the commands and on the subordinates' own decisions.

The *staff's* task is to command and control the organization. This means that they should collect information from the subordinates so that they acquire a shared situation awareness. On this basis they should plan and transmit orders to their subordinates in order to direct and co-ordinate actions between the subordinate units. The staff functions as decision-maker only and does not operate directly on the target system.

13.3.1.1. Complex dynamic systems

Emergency management systems and military systems have two important properties: they are both complex dynamic systems and they are both controlled by distributed decision-making. The complexity and the dynamic and autonomous behaviour of the target system and the emergency organization make them difficult to predict and control. The states of the system are changed both autonomously and as a function of the actions that the decision maker makes. The control of the systems has to occur in real-time and assessing a complete current state of the system is difficult because the dynamics of and the relations within the system are not visible. Brehmer (1994) defines a complex dynamic system by the following criteria.

1. Its *complexity*: there exist a set of disjunctive goals and a set of related processes in the system.

2. Its *dynamics*: the states of the system are changed both autonomously and as a function of the actions that the decision-maker takes. The decision-makers have limited time to make their decisions.

3. Its *opaqueness*: it is difficult to see the current state and what relations exist in the system.

13.3.1.2. Distributed decision-making

The decision-making in an emergency organization and military systems has been classified by Brehmer (1995) as *distributed decision-making* or *team decision-making*. This means that the decision-making is distributed among the actors in the organization. Emergency systems are also often based on a hierarchical organization where the decision-makers work on different *time-scales* (Brehmer & Svenmarck, 1995). The members of the staff work on a higher time level than the subordinate decision-makers, and are responsible for the strategic decisions.

The distributed decision-making in an organization makes it important to train communication and understanding of shared frameworks and goals. *Team decision-making* can be viewed as distributed decision-making where the co-operating actors have different roles, tasks, and access to items of information in the decision process (Klein & Thordsen, 1989; Orasanu & Salas, 1993).

One way to view decision-making in real-world tasks for a commander and staff in an emergency organization is as a tactical reasoning process. This was the approach taken by Rogalski & Samurçay (1993), who described the activity and information flow in a three-level hierarchical emergency organization (see Fig. 13.2).

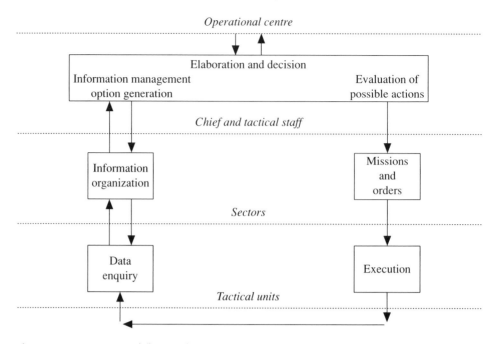

Figure 13.2. Operational flow and task distribution in emergency management.

They also describe the commander and staff's work of assessing the situation and co-ordination of actions by the method of tactical reasoning (MTR) (Samurçay & Rogalski, 1991) (see Fig. 13.3). The staff should collect information from the emergency organization and the other information resources so that they achieve a situation awareness and understanding of the risk status. On this basis they should define the task, plan and transmit orders to subordinates in order to direct and co-ordinate actions between the subordinate units.

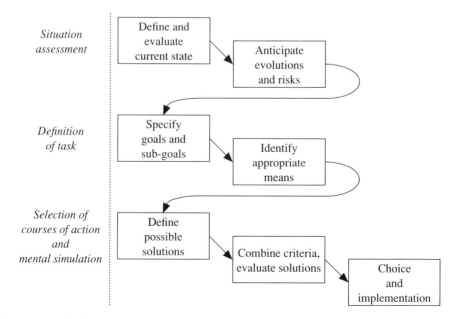

Figure 13.3. The basic steps in the model of tactical reasoning (MTR).

13.3.2. Training emergency management

The goal of training systems for commanders and staff is usually to gain experience-based knowledge. *Experience-based knowledge* is knowledge about how it is to work in real situations and cannot be learned without experiencing the behaviour patterns of the system and the work involved. Berkum & Jong (1991) point out that this kind of know-ledge can be a good target for simulation-based learning environments. They refer to it as *compiled conceptual knowledge* and view it as "getting a feel for the underlying model" (without needing to be able to articulate its internal workings). Another way to describe such knowledge is in terms of Rasmussen's three levels of human action control: knowledge-based behaviour, rule-based behaviour, and skill-based behaviour (Rasmussen, 1983) (see Fig. 13.4).

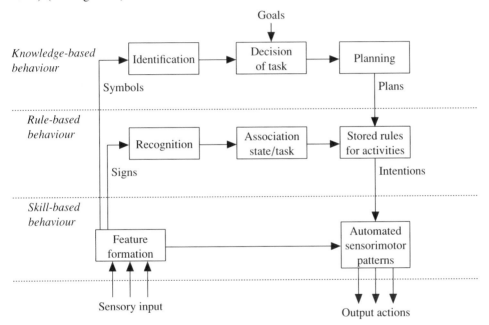

Figure 13.4. A three-level description of human action control.

The *skill-based behaviour* represents sensorimotor performance during acts or activities that, after a statement of an intention, take place without conscious control as smooth, automated, and highly integrated patterns of behaviour. The *rule-based behaviour* represents conscious activities controlled by stored rules or procedures that may have been derived empirically on previous occasions. Performance is goal-oriented, structured by feed-forward control through stored rules. Often the goal is not explicitly formulated, but is found implicitly in the situation releasing the stored rules. The *knowledge-based behaviour* represents activities that are activated by conscious plans from explicit goals and mental models of the problem.

A common view on the differences between a novice and an expert is that the expert can select and use the relevant information, and works with signs and symbols in an efficient way. It is also common to say that an expert has more *compiled knowledge* about a given task and system. This means that the expert works more on the rule- and skill-based behaviour level. The goal of training in an emergency management training system is often to let the trainees experience the system so that they develop more compiled knowledge about their tasks and the system.

13.3.2.1. Training goals

The knowledge gained when using typical emergency training systems can be in the form
of experiencing some dynamic behaviour of the target system or the emergency organization, and learning how to perform planning and co-ordination of actions. Examples of
common training goals can be described by knowledge about the target system, the
controlling system, the tactical reasoning and the work situation.

Target system: To know the concepts and the relation between the concepts, and to
experience the dynamic behaviour of the target system. To be able to assess the current
state of the target system and predict the effects of alternative actions.

Controlling system: Understanding the architecture of the emergency organization.
Knowing how to use the organization to get information and how to use and co-ordinate
the resources so that they regulate the target system. Understanding other persons' needs
and goals, and understanding the importance of shared frameworks and goals.

Tactical reasoning: Understanding the doctrine and the goals of their work, common
strategies to solve the tasks, work procedures, how to interpret and understand the current
situation, i.e. "situation awareness", identifying future critical situations and suchlike.

Work situation: to experience how it is to work under time pressure or with a high
information load, or how it is to work with inconsistent or missing information.

13.3.2.2. Simulation in training systems

One important problem with this type of training system is that the simulation of the
surrounding world should be so realistic that it generates the same behaviour pattern as
the real world. The decision maker in the staff uses the behaviour pattern to generate a
mental model of the world. It is therefore important that this behaviour pattern describes
the dynamic behaviour that exists in the real world system. There is always a risk for the
students to create a mental model of the system that does not correspond to the real
world, by learning some simulation-specific behaviour (Gestrelius, 1993). The problem
with the simulation is that real-world systems are often based on *co-operating actors* in
a complex system. Three important problems are as follows.

1. *Natural language interaction:* the interaction between the staff and the co-operating
   actors in the emergency organization should in many cases mirror real situations,
   which means complex nature language sentences. A common way to solve this simulation problem is to simplify and restrict the type of communication, or to use role-
   playing human actors that play the role of the different co-operating actors in the
   environment.

2. *Activity simulation:* the activity descriptions of the actors in the emergency organization and the target system are often complex and are therefore difficult to simulate.
   The modelling of an actor can be simplified for a certain training goal or the actor can
   be simulated by a human role-playing actor. One goal of activity simulation is that the
   combination of all activities should generate the same dynamic behaviour patterns as
   the real-world system.

3. *Training session control:* the simulation should have a control structure that can be
   adapted to support the pedagogical strategy. The simulation of the activities and the
   communication should vary depending on training goals, the knowledge of the students, and the commander's and the staff's operations.

13.3.2.3. Training organization

A common simulation strategy in this type of training system is to have a training organization that consists of training manager, role-playing training assistants and some computer simulation support (see Fig. 13.5). The tasks in this type of training system can be described as follows.

Trainee: The trained staff should work in their normal environment. They should use the same tools in a training session as in a real situation.

Training assistants: Their task is to perform a realistic role play of the actors that exist in the simulation. The training assistant should follow an abstract scenario, communicate with the staff, react to the commands from the staff and to the information they get from the computer simulation, and follow the commands from the training manager. The idea is that when some event occurs, they use the computer simulation and/or start a *mental simulation* of the activity. The main problem for the training assistant is to perform a good mental simulation of their units in the world. One problem is to keep all the processes in mind and not to forget any important response from these activities. There is always a risk that the training assistant becomes overloaded when he or she is responsible for simulating a large part of an organization.

Training manager: The training manager should follow the activity of staff and direct the session so that it generates a proper training session for the staff.

Computer simulation: The training assistants and the training manager should have a computer system that helps them to simulate physical items and store data about the world. In more advanced simulations the computer can also have simple models of human actors so that it can generate a simple simulation of actors that exist in the world.

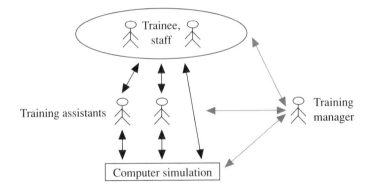

Figure 13.5. A common training organization.

13.4. A TRAINING SYSTEM EXAMPLE

The decision training system, InfSS Borensberg, is a good example of a training system for commanders and staff. The Swedish military personnel who are using this system refer to it as a tactical training system for training military infantry battalion commanders and staff (TRACCS, 1990). The training aims at enhanced team work capacity, where the trainee staff should train in acting and understanding the situations that are common in their work. The training should provide realistic battlefield conditions and sequences of events.

The training system is a tactical training centre for training military staffs that command and control a military infantry unit of the size of a battalion (800 people). This type of staff consists of approximately five persons working in a special commanding and controlling vehicle, communicating with the surrounding world through radio and computer links. In this tactical training system the surrounding world is simulated, but the controlling vehicle in which the staff work is their own off-road personnel carrier, with complete field equipment. They communicate with the subordinate units through the battalion's standard communication equipment. The simulation is made by a group of training assistants, nine persons, who use a computer system to simulate and store data about the physical environment (see Fig. 13.6).

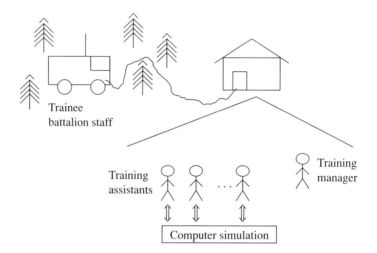

Figure 13.6. InfSS Borensberg, an example of a decision training system for commanders and staff.

The task of the training assistants is to participate in role-playing in which they play the units that the battalion is commanding and controlling, the superior to the staff and all the other surrounding entities in the world. The communication between the battalion staff and the training assistants is meant to be carried out just as in a real situation.

13.4.1. Training description

A training session in the training system at InfSS Borensberg can be described in three phases: game preparation, game phase, and game evaluation.

13.4.1.1. Game preparation

Game preparation starts with a meeting between the chief of the battalion staff who are to be trained and the training manager. At this meeting they define the training session goals. Usually the goals are abstractly defined. Based on these goals they define the game situation and draw up a game plan. They select the geographic area, the hostile activities, their own resources, communication conditions, weather and times of different events, for example. This data can be taken from a dedicated database and specified for the current training session. The staff's resources that are to be simulated are defined in free granularity in terms of a hierarchical organization based on battalion, company, platoon, and squad units. The training manager can also enter a scenario that can contain chains of activities, such as marching activities or combat activities for each defined unit. Based on this information the battalion chief writes a military situation description for his staff, where he describes the current start situation and the current war plans. The trainees also go through a briefing where they are informed about the training goals and training plans. The training manager informs the role-playing assistants of the abstract goal of the training session, the current start situation, and how they should play their role. A game can be used more than once. This means that a number of suitable standard games of varying degrees of difficulty can be stored in the system.

13.4.1.2. Game Phase

In the game phase the *trainee staff* experience the work situation produced by the role-playing training assistants and the computer simulation. The goal is that the staff should work in their normal environment and react to the information they get from the role-playing training assistants. The *training assistants'* task is to play realistically the role of actors that exist in their company. There is one training assistant for every company that exists in the battalion. The training assistants' main task is to react to the commands from the trained staff and the information they get from the computer simulation. When they get a command from the trained staff, they start a mental simulation of the activity and give the computer simulation the important information about this process. (By mental simulation I refer to the process in the training assistant's head when he or she thinks about the activities that normally occur in the company when they are working on a task. This means that they must build up the activity in their mind and think of what probably happens in the world.) Here it is important that the training assistants have a good understanding of how the company that they are supposed to simulate works. The assistants also follow the abstract game scenario received orally from the training managers. The *computer simulation* simulates the physical aspects of the units involved in the training session (e.g. unit position, fuel count-down as consumed). The main task for the *training managers* is to keep the training session on track. This means that they communicate with the training assistants and describe what important activities are going to happen. The training manager can also halt the exercise at any time to give comments on action taken by the trainees.

The basic event steps in the environment simulation can be described thus. When the trainee staff react to their environment, they can give some orders to some subordinate unit. This order will be received by a training assistant. The unit confirms the order, starts the mental simulation, and enters it into the computer simulation. The computer simulation will then start necessary simulations and give an alarm signal to the training assistant if some special event occurs. This helps the training assistants to act as realistically as possible. Examples of alert signal situations are when friendly and hostile units are in sight, or when some resources have dropped below some threshold limits.

13.4.1.3. Game evaluation

In the game evaluation phase the trainee and the training manager perform a debriefing of the game phase. The entire sequence of events is recorded in the training system. This means that any game situation can be replayed and analysed. During the debriefing they discuss orders and actions taken during the game phase.

13.4.2. Reflections on field study

Three important reflections on this system are the characteristics of the session goal, the complexity of the real-world simulation, and the computer simulation system.

The *session goal* is defined in the abstract, often with a main goal of letting the trainee staff experience their task environment. An example of a goal can be to let the trained staff "get to know each other" in their task environment. This can be an important goal, but can also be classified as an abstract goal when we discuss the problem of teaching someone to control a complex system. This abstract goal and the current start situation are given to the training assistants orally. In the game the trainee staff and the training assistants also get a written war plan that can be seen as instructions on how they are supposed to perform their task. Hardly any formal definition existed as to how the training goals are supposed to be achieved. In the training sessions studied, I think that the training assistants get too little direction on how they are supposed to act in their role-playing. They also get little or no information on what type of information or situations are important. This makes it hard for them to know what to do and provides little self-confidence in their acting. Getting support is also important if they have little experience in the role that they are supposed to play. It seems as though the training assistants should be given some information about how the training goals are supposed to be fulfilled, and how they should act to support the pedagogical strategies.

The *simulation complexity* can be seen as one other important characteristic in this type of training environment. The simulation of the surrounding world should be so realistic that it generates the same behaviour pattern as in the real world. This has been solved by using role-playing assistants with their mental simulation and computer simulation modelling for the physical aspects of the units. The main problem for the training assist-ants is that they need to perform a complex mental simulation of the activities that are going on in the world. The problem is to remember all the important properties in the activities that they are simulating and to keep track of all the parallel activities. They should keep all the processes in mind and not forget any important responses. In the sessions studied the training assistants often used the mental simulation as a basis for the simulation and used the computer simulation only as a tool to store data about the units. The computer simulation was not often used by the training assistants, but the geograph-ical maps and data about the unit's position were used and required for the success of the training session.

The *computer simulation system* that is used in the training system seems to have a problem with the connection between the level of simulation abstraction and the user interface. The simulation model consists only of the physical aspects of the world and is described in terms of a causal relation between objects and events in a quantitative way. The main problems with this type of model are that they are usually detailed and com-plex. In InfSS Borensberg it seems as if the training assistants did not use the computer simulation as much as the designer had hoped. The user interface seems to be unsuitable for the training assistants' task. The training assistants could only manipulate the informa-tion in the simulation model at a very detailed level. The granularity and complexity of these models make them hard or even impossible to use and be understood by humans. To experience the proper use of a simulation system they need to have a user interface at the abstraction level at which the user works and thinks. My conclusions on important problems are these: first, the computer simulation interface deals with information that is too detailed; it requires too much work to use the simulation when a user interface does not exist at a proper abstraction level. Second, the computer support and simulation models do not contain any information about the pedagogical strategies or any guide as to how the role-playing training assistants are supposed to act.

13.4.3. Concluding requirements of the simulation

This type of training system can be described from different viewpoints: that of the trainee staff, that of the training manager and that of the training assistants. Requirements that seem important for the services delivered by a computer-based simulation seen from these points of view include the following. First, a *requirement from the trained commander and staff* is that the system should generate proper task environment behaviour. The trainees will, on the basis of this behaviour, create mental models of the task. In time learning will occur and these mental models will then be transformed to compiled knowledge (professional know-how and skill) (Rasmussen, 1993). It is therefore crucial that what is important in the training has the same behaviour as in the real world (Gestrelius, 1993). To provide good training it is also important that the training session consists of sequences of situations that support the pedagogical strategies (Reigeluth & Curtis, 1987). Second, a *requirement from the training manager* is that the system has a control functionality that makes it possible to define a pedagogical strategy for the training session. In the planning process the training manager should be able to define some kind of scenario that describes the main training issues, important situations and activities, and the pedagogical strategy. During a training session the training manager should be able to follow and direct the training towards the situations aimed at. Three, a *requirement from the training assistants* is that the computer simulation system should be able to help the training assistants to simulate the activities in the real world. This means that the computer simulation should consist of the actors and objects that the training assistants are supposed to simulate. To achieve the proper use of simulation the user interface needs to be at the abstraction level at which the user works and thinks. The computer support should also help the training assistants to understand the pedagogical importance of the simulated activities and the computer simulation system should help the training assistants to co-ordinate their activities.

13.5. THE C³FIRE PROJECT

The results of our studies have encouraged us to develop a microworld simulation system. A microworld can be used to show how a computer-based simulation system can be developed and used for emergency management training. When using a microworld we can select the important characteristics of the real world that we want to model and create a small and well-controlled simulation system that retains these characteristics. The advantage of using a microworld is that the complex, dynamic and opaque characteristics that can be generated by a proper microworld can generate similar cognitive tasks to those that people normally encounter in real-life systems. The basic idea behind C³FIRE is that the system should generate a task environment for an emergency management staff. The goal of this project is to examine how a proper information flow, in a microworld, can be generated by simulated agents to support training of *situation awareness* in emergency management organizations. The domain of C³FIRE is forest fire emergency management. It should be seen as an example of an emergency management task. The goal of the project is to show how situation awareness in emergency management can be practised, not to show how training can be performed for this specific domain.

C³FIRE can be viewed as a command, control and communication experimental simulation environment in a forest fire domain. It is based on the D³FIRE microworld, which is a microworld system for studying distributed decision making in dynamic environments (Svenmarck & Brehmer, 1991). C³FIRE can be used for the generation of training sessions where a forest fire organization can practise commanding and controlling fire-fighting units. The C³FIRE simulation includes a *forest fire*, an environment with *houses*, different kinds of *vegetation, reconnaissance persons*, and *fire-fighting units*. The people who run the system are part of a fire-fighting organization and are divided into the staff to be trained and two fire-fighting unit chiefs who are the training assistants. The task of the staff is to gain an overview of the situation, and to co-ordinate and schedule the fire-fighting units so that they can extinguish the fire and save the houses. The training assistants communicate with the staff (trainees) and the computer-simulated fire-fighting unit and reconnaissance persons. The trainee can see the world through information coming from the training assistants. Fig. 13.7 shows the C³FIRE training environment. A detailed description of the C³FIRE microworld is given in chapter 8.

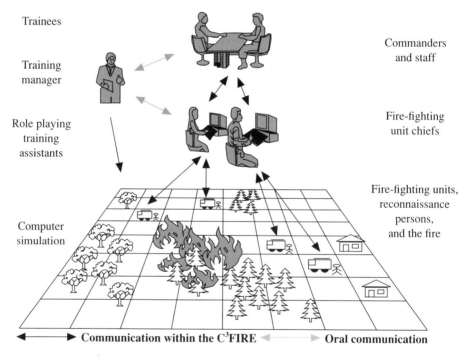

Figure 13.7. The C³FIRE training environment.

13.5.1. Requirements

The requirements met by C³FIRE can be described thus: the *task environment requirements, computer-based simulation support* and *session control.*

13.5.1.1. Task environment requirements

The task environment is the environment in which the team decision-making is performed. The goal is to simulate a task environment that has the same important properties as the real world system. The important properties – ones that the emergency organizations and military systems studied have, and which we want to incorporate in our task environment – are a dynamic context, distributed decision-making, and time-scales. *Dynamic context*: the decision-making should be performed in a dynamic context. Both the target system and the emergency organization should be complex dynamic systems which change both autonomously and as a consequence of actions performed on them. *Distributed decision-making*: the decision task in the emergency organization should be distributed over a number of persons, located as members of the staff and their subordinates. The decision-making should be classified as *team decision-making* where the members have different roles, tasks, and items of information in their decision-making process. *Time-scales*: as in most hierarchical organizations, the decision-makers should work on different time-scales. The staff should work in a high time frame and are responsible for the strategic thinking and the co-ordination of their subordinates. The staff's subordinates should be responsible for the low-level operations, such as performing some concerted task on the target system, which is done in a short time-frame.

13.5.1.2. Computer-Based simulation support

To create a proper task environment simulation the role-playing training assistants need to have some computer-based simulation support. The basic idea behind the task environment simulation is that it should simulate a hierarchical organization. This means that a computer-based simulation can support the role-playing training assistants by simulating the subordinate units.

13.5.1.3. Session control

To create a proper training session or study session the task environment simulation should in some way be controlled to generate the required situations. The session control should help the training manager to define what type of situations the task environment should generate.

13.5.2. Training goals

The training goals that were in focus while developing the C³FIRE microworld are based on *situation assessment* in the tactical reasoning process. The goal is that the trainee should experience the behaviour of the fire, how the fire-fighting organization works, how they can search for and acquire information about the systems. Fig. 13.8 shows the situation assessment processes in Klein's recognition-primed decision (RPD) model (Klein, 1993). When the staff receive information about the target system and the controlling system, they assess the situation in terms of a situation awareness. The goal is that the system should give the trainee information that supports some pedagogical strategy based on this decision-making model.

This situation assessment process can be described in three tactical reasoning phases: current state, evolution possibilities, and risk analysis. The *current state* consists of information such as where the fire is, information on the geographical environment in the area and the weather, and where the fire-fighting units are and what their status is. The *possible evolution* of the fire describes what areas may be burning in the future. The

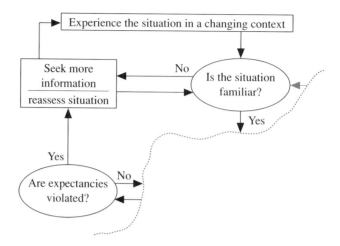

Figure 13.8. Situation assessment steps in the RPD model.

spreading speed and the spreading direction of a forest fire basically depend on two factors, the vegetation and the weather. In the *risk analysis* phase it is important for the staff to have the ability to analyze the situation and identify the risks that exist in that situation or risks that may occur in the near future.

In the experimentation series performed with the C³FIRE environment we defined a task environment in which the trainee could experience the steps in the tactical reasoning process. Examples of defined tasks are risk analysis and selecting a proper solution strategy. In the *risk analysis phase* they should identify future critical situations by studying the vegetation type and wind. They should learn to collect information from the fire-fighting unit chiefs, use the reconnaissance persons in a proper way, and gather and sort out relevant and consistent information about the target system. Fig. 13.9 describes an example where there are two houses surrounded by different kinds of forest. The house in position H2 has a pine tree (fast burning) in front of it and the other house has a birch tree (slow burning) in front of it. The staff should realize this risk situation as early as possible to be able to prevent the house at position H2 from burning down. In the *solutions selection phase*, the subjects were given instructions that the fire extinguishing technique that can be used in C³FIRE is to create fire breaks (see Fig. 13.9).

A fire break is created in C³FIRE by extinguishing the fire so that a line of closed-out fire is made with the fire on one side and non-burning forest on the other side.

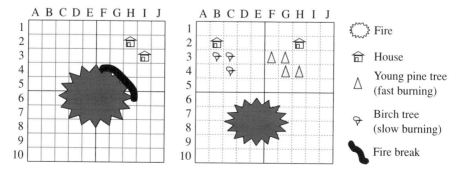

Figure 13.9. Training goals, creating fire breaks and identifying future critical situations.

Besides these tactical reasoning steps, the experiment sessions were designed so that the trainees also experienced different levels of *information load*, and how this influences the time pressure in their work. The information load is achieved by varying the number of messages sent from the simulated reconnaissance persons to the fire-fighting unit chiefs.

13.6. SYSTEM DEVELOPMENT

The design can be completed in three parts:

1. to create a simulation system and organization that generate the *task environment* for the trained staff
2. to define the *information flow* that will generate the training situations for the trained staff
3. to design the control functionality and session recording facilities.

13.6.1. Task environment simulation in C³FIRE

The simulation responsibilities in the C³FIRE training environment are split between the computer simulation and the role-playing training assistants. The simulated entities in the C³FIRE training system are:

- forest fire, performed by the computer simulation
- fire-fighting unit, performed by the computer simulation and the training assistants
- reconnaissance person, performed by the computer-simulated agents
- fire-fighting unit chief, performed by the role-playing training assistants
- civilians, performed by the computer simulations.

The main idea is that the computer simulation should support the role-playing training assistant with a proper flow of information. The task of the role-playing person is to play the role of the fire-fighting unit chief. In this role the training assistants are responsible for acting as a typical fire-fighting chief. They should use the computer simulation to gather information about the target system, and to command the computer-simulated subordinate units (the fire-fighting units and the reconnaissance persons).

13.6.2. Agent simulation

The computer-simulated actors can be characterized in three different classes. The classes are defined by the agents' ability to take commands from the trainee and their ability to change the target system. All agents can give information about the target system (see Fig. 13.10). The classes are as follows.

- Actors who can take orders, change the target system and report some state of the target system. This class is represented by the fire-fighting unit in the simulation. The fire-fighting unit can extinguish fire and report on the fire states of the target system. The movement is controlled by the trained people.
- Actors who can take orders and report some state of the target system. This class is represented by the reconnaissance persons in the simulation. They can give information about the fire and the geographical environment, such as vegetation type and house positions. The movement can be controlled by the trained people.

■ Actors who can only report on some state of the target system. This class is represented by the external agents in the simulation.

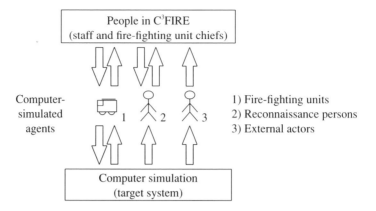

Figure 13.10. Simulated agent classes in C³FIRE.

13.6.3. Information generation

In C³FIRE the information-providing processes consist of two main classes: statically and dynamically controlled processes. The *static* information generation processes are processes that do not change their behaviour according to the current situation in the training session. It is the same process that generates the messages throughout the whole training session. The *dynamic* information generation processes are the processes that change their behaviour depending on the scenario and the current situation in the training session. This dynamically generated information is often connected to the information that is responsible for generating the information situations that are specified by the training goals. Besides the dynamic and static definitions of information generation processes, information is divided into four classes (see Fig. 13.11). First, *normal information* that is generated by the simulated actors without any (dynamic) reflection on the training goals. The goal of this information is to build up the normal information flow that exists in the task environment. Second, *help information* is information that helps the trainee in the decision process. Third, *problem-making information* is information that creates some kind of decision problem for the trained staff. Fourth, *knowledge-check information* is information that can be used for checking the knowledge status of the trainee.

In C³FIRE the help, problem making, and knowledge-test information have the same format as the normal messages. It is important to note that the information we are discussing here is the information that is generated in the staff's task environment, and that trainees should not be able to distinguish the classes. This means that when the trainee gets the information, such as "there is a fire at pos. *x, y*", they should not be able to distinguish what type of information it is.

13.6.4. Session control

The main idea behind the control structure in C³FIRE is that it should be used to define and guide the training session towards some specific training goals, where the following mechanisms are used.

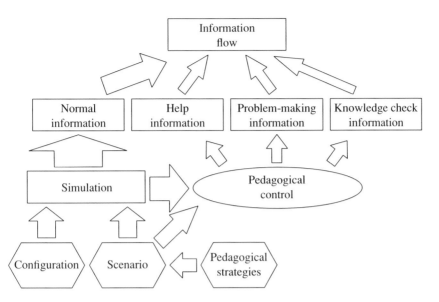

Figure 13.11. Information generation flow.

Scenarios: System behaviour during a session is controlled from a scenario. It controls, for example, the weather and the behaviour of reconnaissance persons. The scenario may also contain textual messages that can be sent from some reconnaissance person or some external actor outside the fire-fighting organization at some specified time.

Simulated reconnaissance persons: These are computer-simulated and their task is to give information about the world to the training assistants. They should help the training assistants to perform a proper simulation of the activities and help them to generate proper pedagogical training situations. The behaviour of computer-simulated reconnaissance persons can be manipulated by changing three main parameters: the information contents, the information load, and the information error. The *information load* parameter defines the number of spontaneous messages sent from the reconnaissance persons. With this parameter the system can change the information load for the trainee. The *information error* parameter defines the truth value of the messages. With this parameter the reconnaissance person can send a message with some special type of error to the fire-fighting unit chiefs.

Scripts: In the current version of C³FIRE there are some statically coded scripts that can be activated by a scenario event. The script is a procedural event description used by the simulation which reacts to the activity of the fire-fighting units and reconnaissance persons. The script activates static text messages that will be sent from some simulated actor, if some special event sequence occurs.

13.6.5. Development results

Three important aspects of modelling complex social systems experienced during the design and implantation of the C³FIRE are the abstraction level, variable definitions and behaviour verification.

Abstraction levels: a simulation cannot include all potentially relevant variables, there exist no clear-cut rules telling us what to include and what to leave unspecified. We must choose a subjective description of our world at a satisfactory decomposition level. Experience tells us that a cut on a wrong level or an ill-defined variable can change the behaviour of the simulation in a major and unexpected way.

Variable definitions: a simulation cannot remain in the abstract; it needs actual concrete values for each of the variables in the simulation program (Brehmer *et al.*, 1991). We experience that at the start of a model construction; the models are often very abstract and designed by people with good knowledge of the real world. After this phase the responsibility of implementing the model goes to a programmer, with less experience of real-world models. The problem is that the variables defined deep down in the models can have a large impact on the simulation behaviour. In other words, we can say that it is difficult to separate the model design from the simulation construction. This indicates that the model designer, with good real-world experience, should work close to and interactively with the simulation implementers.

Behaviour verification: One problem with simulation systems, KBS architectures, and other complex computer systems is their lack of transparency. The causal models in a simulation system are also often of a prototypical nature. This means that behaviour verification is an important step because it is a hard task to define a model that will generate dynamic behaviour. Davis & Blumenthal (1991) state: "When we are trying to create models that are describing a complex system, the interactive development with empirical verification is an important and necessary way to work." Common strategies to verify the model are to focus on functional validity of various system characteristics such as feedback delays and verify them in an *ad hoc* manner that demonstrates that it works on some examples (Brehmer *et al.*, 1991). In the C³FIRE development and experimentation the problem with the model development was so large that it was impossible to predict the generated simulation behaviour without testing it with an interactive test evaluation strategy.

13.7. AN EVALUATION OF C³FIRE

We have performed one study where 15 groups each worked for 2 hours with C³FIRE. The goals of the experiment were to study how the distributed decision-making changed depending on different communication strategies within the emergency organization and to see how the C³FIRE environment behaved. The goal of the system evaluation of C³FIRE as a training system is mainly to study the information flow from the computer simulation to the trained staff. The objectives for the C³FIRE evaluation are as follows.

- Does the generated task environment in C³FIRE create proper decision situations for the staff and the emergency organization?

- How are the messages generated by the reconnaissance persons treated in the C³FIRE environment?

13.7.1. The task environment

The experiment sessions did, in fact, clearly show that the C³FIRE microworld generated the criteria that we defined for a proper task environment. It generated a dynamic context and a distributed decision-making environment. It also generates two time-scales, the staff's level and the fire-fighting unit chief's level. The fire evolution went as planned and the position of the different vegetation types and house supported our planned tactical reason-ing task. The problem with the target system was perhaps that the fire-extinguishing task was too difficult. The fire-spread parameter was probably too high. This should have been observed in the important pre-experiment. It seems as if our minimal task environ-ment generates the decision situations that are needed to perform tactical reasoning. The quality of the subjects' tactical reasoning during the experiment sessions is hard to evaluate and will not be discussed in this work.

For some subjects the technique of *creating fire breaks* was hard to understand. The fire-fighting unit chiefs that did not understand this technique did not close out fire squares at the front or on some flank. The problem they had was that they did not understand the dynamics of the fire evolution and the speed of the extinguishing task. For the groups that had a fire-fighting chief who was responsible for the north-east area and was not able to create the fire breaks, the simulation always led to the state where almost all the forest burned down.

Thematic vagabonding can be seen as a phenomenon where a subject does not have any structure in his attempt to control a target system (Dörner, 1980). This has been observed for some of the fire-fighting chiefs and was often the case when the subjects did not use the fire break technique correctly. The conclusion is that an environment like this can be used to generate a good task environment for some real-world tasks, but to ensure that such a system has some strong real-life connection is a hard task, and this will not be discussed further here.

13.7.2. Information flow

The main goal of the information control was on the one hand to change the information load, and on the other to generate help, problem-making and knowledge-check information.

13.7.2.1. Information load

The goal of changing the amount of information is to change the work pressure in the task of analyzing the information. The messages generated a high workload for the fire-fighting unit chiefs as planned, but the amount of information in the high workload time interval did not increase as much as the number of messages. This led to the information quality in the messages, in the high workload intervals, becoming so low that the people that received the messages thought that the system generated many inappropriate mess-ages. The average message flow during the two sessions for the 15 groups is shown in Fig. 13.12. These figures show how the information load changes during the time interval

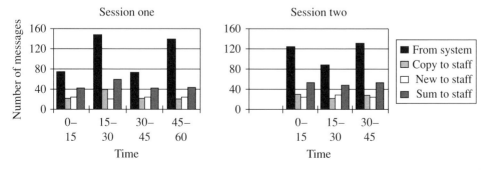

Figure 13.12. Amount of information in sessions one and two.

in the sessions. "From the system" means the number of messages sent by the simulated reconnaissance persons to the fire-fighting unit chiefs X and Y. "Copy to staff" means the number of messages received by X and Y that are directly copied and sent to the staff. "New to staff" is the number of messages that are created by X and Y and sent to the staff. "Sum to staff" is the total number of messages sent to the staff.

We can see that the number of messages generated by the reconnaissance persons follows the scenario goal, but the number of messages sent to the staff does not change much during the different time intervals. What we can see in the experiment is that the fire-fighting unit chiefs perform their work as they are supposed to do: they filter the messages so that the staff only get the messages they need. The conclusion to be made is that if we want to change the information load for the staff, then the system should generate new and important information in all messages so that the information is not filtered away by X and Y.

13.7.2.2. Help, problem-making and knowledge-check information

The main observation is that the staff received the majority of these messages. Messages that contain important information for the tactical reasoning, such as information about houses or fire at new and strange places, was most of the time copied to the staff. On the other hand, the messages containing error information about the practical work, such as information about the fire near the fire-fighting units, were almost never sent to the staff. During the simulation we observed that the pedagogical-controlled messages that had a textual structure which differed from the normal messages more often reached the trained staff. This can be explained by the fact that during the session the fire-fighting unit chiefs received many "normal" messages generated by the simulated reconnaissance persons. The messages that have the same structure as the normal message run a greater risk of disappearing in the large number of messages generated by the simulated reconnaissance persons, while the messages that differ from the large flow of messages will therefore be noted by the fire-fighting unit chiefs.

One important observation during the experiment sessions was that the persons that were playing X and Y never knew when messages generated by the system were important for the pedagogical training strategies. This means that X and Y filtered away some messages that were meant to go to the staff. So if we have a training system where we want to train the staff, then the messages generated by the system should also contain the intention of the messages. This intention should be visible for the training assistants and it should contain information that tells them why it should be sent to the staff.

13.7.2.3. Message flow

To make a qualitative analysis of the message flow in the system is an advanced and demanding task. One way to make a simple analysis is to analyze the number of different types of messages sent in the system. This method may give some hints on what is happening in the organization. Message-flow diagrams for the 15 groups are shown in Figs 13.13 and 13.14, which show the average number of messages each minute during the session for each group. Groups 1 to 15 are sorted by score. Group 1 has the best result. The "Messages sent from system" diagram shows how many messages are sent from the computer simulation. The "Messages sent to system" diagram shows how many orders are given to the simulated reconnaissance persons by the fire-fighting unit chiefs.

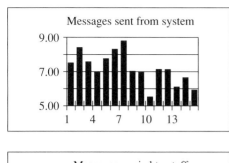

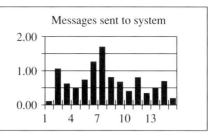

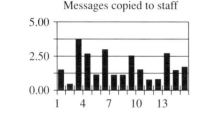

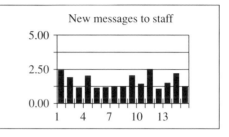

Figure 13.13. Message flow in session 1.

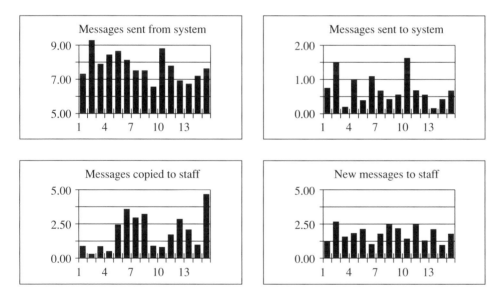

Figure 13.14. Message flow in session 2.

The "Messages copied to staff" diagram shows the number of messages received by X and Y that are directly copied and sent to the staff. The "New messages to staff" diagram shows the number of messages that are created by X and Y and sent to the staff.

It is hard to infer anything from analyzing the number of messages sent in the organization. What we may see is that the groups that got a good score result worked in such a way that the computer system generated more information. We can also see that the groups that got good score results during the second session did not copy as many messages as the other groups. This indicates that the fire-fighting unit chiefs for the first four groups had learned that they did not need to send all the messages to the staff. For the other diagrams it is hard to see any indication of any phenomena based on the number of different message types sent in the system.

13.8. CONCLUSIONS

The objectives of this work have been to study the characteristics and possibilities of supporting emergency management training using computer simulations. The work has focused on team decision training supporting the training of situation assessment in a tactical reasoning process. Possible solution strategies are presented by the development and experimentation of the C³FIRE microworld. The C³FIRE development and experimentation focus around the problem of construct simulated agents with the goal of generating an information flow that will support the training of situation assessment. The training domain, which in this case is co-ordination of forest fire-fighting units, is of less interest and has been used to demonstrate the principles. The results from this development can be generalized for this kind of training environment and used in future research or system development projects.

13.8.1. Microworlds

The development of the C³FIRE microworld indicates that it is possible to construct training and experimental environments that support co-operative work in a simple task environment. The generated task environment in C³FIRE has some of the basic characteristics that exist in a real-world emergency management task. The basic characteristics of the task environment are that it generates a dynamic context and a distributed decision-making environment. It also generates two time-scales, the staff's level and the fire-fighting unit chief's level. It appears that our minimal task environment generates the decision situations that are needed to perform tactical reasoning and team decision-making.

One of the basic problems discovered during the development and experimentation with the C³FIRE microworld is that of defining and discovering the training situations that are generated in the task environment. During the design, one main problem was to define what kinds of situations the system should generate. First a high-level abstraction definition must be made that allows the users to understand the goal and the properties of the required situations. Then this high-level, abstract situation description must be transformed to detailed descriptions that describe this situation using computer simulation data. During the experimentation and evaluation of the C³FIRE microworld one important problem was to identify what situations have occurred. The problem is to be able to catch the high-level abstract situations, from the low-level simulation data that exist in the computer simulation. We think that the recording functionality of a microworld system should be able to detect the defined situations that occur in a training session. This should be an important aid for the training managers who are responsible for evaluating the session.

13.8.2. Pedagogical session control

Common training goals in emergency management training are to train co-ordinated plans, co-ordinated actions, communications and task knowledge (Dowell & Smith, 1996). The experience from our experimentation is that to be able to create a good training environment for some of this training task some session control functionality must be used. In the development of the C³FIRE microworld an important goal was to see how the environment could be controlled so that it generates the required situations. Our focus was on examining the possibilities of using simulated agents to support the training of situation awareness. The goal was to generate a specified task environment with some chaining behaviour. The control functionality in C³FIRE was based on configuration data, on scenario data and on situation-describing scripts. The evaluation of the experimental sessions shows that the configuration data and scenario data did, in fact, generate a task environment that supported the team decision-making study.

The simulated agents that exist in our microworld are mainly controlled by the scenario and by the situation-describing scripts. The goal is that they should generate messages that contain information about the target system that will build up the trainees' mental picture of the simulated world. The message types are normal, problem-making, help, and knowledge check. The normal information can be seen as the information that builds up the basic task environment. The problem-making, help and knowledge-check information are used by the system to support some pedagogical training strategy. The goal of this information is to create problems, to help the trainee and to help the training manager to analyze the trainee's knowledge. Figure 13.11 shows an abstract view of the information generation in our system.

The evaluation of C³FIRE indicates that this kind of information classification can be suitable for use when defining pedagogically controllable training situations. The experience from the sessions is that it was possible to generate an information flow that supported our session goal. One problem we had with the generated information flow was that in some of our defined training situations the generated messages had an information quality that was too low. This happened when we intended to generate a training situation where the trainee should experience a high workload situation. In this situation the agents generated a large quantity of messages. The problem was that information flow did not increase as much as the number of messages. The trainees experienced this phenomenon as if the information quality was too low. Another important observation made during the experimental sessions was that the training assistants never knew when messages generated by the system were important for the pedagogical training strategies. This meant that the training assistants filtered away some messages that were meant to go to the staff. So if we have a training system where we want to train the staff, then the messages generated by the system should also contain the intention of the messages. This intention should be visible for the training assistants and it should contain information that tells them why it should be sent to the staff.

The main experiences from our development of the C³FIRE microworld are that training system should have the following characteristics:

- it should help the training assistants to understand the pedagogical goal of the generated messages
- it should help the training manager to detect what training situations have occurred during the session
- the information quality in the generated messages must be sufficiently high and must support the trainees' cognitive processes.

13.9. REFERENCES

BERKUM, J.J.A. VAN & JONG, T. DE (1991). Instructional environments for simulations. *Education & Computing*, vol. 6, 305–358.

BREHMER, B. (1991). Organisation for decision making in complex systems. In J. RASMUSSEN, B. BREHMER & J. LEPLAT (Eds), *Distributed Decision Making: Cognitive Models for Co-operative Work*. New York: John Wiley & Sons, 335–347.

BREHMER, B. (1994). Verbal communication at a seminar on distributed decision making, 4 Feb. 1994, in the Higher Psychology course at Linköping University, Sweden.

BREHMER, B. (1995). *Distributed decision making in dynamic environments*. Uppsala University, Sweden. Foa Report.

BREHMER, B., LEPLAT, J. & RASMUSSEN, J. (1991). Use of simulation in the study of complex decision making. In J. RASMUSSEN, B. BREHMER and J. LEPLAT (Eds), *Distributed decision making: cognitive models for co-operative work*. New York: John Wiley and Sons.

BREHMER, B. & SVENMARCK, P. (1995). Distributed decision making in dynamic environments: time scales and architectures of decision making. In J.-P. CAVERNI, M. BAR-HILLEL, F.H. BARRON & H. JUNGERMANN (Eds), *Contributions to Decision Making – I*. Amsterdam: Elsevier Science.

DAVIS, P.K. & BLUMENTHAL, D. (1991). *The base of sand problem: a white paper on the state of military combat modelling*. RAND report, N-3148-OSD/DARPA.

DÖRNER, D. (1980) On the difficulties people have in dealing with complexity. *Simulation and Games*, vol. 11, No. 1, March, 87–106.

DÖRNER, D. & BREHMER, B. (1993). Experiments with computer-simulated microworlds: escaping both the narrow straits of the laboratory and the deep blue sea of the field study. *Computers in Human Behaviour*, vol. 9, 171–184.

DOWELL, J. & SMITH, W. (1996). Coordination training for distributed worksystems in emergency management. In *Proceedings of the ECCE-8, Eighth European Conference on Cognitive Ergonomics*, University of Granada.

GESTRELIUS, K. (1993). Pedagogik i simuleringsspel: erfarenhets-baserad utbildning med överinlärningsmöjligheter. *Pedagogisk Orientering och Debatt*, vol. 100, Lund University, Sweden.

HUTCHINS, E. (1990). The technology of team navigation. In J. GALEGHER, R.E. KRAUT & C. EGIDO (Eds), *Intellectual teamwork: social and technical bases of collaborative work*. Norwood, NJ: Ablex.

KLEIN, G.A. (1993). A recognition-primed decision (RPD) model of rapid decision making. In G.A. KLEIN, J. ORASANU, R. CALDERWOOD & C.E. ZSAMBOK (Eds), *Decision Making in Action: Models and Methods*. Norwood, NJ: Ablex, 138–147.

KLEIN, G.A. & THORDSEN, M. (1989). *Cognitive Processes of the Team Mind*. Ch2809–2/89/0000–0046, IEEE. Yellow Springs: Klein Associates.

ORASANU, J. & SALAS, E. (1993). Team decision making in complex environments. In G.A. KLEIN, J. ORASANU, R. CALDERWOOD & E. ZSAMBOK (Eds), *Decision Making in Action: Models and Methods*, Norwood, NJ: Ablex.

RASMUSSEN, J. (1983). Skills, rules, and knowledge; signals, signs, and symbols, and other distinction in human performance models. *IEEE Transactions on Systems and Cybernetics*, vol. smc-13, No. 3, May/June.

RASMUSSEN, J. (1993). Deciding and doing: decision making in natural context. In G.A. KLEIN, J. ORASANU, R. CALDERWOOD & E. ZSAMBOK (Eds), *Decision Making in Action: Models and Methods*. Norwood, NJ: Ablex, 158–171.

REIGELUTH, C.M. & CURTIS, R.V. (1987). Learning situations and instruction models. In R.M. GAGNE & R. GLASTER (Eds), *Instructional Technology: Foundations*. Hillsdale, NJ: Lawrence Erlbaum, 175–207.

SAMURÇAY, R. & ROGALSKI, J. (1991). A method for tactical reasoning (MTR) in emergency management: analysis of individual acquisition and collective implementation. In J. RAMUSSEN, B. BREHMER & J. LEPLAT, *Distributed decision making*. Cognitive models for co-operative work, 287–299.

SAMURÇAY, R. & ROGALSKI, J. (1993). Co-operative work and decision making in emergency management. *Le travail humain*, vol. 56, nr. 1, 53–77.

SAMURÇAY, R. & ROGALSKI, J. (1993a). A method for tactical reasoning (MTR) in emergency managment: analysis of individual acquisition and collective implementation. In G.A. KLEIN, J. ORASANU, R. CALDERWOOD & E. ZSAMBOK (Eds), *Decision Making in Action: Models and Methods*, 287–298. Norwood, NJ: Ablex.

SAMURÇAY, R. & ROGALSKI, J. (1993b). Analysing communication in complex distributed decision-making. *Ergnomics*, vol. 36, 1329–1343.

SVENMARCK, P. & BREHMER, B. (1991). D³FIRE: An experimental paradigm for the studies of distributed decision making. In B. BREHMER (Ed.), *Distributed Decision making*, Proceedings of the Third MOHAWC workshop.

TRACCS (1990). Training Centre for Commanders and Staffs. *A system description*. Produced by CelsiusTech, Sweden.

PART FIVE

Computer Artifacts

CHAPTER FOURTEEN

In search of organizational memory in process control

ESA AURAMÄKI AND MIKKO KOVALAINEN

14.1. INTRODUCTION

Work in process control requires successful co-operation between different partners such as production planners, supervisors, shift foremen, operators, and maintenance personnel. The work is done in more or less "official" teams. As one of the interviewees told us (at least this has become "true" during the industrial phase of paper production): "Nobody has ever made paper alone."

A large body of fragmented expert knowledge is needed to manage the production process successfully. In the mills, knowledge is exchanged during meetings, discussions, and informal interactions, but it is often not stored anywhere. A great part of the knowledge needed in process control is learned by doing the job. Learning includes learning both from one's own experience and from the experiences of others. The expertise includes both conceptual and procedural knowledge. It is often expressed only as patterns of actions, and the utilization of this knowledge depends on the expert's ability to remember, interpret, and represent matters.

In this chapter we characterize the group memory in process control. Our approach is based on the concepts of organizational memory, organizational interaction, and organizational learning. One goal of the chapter is to present concrete examples of the organizational memory in a special setting – process control. We search for where the organizational memory resides and in what forms it is presented. Several issues in process control, such as the work itself, modes of interaction and learning, breakdowns, the nature of expertise, and remembering are discussed. We characterize the importance of memory and remembering to the crews, and illustrate ideas that could make the organizational memory more "visible", easier to access, and easier to maintain. We also present some ideas of how to support the organizational memory with computerized tools.

First, we present our research setting and research methods. In section 14.3 we give a short introduction to the "theory" of organizational memory. Section 14.4 characterizes the work and organizational memory in paper mills. In section 14.5 we give a short outline of tools developed for supporting organizational memory, organizational learning, and organizational interaction. We also present our prototype tool to support the organizational memory in process control. Finally, we present our conclusions, and ideas for further work.

14.2. RESEARCH SETTING AND RESEARCH METHODS

The study was conducted at several sites: a process automation company, a paper machinery company, six paper mills, one oil refinery, one pulp mill, and one test paper mill. Data for the study were collected in summer 1994 and autumn 1995 by interviewing and observing. Sixty workers, foremen, edp-people, trainers, project managers, and system developers were interviewed.

The work in process control was observed over a period of one month (about 30 hours, summer 1994) including normal state, disturbances, shift changes, a process shutdown, and maintenance work. Based on the initial observations and interviews in summer 1994 we outlined a set of tools that could help to collect and transmit expert knowledge. We found that the concept of organizational memory (group memory) could be useful, and that some of the fragmented expert knowledge could be stored in a computer-based group memory (Paunonen, 1995; Auramäki, et al., 1995). The memory is a communication and knowledge-sharing tool for maintaining situation awareness among experts and for recording experiences for later use.

Based on the initial studies in 1994, we constructed in our SHAMAN-project (SHAring and MANaging expertise in process control) a prototype system that was used later as a tool for supporting the interviews in autumn 1995. In these interviews we first gathered data concerning the contents of knowledge inherent in process control, organizing of the work, the exchange of information, the expertise learning, training, importance of experience, importance of remembering, systems used, and so on. After the initial interviews we introduced our software prototype and collected attitudes of the interviewees towards such a tool. The prototype system also seemed to stimulate further discussions, especially, the issues of remembering and information-sharing emerged again.

14.3. ORGANIZATIONAL MEMORY, LEARNING, AND INTERACTION

There are several definitions or characterizations of organizational memory, such as "record of an organization that is embodied in a set of documents and artefacts" (Conklin, 1993), "stored information from an organization's history that can be brought to bear on present decisions" (Walsh & Ungson, 1991), "means by which knowledge from the past is brought to bear on present activities, thus resulting in lower or higher organizational effectiveness" (Stein & Zwass 1995), "collects shared and stored understandings and beliefs and forms the basis for organizational sense-making and social construction of reality" (Kim, 1993). The organizational memory is not a passive storage of information, but rather an active process of remembering and forgetting (Engeström et al., 1990). Active memory defines what an organization pays attention to at the moment, how it chooses to act and what it chooses to remember from its experience (Kim, 1993). Organizational memory consists of several kinds of items such as events or episodes, experiences, routines, stories, and decision rationales. Some knowledge is well-defined, formal, concrete, and operational while some knowledge is informal, conceptual, and abstract.

Organizational memory is not constructed only by adding together the individual memories, but is rather a result of shared interpretations, and negotiations (see Kim, 1993). Understanding both the role of a single person in producing the contents of the organizational memory and the role of interaction in producing the shared understanding and interpretations is crucial.

Basing action on memory can be dysfunctional or beneficial. Without memory organizations can repeat old failures. On the other hand, memory can be an "enemy" of learning, it can lead to the repeating of old unsuccessful "solutions", and prevent creativity. So, the memory must not be used in a mechanistic way. Organizations must be capable of evaluating what is useful in the history and decide how to use the memory as a source of learning and creativity: they have to learn to learn.

Learning means the acquiring of knowledge or skills. It means "increasing one's capacity to take effective action" (Kim, 1993). Huber (1991) emphasizes the change in the "range of . . . potential behaviors". Organizational memory and organizational learning are closely related to each other. Actually, they cannot exist without each other. As Kim (1993) states, "memory affects what we learn and what we learn affects the memory", and "memory plays a critical role in linking individual to organizational learning". The individual and shared mental models provide the means through which the individual learning links to organizational learning (Kim, 1993). Levitt & March (1988) characterize organizational learning as routine-based, history-dependent, and target-oriented activity, and see organizations as "learning by encoding inferences from history into routines that guide behavior". Organizational learning requires interpretation, and the interpretation schemes' effect on what is learned, not only history (Levitt & March, 1988).

The *distribution* of knowledge, experience, and information between people is an important feature of organizational learning (see for example Huber, 1991). In recent studies not much emphasis has been put on the communicative aspects of organizational memory. Stein and Zwass (1995) mention in their valuable survey of work on organizational memory the works of Krippendorf, where organizational memory is characterized as a communication process, and a by-product of encoding/decoding. The communicative aspects have been raised again by Tuomi (1996), who sees the memory as the "totality of processes that reproduce organizational structures, including its cognitive structures, routines, institutions, and power structures". In this view, intersubjective languages and co-ordinated action are also emphasized as the characteristics of organizations.

14.3.1. The SHAMAN view of organizational memory

We base our concept of organizational memory on the definitions of Stein & Zwass (1995) and those of Kim (1993). The former seems reasonable, because it characterizes organizations as arenas of action, not only decision-making, and because it also stresses the impacts (effectiveness). The definition of Kim is important, because it emphasizes the formation of shared interpretations and shared understandings.

To us it seems that there are three interrelated *organizational processes* which should not be separated:

1. organizational remembering/forgetting

   ■ without remembering there will be no learning

   ■ we cannot forget forgetting, because it happens anyway, and it is needed in making abstractions from our experiences

2. organizational learning/unlearning

- without learning there will be nothing to be remembered
- experiential learning is an important form of learning (learning from one's own experiences and learning from the experiences of others are both important forms of learning)
- without unlearning we can not make substantial changes to our behaviour

3. interaction (communication)

- without interaction (communication) there will be no shared interpretations/ understandings
- without communication what has been learned cannot be transmitted to others.

We adopt the structural classification of organizational memory presented by Walsh and Ungson (1991). They discuss various "storage bins" where the organizational memory is retained:

- individuals (direct observations, experiences)
- culture (symbols, stories, grapevines, former experiences, etc.)
- transformations (logic of how input is transformed to output; the knowledge concerning previous transformations guides the new ones)
- structures (organizational structures)
- ecology (physical structures such as the floor plans, furniture, etc.)
- external archives (such as previous employees ("old hands"), government reports, competitors, media)
- information systems (addition by, for example, Stein & Zwass (1995), Ackerman (1994)).

All these interrelated 'bins' are of importance. They are interrelated in the sense that the people create most of the other structures, and these structures have influence on the behaviours of people.

The major processes related to organizational memory (OM) are *organizational remembering, organizational learning,* and *organizational interaction.* They include the processes of *creating shared interpretations* and *understandings.* The "technical" processes towards OM include acquisition of knowledge, retention of knowledge, search and retrieval of knowledge, and maintenance of knowledge (Walsh & Ungson, 1991; Stein & Zwass, 1995).

The SHAMAN view of organizational processes is depicted in Fig. 14.1. The view connects the organizational processes and the organizational memory. In our model we combine ideas of organizational memory, organizational learning, and organizational interaction. We emphasize the experiential learning models and represent an explicit learning model based on the models of Lewin and Kolb (Kolb, 1984). Accordingly, we think that people (the *actors*) are *doing* things (acting) both individually and in co-operation with others. While acting they get *experiences,* and *learn* from them. In their *interaction* they create *interpretations,* they share them with each other, they *acquire* knowledge both from inside the organization and from external sources. They *observe* the actions within the organization and they observe the behaviour of the environment. They *reflect,* i.e. they relate their current experiences to their earlier experiences. Sometimes they make deeper *analyses* of their knowledge and skills. They also make *abstractions* from their experiences. During their action the actors and groups of actors create knowledge in the organizational memory, and also maintain and use it.

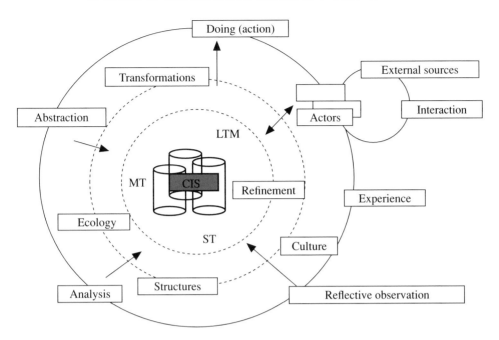

Figure 14.1. Organizational remembering, learning, and interaction.

The learning cycle presented in Fig. 14.1 is not a result of any "scientific" evidence gathered from our studies. It seems, however, that there are occasions where the different "phases" can be "seen".

We make a distinction between "levels" of organizational memory according to two dimensions: representation and temporal aspect. The representation dimension is depicted in Fig. 14.1 by a dotted circle. The area inside the circle presents "objects" that can be more or less easily represented (representable area), and the area outside it "objects" that cannot be represented. The innermost part of the representable area points to computerized information systems (CIS). By making this distinction we want to emphasize the fact that only a small portion of an organizational memory is usually visible and explicit, and it can be difficult to represent some of the knowledge. Several types of "representations" and representation formats have been discussed in the literature, such as cognitive maps, frameworks, stories, procedures, and programs. Different storage "bins" might require different representations; for example transformations can be presented in procedural descriptions, mental models of actors as cognitive maps, some episodes in the action, or in culture as stories.

The temporal dimension depicted in Fig. 14.1 illustrates the duration of organizational memory. The temporal dimension seems reasonable, because organizations deal with information with different durations. Some parts of the knowledge are valid or important only temporally (e.g. some temporary orders), while others can be important and valid over many years or decades (e.g. "missions" of organizations). We have found it important to deal with the duration of knowledge, because it provides a basis for the *refinement* of information. In this sense it deals with the *abstractions* inherent in organizational learning. In the short-term memory (STM) we have knowledge for immediate use (for example, what should I do next?). The medium-term memory (MTM) is used for refining the information into a more context-independent form (for example, an abstract description of a single event). The long-term memory (LTM) contains more general rules and frameworks that help the understanding of the organizational work and its environment (for example, quality policies in the *Quality Handbook*). In the course of time one can make abstractions on single episodes, and these refinements can be supported by the evidence of the episodes.

Several modes of interaction can be identified, such as interaction through communication, gestures, and shared materials. Communication is needed for building shared mental models and interpretations, for transferring experiences and knowledge, for learning concepts and routines, and for creating knowledge in OM. Communication is not the only means for enchancing learning; people can learn also by observing and imitating the behaviour of others. Co-operation and co-ordination can be based on other media too, especially on shared materials (see Sörgaard, 1987).

Several means of interaction can be found in organizational life such as face-to-face communication between two actors, communication between several people, and communication through various media independent of space and time. These interactions are needed in co-operative functions such as co-ordinating, creating ideas, creating shared understandings, and making decisions.

14.4. ORGANIZATIONAL MEMORY IN PROCESS CONTROL

This section presents our findings characterizing organizational memory in process control, mainly in paper mills. We first provide a characterization of work in process control. Second, we discuss the expertise and learning of the people involved in process control. Third, we present some findings related to remembering. Fourth, we characterize the memory "bins". Fifth, a short characterization of breakdowns and their "meaning" are highlighted. Sixth, some of the interactions in process control are discussed. The last part of this section raises the issue of dynamics in process control.

14.4.1. The work in process control

Work in process control requires successful co-operation between different partners. The work is done in more or less explicit teams. It requires communication and distributed decision-making in real time. For example, problem-solving situations may require the knowledge and information of operators, their foremen, superintendent, production management, research, laboratory, maintenance and adjacent departments. The work in paper mills and in any production organization calls for quick decisions and actions. The process demands continuity. This work consists of both preplanned tasks and unplanned disturbances.

Working in shifts is a typical feature in process control. Usually there are five shift crews; three shifts per day, eight hours each. In addition to the shifts, there are several other people and groups of people on daily work. Working in shifts has some consequences discussed later in this chapter.

In paper mills a great deal of an operator's work consists of monitoring the process. Monitoring includes sparse interventions to keep the process within nominal values or to make it function more efficiently. In practice the process is left untouched if everything goes well. Expertise is needed when monitoring the process to interpret whether the situation is normal or whether it calls for intervention. The task relies heavily on human action, and not only on automatic alarm systems. This is because the "recognizing" of the normal state of the paper process is too complicated for traditional alarm systems.

Dealing with disturbances has demanded an ever greater proportion of the work, because routine tasks have decreased along with increased automation. The handling of these quick and unknown situations requires deep knowledge about the process.

14.4.2. The expertise and learning in process control

Part of the expertise is created through formal methods: training, documentation and guidance. This could be called design knowledge (Croon, 1994). The remaining part of the expertise is created when doing the job, for example when solving disturbances, in formal or informal meetings, and other interactions. Baerentsen (1991), in his study on power plants illustratively describes how the expertise is spread through "war stories" told in the organization and how these stories are implicitly used to form generalized knowledge about the process behaviour.

In our study several classes of knowledge used in work have been recognized: former incidents and actions, present situation, future tasks and incidents, process and equipment, normal situations, good control methods, disturbances, and general knowledge about automation and information systems. At the moment this expertise is mostly in the heads of the workers and it is exchanged in discussions. It is rarely written down.

The educational backgrounds of the people involved in process control vary widely. There are "men of the long line", who have gained the major part of their expertise through their own experience. On new machines the factories pose more educational requirements for the employees. Most of the employees in "higher positions" have gained their basic knowledge from technical schools, and on the "manager" level often from institutes of technology.

The vendors of the machines and information/automation systems train the employees, especially when new machines are installed or when substantial changes are made to the existing machines and systems. However, often the training of the vendors concentrates more on the technical questions, and also on questions concerning general features of the machines. In many mills the workers felt that the training focuses more on the service and maintenance than the production of paper.

> The vendor tells us what a fine piece of equipment this is. It has these types of bearing, and they should be greased this way, but the user viewpoint – that is, how to operate it, what pressure has to be used – that is not brought out as well.

For internal training the mills have various training systems such as professional examinations and "entry vacancies". Through the entry vacancies and the examinations the employees proceed to more demanding positions.

The most important form of learning seems to be learning by doing: learning from one's own experience as well as from that of the others.

> There are not training systems for training precisely how to produce paper . . . how one makes right decisions in that huge information flow . . . it is the "feel" for the machine. . . .

> The basis for the "paper man" is the instinct of how to run the machine, and it should never be forgotten. One must always use common sense. One must have the "sense" with him, and one must master the process as a whole.

In this sense the most efficient training system is the work itself, and the mastering of the work involves the interactions between the workers.

One has been here for over twenty years, so that is the training, the best school of all.

The work group itself knows best, how to cope with them (the disturbance situations). We try to gather information from it and then try to distribute it to everyone.

14.4.3. The need to remember

Remembering is an important issue in paper mills. The short case descriptions below illustrate the need to remember and to interpret the history.

Case 1 (serious quality problem, identified a long time after it happened). In one mill a customer reclamation caused much work and data searching. Several weeks' work needed to be done. The history information existed, but it was in such a form that it took a lot of effort and time to find the data concerning the mass, additives (chemicals), parameters, and so on.

Case 2 (serious runnability problem, recurred several times during a period of eight months). In one mill a serious breakdown occurred. After a violent shutdown of the machine and the maintenance procedures, the process did not behave as expected. Several recurring paper breaks were encountered. A lot of work had to be done to find the causes of the break. During the problem-solving similar "cases" from the history were recalled. Those cases helped in finding the solution, although the history did not reveal a strict solution. However, the new solution also seemed to fit the cases in the history. The new solution was recorded, and the old case and the current case were used as evidence (episodes) for the solution ("stories" about problem-solving).

In problem solving the knowledge and experience of several people are needed:

It is recalled from tradition when and where a similar issue was encountered. Traditional (known) problem positions are checked first. Sometimes we scan the electronic diary, earlier we looked at the paper-form diaries.

Remembering requires cooperative efforts but, at the same time, the knowledge of individuals is important:

Someone remembers certain matters better, someone has the knowledge. This is an extremely positive thing you have here (the database) . . . what has happened in year X, when that person is not available here anymore.

The dangers of placing too much trust on (computerized) memory were also understood:

One day we have this opinion, on another day another. Then we write a long list of items there (into the database), and they are valid one day and another day they are not. And the conclusion can even be totally wrong.

14.4.4. Where is the organizational memory in paper mills?

The organizational memory in paper mills is retained mostly in **individuals**, but because industrial paper production has always been group work it is also retained in **culture**. The experience of individuals forms an important source of knowledge needed in the operation of the machine. Many mills have been doing a lot of work to implement "teamwork" in the action. It seems to provide a better basis for "information-sharing", which seems to be an important condition for the "improvement" of organizational remembering. The **transformations** also form an important "bin", but they seem to be related to the culture (different shifts have their own views of how to make paper). Organizational **structures** also retain parts of memory (e.g. the floorplans). There is also information in the machinery (**ecology**); the different parts of the machine and the process provide a basis for the division of work, and the stream of the paper produced co-ordinates the work. For example, when the tampuuri (a roll collecting the paper) gets full, the winderman has to set up a new tampuuri. Information from the physical structures and transformations is also produced through the automation and information systems. There are many probes and measurement devices located all around the machine feeding data to the automation and information systems. **External archives** are also needed. The expertise from the suppliers of the different equipment is needed occasionally (for example, start-up engineers from paper machinery companies may be called in severe disturbances that cannot be solved with the company's own personnel). Many types of information and automation **systems** are used in mills, such as fault diagnosis systems, automation systems, and laboratory systems.

14.4.5. Breakdowns

The skills and experience of the workers are particularly tested in breakdowns – process disturbances. The semantics of the term varies; in some mills they talk about challenges rather than disturbances or problems. In some mills they prefer the term "exception". It seems that this variation is not only a naming "trick"; it also reflects the attitudes towards these breakdowns.

The typical breakdowns in paper mills are paper breaks and machine breaks. A third important issue that can cause a breakdown in the production derives from quality factors. The paper breaks are a normal part of the functioning of the mill: they cannot be totally prevented. "Normal" paper breaks are handled quickly in a routine way: the paper is "put" on without stopping the machine. General causes for the breaks are dirt somewhere in the machine, and a quick cleaning can solve the problem. Several quality problems (such as holes in the paper) can often be handled on the floor. All these "normal" breakdowns are handled by the operators. More severe problems with the paper or machinery might require the knowledge of other experts such as the shift foreman and the superintendent. Sometimes help is needed from external sources, for example the start-up engineers from the machinery vendors.

Breakdowns are an inherent part of the work in process control. They start many kinds of co-operative processes in which new knowledge is created, and old knowledge is evaluated and used. Because the breakdowns cost a lot of money, they are a major focus in the process control. The goal is to produce good quality paper, to produce it at a high speed, to avoid breakdowns, and to keep the efficiency level high. In this sense the management of distributed knowledge in the production and process control is crucial.

14.4.6. Interactions in process control

The work in the process industry is usually organized as shift work. Working in shifts has its own impact on expertise and the process of creating the organizational memory. The process runs continuously but the crew changes every eight hours. One important feature of shift work is that the whole expertise of the organization is not available for operators working outside office hours. If there is a problem during the night shift, the operators and shift supervisors have to manage on their own.

Usually the new crew only comes into brief contact with the previous crew. During the shift change a short discussion is conducted regarding the present situation and the incidents that have recently happened. The success of information exchange during the shift change depends on the people and the culture. In some mills there are not major problems in information exchange; in some other mills they see it as a subject "of constant complaints". The long free times inherent in shift work cause problems: when a worker comes back to work after six days off, it is difficult for him to find out what has been happening, and what the current situation is. The notes on the control desk can be lost, and face-to-face informing can be haphazard.

In the mills which we visited the morning meetings seemed to play an important role in exchanging expertise in the organization. In these meetings the production management, operation supervisors and maintenance personnel discuss and analyze past incidents, the current situation, and future actions. Issues discussed include, for example, production levels, problems, service and maintenance, quality, planning, and sales. The meetings are usually arranged in a special meeting room. The morning meetings are an important arena for exchanging ideas and information. In most mills the meeting minutes are recorded, and in some mills they are also distributed to all involved persons. Some mills use computers to record and distribute the minutes of the meetings.

> . . . anyway, we communicate so . . . that we arrange this morning meeting every morning. The most important issues and activities are recorded there. They can also be viewed on the terminal, readable by all.

Exceptions are a central issue in the morning meetings (problems, disturbances, quality exceptions).

The diaries and reports of the crews and their foremen are important sources of information. Most of the staff fill shift/daily reports concerning their responsibility areas. The conventions of the diaries and reports vary. In some mills forms are used, in some others they are more unstructured. In some mills the diaries are computerized: the records of interesting incidents are stored in the information systems. Breaks are also reported. In some mills formal methods are used for collecting the breakdown reports and in other mills the information is found only from the diary of the shift foreman:

> If it is recorded only in the diary of the foreman, it is hand-written, in some pile; it is not shared that way: it is in the heads of people, this information . . . There can be a lot of knowledge that is only in the head of X or in the head of Y. The distribution of the information happens then through X.

Recording events in diaries and reports is not always easy. It requires time, and it also means some kind of risk or revelation of one's own opinions:

> Writing matters up is a very difficult thing, because it puts something on hand: my opinion, what I have thought. You then risk the so-called "cover my ass" issue all the time. . . .

14.4.7. Dynamics of process control

The people involved in process control live under continuous change. The requirements of the customers vary, the different shifts have their own ways of producing paper, breakdowns emerge, and some parts of the machines wear out. Also, the process is not fully predictable; for example the mass and the chemicals affect the process in unpredictable ways. There is some general knowledge about the process and the machine, and the automation system handles a great part of the control. However, as the interviewees told us, a successful operation depends on the expertise and continuous learning of the crews and their foremen: their "feel" for the machine and the process:

> That (paper production techniques) can actually not be written down, it depends on chemicals, it depends on the product we are working on, raw materials used, so it is quite unique. . . .

As Paunonen (1995) points out, the mental models of the operators are important, they form the basis for decision-making and action. In the dynamic situations the mental models are both produced and used.

> I come here, still sleepy, and then we are trying to "practise" paper making, and then, suddenly we find out that: Hello, here it is . . . so it exists here in my head, if I can just get it out.

As we have noted earlier, the mental models are also a crucial factor in learning both on an individual and on a group level. The mental models include general goals ("I have to keep this process running no matter what"), beliefs ("I can handle this situation by experience"), evaluations ("The machine is getting dirty"), process dependencies ("Changing the mix of mass improves the quality of the paper"), and so on. The dynamics of the work environment require the constant recreation of some of the mental models, and also the recreation of the shared mental models.

14.5. TOOLS FOR ORGANIZATIONAL MEMORY

Several types of tools have been developed to support organizational memory. They can be classified into:

- organizational or group memories
- meeting support systems
- systems that support organizational or group learning
- communication/co-ordination support systems
- case-based reasoning (CBR) systems
- others – group editors, information-sharing tools.

14.5.1. Tools for organizational memory, learning, and interaction

Only a few systems are called *group memories, team memories, corporate memories, or organizational memories*. Perhaps the most well-known of these are gIBIS and its predecessors, Quest Map (Conklin, 1993), SIBYL (Lee, 1990), Answer Garden (Ackerman, 1994), and ASSIST (Ackerman, 1995). Also, several experience databases have been developed. gIBIS and SIBYL are tools that provide semiformal structures for representing design/decision rationales. They provide means for structuring information in the organizational memory. They suggest structures for both interaction and representing the results of that interaction. The basic concepts of gIBIS-structuring are "Issue", "Position", and "Argument". In Quest Map the concept "Decision" is also supported. Answer

Garden offers a database that contains answers to frequently asked questions. It provides a network that helps the users to find answers to their questions. If the answers cannot be found from the database, the system forwards the questions to human experts, and adds the questions and their answers to the database after the answers are found. ASSIST is a "small-scale" organizational memory which combines the organizational memory and task performance. It provides a task-based memory for astrophysicists all over the world. ASSIST retains both data and computing resources (questions and answers, research data, data analysis packages and so on).

Spider (Boland *et al.*, 1994) and CLARE (Wan & Johnson, 1994) are examples of systems that *support group/organizational learning*. Spider supports distributed cognition, which is closely related to organizational learning. Spider is "advertised" as a tool for active thinking. The developers of Spider emphasize individual interpretations and group dialogue. Spider helps in generating ideas and analyzing situations. One can use it to clarify and analyze ideas by using several kinds of representations such as cognitive maps (e.g. cause maps), graphical presentations, and annotations. The emphasis is on a single actor, but Spider also helps the actors to exchange the representations, examine the assumptions behind them, build new constructions, and discuss the representations. CLARE is a computer-supported learning environment that supports learning through collaborative knowledge construction. It is based on the schema theory of cognitive psychology. It provides a semiformal representation language (RESRA), and a model of learning process (SECAI). RESRA (REpresentational Schema of Research Artifacts) supports the collaborative learning of scientific text. The structures of RESRA include nodes, links, and canonical forms. The nodes (e.g. claim, evidence, problem) represent thematic features and learner views of the object. Links represent associations between the nodes, for example a claim must be "supported by" evidence. SECAI presents an explicit model for the learning of scientific text: Summarization, Evaluation, Comparison, Argumentation, and Integration. During the first two phases – summarization and evaluation – the learners produce their individual representation and evaluation of the object under study. During the last three phases they compare their representations, criticize them, and in the integration stage they can build explicit links between their representations.

Several *communication/coordination support tools* have been developed, such as Coordinator (Winograd & Flores, 1986) and Information Lens (Malone *et al.*, 1993). In a sense they have been advanced tools that have contributed to the development of modern e-mail, workflow, and task-management tools. The problem of the standard e-mail as a tool for supporting organizational memory is that usually e-mail is used as a personal tool, and the means for supporting the organizing of e-mail messsages have been quite poor (see Conklin, 1993). Information Lens supports "intelligent information-sharing" and communication. It provides tools such as semistructured messages, filtering tools, and agents for searching information from the network. Co-ordinator combines functions from e-mail and calendaring. Co-ordinator is based on the language/action view, which views action – for example office work – as a network of commitments. It offers a structure for a special conversation type: conversation for action (CfA). It guides the users according to the CfA model, and offers the discussant "rational" alternatives in each conversation state. It also helps the users to keep track of the state of their commitments (e.g. promises I have made).

Meeting support systems can also be seen as tools supporting organizational memory (Nunamaker *et al.*, 1991). Meetings are an important part of the functioning of organizations. During and between meetings many kinds of interesting materials are produced, and interesting discussions are conducted. GroupSystems (Nunamaker *et al.*, 1991) is a well-known meeting support tool (GDSS). The system collects and distributes meeting information also to those who could not attend the meeting, and to those who could not participate during the whole meeting. It also helps the users to filter the information, and gives them the possibility to put some information in "wait state" (gives them time to think).

Case-based reasoning offers a new view and several techniques for the management of experience-based knowledge. These systems include an experience base, where the individual incidents are linked to their context, solutions, and their impacts (Stein & Zwass, 1995). The systems "learn" by adding new incidents to the database, and by creating analogies based on the "old" incidents.

Other tools include group editors (e.g. GROVE; Ellis *et al.*, 1991) and various kinds of information-sharing tools (such as Lotus Notes).

14.5.2. The SHAMAN approach

The tools briefly presented in the previous section offer various interesting ideas for supporting organizational remembering, learning, and interaction. Especially, they provide ideas for structuring both the results of organizational processes and the processes themselves. "Capturing" information about the processes is crucial for the development of computer support for organizational memory (see Conklin, 1993).

In our work we try to find structures that help to collect and recall experiences, models, and guidance in process control. Several artifacts are important in the work of the crews and their foremen, such as the diaries, reports of breakdowns, morning meeting reports, training materials, messages, and many kinds of guidance materials. These provide the basis for developing tools that support remembering, learning, and interaction.

By computerizing the memory one can make it visible to the whole organization, provide a permanent and precise record of interesting issues, and support the accumulation of organizational knowledge. The memory can transmit information about changes in process, products and operation methods to all shifts, and keep the shifts aware of the relevant incidents in the previous shifts. The memory could also support the operators in extracting information relevant to the situation, interpreting and judging the situation, selecting corrective actions, and estimating the results of the actions.

In the SHAMAN project we have developed a prototype tool for supporting expertise-sharing in process industry. The prototype includes a case library, disturbance guides, task guides, model patterns, diaries, and a training part. Several media types are supported in the prototype, such as text, voice, graphics, and video.

The basic structure of the SHAMAN prototype is based on the *issues* found interesting during the observations and interviews. Thus the basic issues are disturbances, model patterns and guidelines, diaries, and training materials. The *refinement* of the materials is supported in the prototypes. Single incidents that are "found interesting" are recorded in the diaries. The records also contain notes concerning breaks and other disturbances. Brief descriptions of disturbances that are found interesting can be recorded in an intermediate disturbance storage. The operator may copy process displays representing the situation as attachments. Later these incidents can be handled in the morning meeting, and they can be supplemented by further information. If the case is of interest and has some general implications it is stored in the case library. The information about the case may inspire the production personnel to write a new task or disturbance handling guide or to update old guides. The same kind of refinement can also be used for model patterns, for example "good parameters". Also, temporary guides can be suggested in the intermediate storage. In this way the prototype supports the creation of different types of memories (short/medium/long-term memory).

When the production personnel have a problem at hand they are provided with efficient search mechanisms to retrieve guides for that very situation or accurate knowledge about previous incidents, and "example cases" describing how similar situations have been handled before. The cases provide the users with *context-specific knowledge* and the guides offer more *generalized knowledge* for the situation. The search mechanisms include search based on specified classes, and full-text search.

The prototype implicitly functions as a learning tool. The distribution of the materials through the databases supports the creation of shared understandings, for example about "good methods", about "problems and their solutions", and about "task guides". Additionally, the database can be used explicitly for training purposes. The current training part includes a lot of materials concerning the machines and how to operate them; for example security guides, audio/video material about the performance of some tasks, technical drawings, and photos.

14.6. SUMMARY AND CONCLUSIONS

In this chapter we have briefly described our view of organizational processes: organizational remembering, organizational learning, and organizational interaction. We have presented our framework to illustrate some crucial issues in work practices in process control. Several issues were discovered in the interviews and observations.

The work in paper mills is highly co-operative and requires communication and distributed decision-making in real time. The nature of shift work has an important impact on the exchange of process information, and the improvement of information exchange between shifts is a crucial issue. The experiences of the employees are a major source of knowledge and learning. The employees learn mostly from their own experiences, and from those of the others. Both individual and collective remembering are crucial factors affecting success in their work. The dangers of trusting memory too much were clearly understood by the interviewees. The individuals, culture, automation/information systems, transformations, and the machines seemed to be the most important storage 'bins'. A lot of the information about transformations and machines is mediated through the automation/information systems. Interactions are an important part of the work and learning in process control. Shift changes, breakdowns, and morning meetings are crucial arenas of interaction. They initiate many kinds of co-operative processes that create new knowledge and shared interpretations and meanings. In these processes old knowledge is also used, evaluated and updated. For example, the handling of disturbance requires collective remembering and intensive interaction between different experts.

We have developed a prototype tool for supporting the work of operators and their foremen in process control based on our studies. In our view, the computerized organizational memory is not only a tool for knowledge retention but also a tool for learning and communication: it is produced as a result of learning, it affects what we learn, and it supports the distribution of knowledge and experiences among people. In our prototype we use concepts familiar to the crews in process control, we give them a capacity for refining the information, and for easy and effective search. Different kinds of representation modes are supported, which may help in the interpretations of the contents as well as the context. The representation of procedural knowledge for example, can be presented through video.

We have conducted pilot studies of our prototype at two sites. At the moment we are starting real production use at one site. Through these pilot studies we want to gain a better understanding of the possibilities to support expertise sharing and management through information technology. We also strive to get a deeper understanding of work practice in process control. We will see if the technology helps the workers to share their expertise with each other, if it helps them to learn from one another, if it helps them to find new solutions to problems, and if it supports them to better assess and manage the current situation. We consider group memory in process control not only as technological intervention, but basically a social issue and we hope we can consider it from this kind of viewpoint, too. The staff on our project group consists of people with a sociological background and people with a background in information systems science.

In future work we will try to gain a deeper understanding of the learning processes in process control, and to find new ideas of how to enhance learning through computer support. We will look for ideas of supporting the interaction in a more explicit way, for example by adding discussion support to the databases. Many of the structures suggested by the tools briefly described in the tools-review seem intuitively appealing. Also, workflow approaches will be examined and carefully analyzed in our further studies.

14.7. REFERENCES

ACKERMAN, M. (1994). Augmenting the organizational memory: a field study of Answer Garden, in *Proc. CSCW'94 Conference*, ACM Press.

ACKERMAN, M. (1995). Memory in the small: an application to provide task-based organizational memory for a scientific community. *Proc. 28th Hawaii International Conference on System Sciences*.

AURAMÄKI, E., KOVALAINEN, M. & JA PAUNONEN, H. (1995). Tools for co-operative work in paper mills. In L. NORROS (Ed.), *Proc. 5th European Conference on Cognitive Science Approaches to Process Control*, VTT Symposium 158, VTT.

BAERENTSEN, K.L. (1991). Knowledge and shared experience. *Proc. 3rd European Conference on Cognitive Science Approaches to Process Control*, Cardiff, UK, 2–6 Sept.

BOLAND, R., RAMKRISHNAN, V., TENKASI, V. & DOV, T. (1994). Designing information systems to support distributed cognition, *Organization Science*, vol. 5, No. 3, 456–475.

CONKLIN, J. (1993). Capturing organizational memory. In BAECKER, R. (Ed.), *Readings in Groupware and Computer-Supported Co-operative Work*. San Mateo: Morgan Kaufmann Publishers.

CROON, I. (1994). Future challenges for pulp and paper industry (summary of Session 1), *Control Systems '94*, STFI/SPCI, 31 May–2 June, Stockholm.

ELLIS, C., GIBBS, S. & REIN, G. (1991). Groupware: some issues and experiences. *Communications of the ACM*, vol. 34, No. 1, Jan.

ENGESTRÖM, Y., BROWN, K., ENGESTRÖM, R. & KOISTINEN, K. (1990). Organizational forgetting: an activity–theoretical perspective. In MIDDLETON, D. & EDWARDS, D. (Eds), *Collective Remembering*, London: Sage Publications.

HUBER, G. (1991). Organizational learning: the contributing processes and the literatures, *Organization Science*, vol. 2, No. 1, 88–115.

KIM D. (1993). The link between individual and organizational learning. *Sloan Management Review*, Fall.

KOLB, D. (1984). *Experiential Learning, Experience as The Source of Learning and Development*. Englewood Cliffs, NJ: Prentice-Hall, 37–50.

LEE, J. (1990). SIBYL: a tool for managing group decision rationale. *Proc. CSCW'90*, ACM.

LEVITT, B. & MARCH, J. (1988). Organizational learning, *Annual Review of Sociology*, vol. 14, No. 3, 319–340.

MALONE, T., GRANT, K., LAI, K.-Y., RAO, R. & ROSENBLITT, D. (1993). The information lens: an intelligent system for information sharing and co-ordination. In R. BAECKER (Ed.), *Readings in Groupware and Computer-Supported Co-operative Work*. San Mateo: Morgan Kaufmann Publishers.

NUNAMAKER, J., DENNIS, A., VALACICH, J., VOGEL, D. & GEORGE, J. (1991). Electronic meeting systems to support group work. *Communications of the ACM*, vol. 34, No. 7, 40–61.

PAUNONEN, H. (1995). Decision making tools for changing paper production organizations, the first ecopapertech. *Proc. International Conference on Papermaking and Paper Machine Technology*, Helsinki, 6–9 June.

STEIN, E. & ZWASS V. (1995). Actualizing organizational memory with information systems. *Information Systems Research*, vol. 6, No. 2, 85–117.

SÖRGAARD, P. (1987). A co-operative work perspective on use and development of computer artifacts. In P. JÄRVINEN (Ed.), *Report of 10th IRIS Seminar,* University of Tampere, Acta Universitatis Tamperensis, ser. B, vol. 27.

TUOMI, I. (1996). Abstraction and history – from organizational amnesia to organizational memory. *Proc. 28th Hawaii International Conference on System Sciences*.

WALSH, J. & UNGSON, G. (1991) Organizational memory. *Academy of Management Review*, vol. 16, No. 1, 57–91.

WAN, D. & JOHNSON, P. (1994). Computer supported co-operative learning using CLARE: the approach and experimental findings. *Proc. CSCW'94*, ACM.

WINOGRAD, T. & FLORES, F. (1986). *Understanding Computers and Cognition: a New Foundation for Design*. Norwood, NJ: Ablex.

CHAPTER FIFTEEN

Knowledge management for collective learning and organizational memory

STURE HÄGGLUND

15.1. INTRODUCTION

Most organizations, and especially most companies, are becoming more and more dependent on the body of knowledge that underlies the operation of the organization (Feigenbaum *et al.*, 1988). Thus, not only in consulting firms but also in manufacturing and process control, the competence, experience and general knowledge possessed, maintained and utilized by the employees provide an important ingredient in the successful operation and survival of the enterprise.

Computer-based information systems, in particular knowledge-based systems, promise to improve the possibility to record and communicate qualified competence within an organization and thus to make the organization less vulnerable to losses of specific individuals, who carry important knowledge for the operation of the organizations. In fact, computers and information-processing systems are more and more perceived as media for communication, rather than as systems for computation as such (Wærn *et al.*, 1992). In particular, knowledge-based systems or expert systems are viewed and developed primarily as co-operative systems supporting human decision-makers by providing knowledge and information in such a way as to facilitate the understanding of a given situation and the consequences of a possible decision (Hägglund, 1994).

In the area of collaborative process management, process operators may interact with each other and with the controlled systems through a computer-mediated communication channel. This chapter will discuss information technologies available for managing the knowledge which influences the decision-making and actions of the people involved in running the operations of a given organization.

Technologies concerned range from support for making existing information more easily available to techniques for acquiring and representing knowledge in a deeper sense. These technologies will be reviewed in the perspective of joint learning and joint decision-making in dynamic environments. In general, we feel that in the CSCW research area more emphasis should be given to issues concerning support for team decision-making and knowledge management for co-operating groups of people, in particular for managing a real-time process of some kind. Finally, we will reflect on some consequences of utilizing knowledge-based systems for developing and maintaining the knowledge capital in a given organization.

15.2. KNOWLEDGE MANAGEMENT AND COMMUNICATION

Current research and experience in the area of knowledge management systems emphasize the insight that a combination of various types of information services are called for. Thus advanced reasoning and problem-solving may be required for special, albeit important, situations while efficient information retrieval based on textual matching is more appropriate in other cases. Access to external data repositories, as supported by conventional database management systems, may be important for linking operational data to the decision-making processes. The general technical framework for managing information resources today is provided by WorldWideWeb software and internet/intranet architectures.

Practical work on knowledge management systems thus brings several software technologies together, as follows.

■ Hypertext and hypermedia, where information is stored in a structured network of nodes, which might contain text, formatted data, pictures, programs, etc. Emphasis is on interactive browsing and flexible assembly of excerpts from the network. WWW-type systems support easy building of such information structures and provide a user interface needed to access the information.

■ Information storage and retrieval, based on full text, abstracts and keywords. The system does not interpret anything of the contents of stored information (except for keywords). Emphasis is on support for very large, read-only databases, fuzzy information needs and a pattern-matching strategy for retrieval. Systems typically support iterative query formulation before the user is satisfied.

■ Database management, based on formatted data where the meaning of data is defined (to a certain degree) in the database schema. Emphasis is on large, permanent, mutable and shared databases. Systems support formal set-oriented query languages, which allow efficient processing of database accesses.

■ Knowledge-based systems, where expert knowledge is represented in the system in order for it to be able to reason about problems in a given application domain and come up with reasonable solutions. The emphasis here is on problem-solving based on intensive processing of fairly small resident knowledge bases. Systems directly propose a solution to a given problem or provide assistance for decision-making.

Of special interest to us is the possibility to promote computer-supported co-operative work through knowledge systems technology. Thus the integration of different sources of expertise and individualized distribution to members of a work team responsible for decision-making is a crucial challenge.

15.3. REVIEW OF KNOWLEDGE-BASED EXPERT SYSTEMS

Knowledge-based expert systems emerged originally as an attempt to build software that could compete with humans in solving problems at an expert level in a given domain of application. A typical definition of the term "expert system" emphasizes its character as an intelligent computer program which otherwise uses knowledge and logical inference to solve problems which demand significant human expertise for their solution. Such software systems attempt not only to formalize information from the application domain and the procedures for computing with such representations, but also to allow reasoning about informal and experience-based qualities of decision-making. The key to success in this endeavour seems to be the ability to represent and use within the computer system a wide variety of knowledge from the application domain. The instrumental character of knowledge is emphasized, which means that when we refer to knowledge of the kind that can be symbolically represented in a computing system, we also assume that some generalized procedures are provided for reasoning with that knowledge.

Knowledge-based systems are generally viewed as exhibiting the following characteristics.

■ They provide expert-level problem-solving or decision support for some suitably restricted domain of application.

■ Domain knowledge is explicitly represented within the system and changes in the implemented functions can be accomplished in terms of the domain knowledge.

■ Stored knowledge can be used for inferring facts and solutions to problems in a multitude of ways.

■ Explanations and motivations can be provided in order to elucidate the reasoning of the system and justify its results.

■ The development process and supporting tools tend to promote an improved understanding of problem-solving in the given domain and the nature of the knowledge involved.

Typical applications for knowledge-based expert systems are tasks which involve monitoring, interpretation, diagnosis, design, planning, and so forth. An area where many of these types of task are involved is process control. Knowledge-based systems can at present be used to represent expertise in small but presumably complex domains. They are useful as a means of conveying specialist knowledge to a less experienced user.

One important mechanism for knowledge representation provided by most systems is the use of rules. Rules are conditional structures which can be used to define logical necessity, causal relationships, situation–action pairs and production rules for substitution patterns. It is assumed that there is a well-defined mechanism for reasoning with the rules and facts in the system. This mechanism, or inference procedure, can then establish various conclusions from available facts by identifying and evaluating relevant rules from the knowledge base.

15.4. DISCUSSION

The technologies referred to above provide a spectrum of possibilities in terms of supporting the elicitation of knowledge and experience in an organization and when making this body of knowledge available. This applies to the task of supporting the individual employee in the processes of making decisions and making explicit the facts and experiences which are important for carrying out his or her professional assignments. But it also applies to the organization's need to manage and control the body of knowledge and experience, which might be essential for its operations.

In various application domains, we have been involved in studies where individual experts or a team of professionals were given access to knowledge-based software systems in order to support their decision-making processes. The discussion in the rest of this chapter tries to summarize some issues of importance when advanced knowledge management systems are considered in the context of organizational decision-making.

For instance, one can observe that contrary to the effect of mechanical automation, where human skills were made less important as machines took over most of the work, it is likely that computing and knowledge management support will cause an increased demand for people with professional competence and skills. Computers will not in the foreseeable future be able to process knowledge more efficiently than proficient humans, except in narrow, albeit presumably complex, domains. Thus the strategy for their efficient use in advanced organizations must combine efforts to develop human competence and to provide an efficient knowledge communication network. Such a network should not only be a passive link for conveying information, but provide various knowledge-based services as well.

It seems that a key task here will be the ability to organize systems in such a way that they promote the growth of user competence and counteract the erosion of knowledge within an organization. Of particular importance is the potential of knowledge systems for explicit training in core areas of a profession. Although the use of systems which implement an expert problem-solving capacity for decision-making can be cost-effective in the short run, there is also often a danger that the quality of decisions degrades over time due to changes in the environment. In this case it is especially important that professional knowledge and skills are maintained within the organization, and that knowledge systems can be updated and improved continuously. Research has shown that existing knowledge bases can be utilized for training as an additional service, although more work is still needed in order to make this a common practice (Sokolnicki, 1991).

15.4.1. Knowledge management for individual and organizational learning

The primary motivation for development of expert systems has typically been the desire to support or automate problem-solving processes in the domain of application. However, the explicit representation of knowledge in a system can also serve the purpose of providing the basis for a tutoring system, which can be used to train inexperienced personnel in decision-making, especially for unfamiliar or extraordinary situations. For instance, training simulators should have a great potential for improving decision-making and for developing the knowledge and competence for the actors in, for instance, a CSCW environment (Hägglund & Granlund, 1994).

One possibility for a knowledge-based tutoring and training system is to allow the user to test and train his ability to solve problems in the domain of an existing expert system. The system can then monitor the progress of the user and compare with a parallel internal problem-solving, which uses the strategic knowledge recorded in the knowledge base. Deviations are checked as potential errors, omissions or malpractice. It is also possible for the user to ask for help or hints if needed.

We have previously tested these ideas with some success in the areas of medicine (Elfström et al., 1980) and economy (Hägglund et al., 1987). In a present project, where the aim is to use simulations to train process control operators, we are studying the possibilities to improve the resulting understanding of involved processes by developing an intelligent tutoring system employing a "learning-companion" approach (Ragnemalm,

1996). This work involves a study of what distinguishes an expert from a novice and how the acquiring of proficiency in a given domain can be promoted.

This is an example of a dynamic decision-making situation. Of particular interest is the possibility to relate strategies for explanations to the coaching exercised by the system in a training situation. Such training simulators should have a great potential for improving decision-making and for developing the knowledge and competence for decision-makers.

Thus we can see a potential for using a computer-managed knowledge base in an organization as a tool for individuals to develop their understanding and insight and for the organization to document and preserve the knowledge as such (Hägglund, 1989).

15.4.2. Control of the "knowledge capital"

Many organizations and, especially, many companies are becoming more and more dependent on the body of knowledge which underlies the operation of the organization. In consulting firms, for example, it is obvious that the most important resource is the competence and skills possessed by the employees. It should be a common interest for all concerned parties to develop and maintain this knowledge capital which is working in the organization.

It is noteworthy that little is known about how to treat such a resource from a financial analysis point of view. Continuing education activities and programmes for personal development represent ways of making knowledge investments, but it is also important to consider whether work is organized in such a way that a development of competence and skills is promoted. However, the knowledge capital often leaves a company together with the specialists and experts who carry the knowledge.

Knowledge systems promise to improve the possibility to record and communicate qualified competence within an organization and thus to make the organization less vulnerable to such losses (Sandahl *et al.*, 1991). There seems to be a serious conflict here. The organization ought to have a legitimate right to access and control the knowledge capital built up within the organization. At the same time, a specialist in an area has an obvious interest to maintain and protect this personal competence resource. It is not even obvious that the expert should be prepared to share his capabilities with trainees without a reasonable compensation. Since knowledge systems claim to reproduce the problem-solving capacity of an expert in specific areas and, further, to offer a possibility for less experienced people to increase their own skill in the domain, we could expect to meet serious obstacles in obtaining the commitment from experts necessary for the development of knowledge systems.

It would, however, be naive to conclude that a knowledge system in a particular domain actually makes the expert obsolete. It is not to be expected in the near future that systems can be built that capture more than a small fraction of an expert's knowledge and competence. Further, it is still far beyond the state of the art to build practical systems which could maintain and develop their knowledge by automated learning. Current experiences thus indicate that experts tend to gain an increased importance when knowledge systems are introduced, since the yield of their competence can be multiplied through the systems.

Of special interest is the situation where the knowledge is developed and shared in a group of people. Here the same problems with regard to protection of the right to the knowledge may appear within the group. But at the same time, the need to make the knowledge explicit and to share an understanding within the group promotes a view of the knowledge as an organizational resource.

15.4.3. Knowledge systems and professional integrity

When computer support plays an increasingly important role in decision-making, especially when expert advice is provided by a system, it is only natural that issues of responsibility for decisions taken are raised. With the exception of matters where the decision rules can be strictly formalized, at present there seems to be no justification for removing the responsibility from the human decision-maker. In practice the situation is a bit more complicated. Consider, for instance, a medical diagnosis or a financial advice. Even if everybody agrees that the responsibility be left with the physician or the adviser, it is obvious that it will be very difficult to ignore a recommendation if it later turns out the system was right in the first place. This will lead either to a presumably suboptimal compliance with the system's advice or to a situation where the system is not consulted at all.

In our opinion, this problem is partly the result of a widespread and unjustified confidence in information that has been processed by a computer. Although it is reasonable to believe that this confidence will be reduced to more realistic levels in the future, we have to face the fact that using computer support for decision-making may introduce severe problems in certain cases. The way we choose to organize this support, in particular the division of tasks between the user and the system, will obviously play an important role here. Also, in regard to the situation where a number of people are participating in a computer-mediated co-operation and jointly making decisions, we will find new and intriguing problems with respect to the sharing of formal and informal responsibility for decisions taken.

15.5. CONCLUSION

In this chapter we have discussed a situation where we apply various computer-based techniques, in particular knowledge-based systems, for supporting knowledge management in organizations. These techniques may be instrumental for collective learning and organizational memory, understood as the ability of individuals to develop jointly their knowledge and understanding of subjects crucial for a given organization, as well as the ability for the organization as such to access and manage the same knowledge.

Three specific issues of salience in this context were raised as topics for discussion, as follows.

- How can we devise and use training simulators that allow people to develop jointly insights and understanding of the common knowledge base in an organization?

- How do we control the ownership of the knowledge capital, and which problems may arise from the fact the individuals may have different objectives to the organization?

- What happens to the possibility for individuals to take responsibility for decisions when computer-based decision support is introduced?

These matters are not well understood in general, and viewing them in the context of collaborative work presents additional interesting challenges for research.

15.6. REFERENCES

ELFSTRÖM, J., GILLQVIST, J., HOLMGREN, H., HÄGGLUND, S., ROSIN, O. & WIGERTZ, O. (1980). A customized programming environment for patient management simulations. *Proc. 3rd World Conf. on Medical Informatics*, Tokyo.

FEIGENBAUM, E.A., MCCORDUCK, O. & NII, P. (1988). *The Rise of the Expert Company*. New York: Times Books.

HÄGGLUND, S. (1989). The impact of intelligent systems on office procedures and knowledge management. Invited paper, *Proc Int. Conf. on Opportunities and Risks of Artificial Intelligence Systems*, Hamburg.

HÄGGLUND, S. (1994). Introducing expert critiquing systems. *The Knowledge Engineering Review*, vol. 8, No. 4, Guest Editor's Introduction.

HÄGGLUND, S. & GRANLUND, R. (1994). Computer support for collaborative C3I decision making and training. *SIGOIS Bulletin*, vol. 15, No. 2, 5–7. Presented at the Workshop on Collaborative Realtime Process Management at CSCW'94.

HÄGGLUND, S., HANSSON, C. & SOKOLNICKI, T. (1987). Knowledge-based training of case management routines and emergency procedures. *Proc. 3rd Int. Conf. on Expert Systems*, London.

RAGNEMALM, E.L. (1996). Collaborative dialogue with a learning companion as a source of information on student reasoning. *Proc. ITS'96*, Montreal.

SANDAHL, K., ERIKSSON, H., PADRON-MCCARTHY, T., SOKOLNICKI, T. & ÖSTERLUND, B. (1991). Meeting the requirements of knowledge management. *Expert Systems with Applications*, vol. 3, 259–267.

SOKOLNICKI, T. (1991). Towards knowledge-based tutors: a survey and appraisal of intelligent tutoring systems. *The Knowledge Engineering Review*, vol. 6, No. 2, 59–95.

WÆRN, Y., HÄGGLUND, S., LÖWGREN, J., RANKIN, I., SOKOLNICKI, T. & STEINEMANN, A. (1992). Communication knowledge for knowledge communication. *Int. Journal of Man–Machine Studies*, vol. 37, No. 2, 215–239.

CHAPTER SIXTEEN

Knowledge graphs in group learning

ROEL POPPING

16.1. INTRODUCTION

Learning, acquiring and conveying knowledge can take place in many ways. The best-known way of learning is via the teaching that is undertaken in schools. The concept of self-learning, however, is often used at places where goals are absent or are barely specified, and several methods and systems have been developed to promote this kind of learning.

My interest is in building and representing knowledge. I consider knowledge-building to be a form of group or collective learning, and here one is not confronted with knowledge in terms of who knows about a specific topic or where can one find this and that, but rather with knowledge in the sense of something that has to be created, and how this can be achieved. This presupposes a group at work, and the knowledge the group produces can be considered to be a collective memory. It is knowledge that needs to be represented in a clear way. This knowledge, which can be very complex and sometimes also very dynamic, has to be manageable and the participants in the group should at least be able to understand it. To create this knowledge one can use methods that are comparable with the basic ideas behind self-learning methods. One of these methods, called knowledge graphs, will be discussed in this chapter. Learning is seen as a typical way of structuring knowledge, and knowledge graphs allow the structuring of such knowledge. This method can be very useful in process management, especially where decisions have to be taken at short notice, though it is new and needs to be refined in several respects.

First, the context of the problem will be outlined, and this is followed by some remarks about knowledge-building. The building of group knowledge is connected to learning. Attention is paid to several features that perform a function in these graphs. When this building process has been discussed, attention can then be directed to knowledge graphs, whose importance will be discussed toghether with what needs to be done before they can be used adequately.

16.2. THE CONTEXT OF THE PROBLEM

Today people are confronted more and more often with problems they cannot solve individually. The reason is that these problems either are too complex or are weakly structured. The joint formulation of and consent upon agreement concerning research topics, the development of study plans and the finding of solutions to the research problems often require expertise from different areas and sources. The environment is a concrete example of a problem area. Here one meets several problems that may act world-wide. In firms or services there are many situations where task groups or loosely structured teams fulfil some important function. Their function might be the planning of duty time-tables of complex activities, organizing retraining courses for the staff, the development of strategies for the firm, or finding, analyzing and solving of certain problems relating to quality.

These problems need to be attacked not by one person but by a team, where everybody contributes with knowledge from his or her discipline or experience. In general the task of the group is to solve the problem quickly and well. These kinds of knowledge have to be combined and integrated. People working on such integration, or at least on structuring a problem, have to learn from each other. They also have to identify what the others know that could contribute to solving the problem. They need to establish some common knowledge, for without common knowledge the group members are unable to share views and thus may encounter a range of problems when undertaking their tasks. Delay is possible with regard to reaching the goals; one might only find half solutions, or even fail completely. The negative consequences are demonstrable and can be enormous. It is a problem with which every organization is confronted. The company learns, as do the participating individuals.

Knowledge is a continuing representation of reality in our minds for which many different representation techniques exist. It is the sum of opinions, experiences, procedures that are considered to be true, and which therefore give direction to our thoughts, acts, and communications.[1] Knowledge allows us to give meaning to data and in this way to generate information.

The knowledge that is looked for is passed on from different sites and has to be used by various people. For this reason it should be group knowledge. This might be knowledge that is accessible to each member of the group and that is currently expressible, but it can also be the sum of the knowledge of each of the group members. With respect to the task that is to be performed I emphasize the first view: each of the participants should possess the accessible knowledge.

For the accomplishment of group tasks decisions are to be taken, but other general tasks have also to be performed (McGrath, 1984, p. 61). The decisions are based on a rethinking of the knowledge that has been communicated. In early research much attention was paid to the development of decision-making systems for individuals. These systems are aimed at individuals and concern those parts of a decision-making process where it is possible to choose from different alternatives. The phases preceding the decision, however, need more attention and here the exchange of knowledge is essential (Kraemer & King, 1988).

Due to the complexity of decision-making in organizations, this exchange of knowledge becomes increasingly participatory. To enable a decision to be made, more and more information is needed from an increasing number of specialists, even though the final decision may have to be taken by just one person.[2]

The development of group knowledge includes more than just decision-making. It starts when the first contacts are made between the participants in the group. They have to learn to know each other, and learn how to co-operate. Therefore it is of interest not only for investigators of information systems, but also for investigators from quite separate disciplines such as anthropology, social psychology, ethnomethodology, organization theory and artificial intelligence. Just having group decision-making systems is not suffi-cient to solve problems.

Knowledge-building by a group can be performed in the context of CSCW (computer supported co-operative work). This is a term "which combines the understanding of the way people work in groups with the enabling technologies of computer networking and associated hardware, software, services and techniques" (Wilson, 1991, p. 6).

For the process of knowledge-building, communication between the participants in the group, including all aspects connected to it, is important, and this aspect receives a good deal of attention in CSCW. There is, however, another important aspect that receives less attention, namely that concerning the tools that can be used in knowledge-building. The various opinions should be integrated.

16.3. GROUP LEARNING

"Learning" is described as "increasing one's capacity to take effective action" (Kim, 1993, p. 38). This description contains an operational (the acquisition of skills) and a conceptual (the creation of sense giving knowledge) aspect, and the interest centres primarily on this second aspect. Knowledge that is acquired can be important for both the organization and the individual. Kim (1993) describes the relation between the learning of the two.

The way in which the creation of new knowledge advances within an organization is determined by what is known as the interpretative framework (Tsuchiya, 1993). Here a study is undertaken to ascertain whether such new knowledge is consistent with the knowledge already available within an organization. To achieve this a feedback loop is used that has three stages. In the *dialogue stage* new knowledge is created by discussion. Next, a conclusion is arrived at, or an action is agreed upon in the *decision-making section*. In the *interpretative stage* the decision is confronted with the interpretative frame-work, which gives motivation for a further dialogue. The model by Tsuchiya is related to the model by Daft & Weick (1984) regarding learning behaviour in organizations.

Many ways of learning exist. Some of them are planned, others not. The (planned) method, what is wanted most at a given point of time, is determined by the goal one wants to reach. Projects that have to be completed might, for example, benefit from the knowledge that was obtained in previous projects. If the knowledge gained in these earlier projects is well documented and is easily accessible it can be used. Those who have to perform the projects have to know how to look for the way comparable projects have been approached by using, for instance, an index. Clear catalogues, indexes and search systems have to be developed and implemented.

The computer can have an intermediate function with regard to the resolution of problems if the knowledge domain is structured, the function of variables is known, and a lot of experience exists. Should a new problem arise that can be described by using the terminology of the known variables, one can use "case-based reasoning" to generate an answer to a question (analysis task). It can also be used for tasks demanding a synthesis. This is especially so in the learning situation.

Many problems are such that no structuring exists, in which case it is not known which variables have some function. These problems must therefore be approached in another way, and there are no experts on hand who know the answer to the problem. Neverthe-less, there will be experts in different places who can contribute to the solution. Some-times one might assume that this solution is nothing more than mapping out the field, but the fact is that the knowledge of these experts must be combined. Before this can be discussed, some attention must be paid to the topic of group knowledge.

There is also a management perspective, where the organization for learning and the collection of experience and knowledge is focused (see Levitt & March, 1988). This is usually called "organizational learning".

16.3.1. Group knowledge development

The process of developing group knowledge is especially a process of exchanging knowledge.[3] This occurs mainly in the dialogue section as viewed by Tsuchiya. In the exchange of knowledge an explication process and a sharing process are distinguished. The explication process is the process by which implicit shared knowledge is communicated and so becomes explicit shared knowledge. Shared knowledge is common to all group members or to a subset of group members, either implicitly or explicitly. Unshared knowledge has been experienced by only one group member (it is part of his/her individual knowledge) or by none of them. Implicit shared knowledge is knowledge that group members have in common without knowing this. If the group members know they have it in common, it is called explicit shared knowledge. The sharing process is the process where not-shared knowledge is communicated and becomes explicit shared knowledge.[4]

Group knowledge exists in the minds of the participants, with each participant knowing that other versions of the group knowledge are present in the minds of the other participants. The group knowledge development process involves an individual knowledge development process.

Group knowledge is the sum of individual knowledge possessed by all group members. It can be conflicting where individual members have different opinions. Different types of group knowledge exist:

- group knowledge *before* the sharing process – not-shared knowledge or implicit shared knowledge
- group knowledge *after* the sharing process – explicit shared knowledge.

As it is assumed that the sharing process includes the explication process, knowledge should be explicit after sharing. Note, however, that group knowledge can refer to both the intersection and the union of all individual knowledge.

In the group knowledge development process the participants in the group exchange (clarify) and organize (unify) knowledge. Therefore it is a process of *clarification* and *unification*. The clarification process is part of the development process where group members exchange their knowledge and discuss its meaning and relevance. It consists of two subprocesses: the sharing and explicating processes.

The members of a group share a lot of knowledge, but they are not aware of how much or what they share.[5] The construction of group knowledge has to start by making explicit the relevant knowledge that is being shared. This is denoted as the process of explication. There is also knowledge that is not shared by all participants in the group, but is available to only one participant of the group (it is part of his or her individual knowledge). The group member who possesses specific knowledge might contribute this. Now the process of "sharing" starts. This is the process where not-shared knowledge is communicated and becomes explicit shared knowledge. However, the interpretation of this explicit knowledge varies between participants. Each participant knows that others may have available other interpretations of the explicit shared knowledge, and each may take a different approach to the explicit shared knowledge. One participant may attempt to incorporate this knowledge into his or her own previous knowledge, while others may be satisfied with knowing that another participant can contribute the knowledge required. It is not necessary that agreement exists with regard to the interpretation of the explicit shared knowledge. To reach a specific group goal, however, it is in general necessary that such agreement exists. Fig. 16.1 indicates the various cases of shared knowledge. The knowledge which is shared, whether explicated or not, is drawn as the outer circle. The explicit shared knowledge is a part of this knowledge. The knowledge which is agreed upon is in turn a part of the explicit shared knowledge. The group knowledge development process implies an individual knowledge development process. Group knowledge is the union of the individual knowledge possessed by all group members. It is preferred that this also be the intersection.[6]

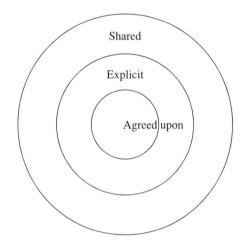

Figure 16.1. Forms of shared knowledge.

So far the exchange of knowledge, the clarification, has been discussed. The new knowledge must now also be integrated with the knowledge already available. The unification process is the part where group members organize their knowledge. Here the knowledge is merged, and synthesized, and an agreement is found on (part of) the knowledge model. This process especially helps the group to achieve its goals and is carried out by all the individual group members. Here they build their (part of the) knowledge model that they may contribute to the group, and the result is agreement concerning (part of) the knowledge model. The process of clarification and unification is very important if the group is to reach its goal.

It is in this process of unification that the participants can receive assistance in building their theories. This help may be provided by a system that ensures that the available knowledge is represented in a clear and structured way.

Without systematic efforts the group knowledge leading to the fulfilment of the group task cannot be developed. Therefore the improvement of group activities has, in principle, several advantages if attention is given to the construction of group knowledge. This process of development may be supported by a (possibly computerized) cabinet of instruments and can also be improved in this way. The model described here fits into the model for the evolution of knowledge according to Tsuchiya. Most of it belongs to the dialogue stage.

16.3.2. Storage of knowledge

The participants in a group are not always physically together; they might even be working on the problem at very different places and times. For that reason, a first requirement to be posed to a group is that it has some medium for storing the available knowledge. One such medium is the minds of the participants, though there should also be some other place where the knowledge is stored. Now one has access to the knowledge that others have contributed and that one does not possess himself or herself yet, without having to trouble the other person. This knowledge can be available in writing or stored in some database, where it is considered as data. Having its common knowledge stored in some way is the most basic requirement that a co-operative group may have. In technical terms, stored knowledge can also be regarded as data (carrying some information that can be interpreted as knowledge[7]). The simplest functions needed in manipulating stored knowledge are thus partly comparable to those of database management systems. Knowledge may also be seen to have various forms of existence concerning its format. The usual meaning of a "knowledge-based" system implies some formalism in expressing knowledge: natural language, formal language, semantic networks, facts, rules, and so on. It is preferable to be fairly open in this respect and allow knowledge to be expressible in almost any form so that it can be stored and transferred between the participants in a group.

Whatever the form in which knowledge is represented, it is usually not possible to manage it without classifying or grouping it into suitable domains. Database systems, or hypermedia or hypertext[8] systems, are suitable as electronic media.[9] The system that is used to store and manage the group knowledge must be able to localize the units of explicit shared knowledge. This can be done by using an index or placing a flag to indicate whether someone has already inspected the newly delivered knowledge.[10] The system itself cannot verify whether the knowledge is agreed upon, and so the group knowledge management system should be able to introduce a domain structure in which the units of shared knowledge can be located. The structure has its main purpose when group members are accessing knowledge; they should be able to restrict their interest in some classes of knowledge, and define personal priorities between classes. Overall this classification property is a key concept in giving a group knowledge management system its characteristic advantage over pure data management.

16.3.3. Knowledge augmentation

Knowledge may originate from different sources. Every new knowledge unit initially belongs to some group member who considers it valuable to the entire group. As a technical issue the transfer of knowledge units from the private environment of a user to the shared knowledge of the group is quite easy even if conversions between different formats of presentation and some means to filter the appropriate information may be needed. The knowledge units may be ready in some documents or edited by a participant just for the situation at hand. Where knowledge management is decentralized the actual transfer is more or less replaced by keeping the participants aware of the existing knowledge, and especially by informing them about the "new" knowledge units.

A crucial question in augmenting knowledge is the issue of retaining its integrity. Some checks against duplicate or contradictory elements might be automated if the constraints needed can be defined in advance. More inherent, however, is an incremental and informal check made by group members when they discover new knowledge and – whether consciously or not – evaluate it in relation to existing knowledge. This process can probably only be supported by giving the participants suitable means of access to knowledge, for example powerful knowledge browsers, and by using visual presentations where applicable.

To be useful, group knowledge has to maintain sufficient conceptual clarity and uniqueness. The personal preferences of the participants and the general, unified, contents of the shared knowledge may occasionally contradict each other. Explanation mechanisms (as well as powerful access means mentioned earlier) will be helpful in this respect. It might also be possible to define some new concepts of knowledge similarity and differences to aid the workable agreement of knowledge within groups.

Earlier in this chapter it was noted that database-like systems are suitable for storing knowledge, though such systems also have several disadvantages that become particularly clear when the growth of knowledge is considered. These systems allow only the physical growth of knowledge. Masses of knowledge are added, the participants in the group have to find their way through it and this means that participants may be confronted with more information than they can handle. When knowledge is outdated, and can therefore be removed from the medium, somebody (the database manager, the group member that contributed the knowledge) must do this. This becomes very important when agreement about some explicit knowledge exists. The steps in between, leading to the result, must of course be kept in some archive, but in the system they are an annoyance.

16.3.4. Knowledge integration

A major problem of group knowledge development is to identify misunderstandings in groups and to establish agreed meanings for concepts in a problem or application domain. At a given moment it should also be clear which concepts exist in a problem or where application domain agreement exists. Several methods for knowledge representation are available which might cover this problem. This is especially true when the method allows knowledge integration.

This brings us back to the participants in the group, who have also been indicated as experts. These experts all can contribute those items of knowledge that in their view contribute to the solution of the problem. These parts need to be integrated into a larger body of knowledge, and this should result in the overall knowledge required. Based on this knowledge, better, or less *ad hoc*, decisions are probable.

One method that permits the integration of knowledge is the use of so-called knowledge graphs. Here the content of a knowledge area is represented in a directed graph, where the concepts constitute the nodes. The relation between a pair of concepts is indicated by their link. Knowledge graphs may represent the knowledge available in some specific field, or the knowledge a scientific investigator has ordered and presented for his or her own purposes, or the knowledge an arbitrary person or organization uses in individual and collective situations of decision-making. The idea of knowledge graphs was originally developed in order to map the (empirically proven) state of art in some area in science. Scientific knowledge is generally found in texts, although the way the knowledge of participants in a group is contributed may not be precisely known. I assume for the moment that it is done by text.

16.4. KNOWLEDGE GRAPHS

Language is still the most important medium in which to represent explicit knowledge. Here some problems can be expected,[11] and the most important one is that language is ambiguous. Concepts can often be explained in several ways (the ontology problem) but when they are defined with as little ambiguity as possible acceptable communication is possible. There is, however, another problem. Text is a static way of representing knowledge whereas knowledge itself is dynamic, with continously changing content. So the computer may allow a less ambiguous and more dynamic representation of knowledge.

Tsuchiya (1993) indicated that information technology has an important function in the model for the evolution of knowledge in that it is situated between the phases of building or creating knowledge and decision-making. It is here that knowledge graphs can be situated.

One way of representing knowledge using computers is by knowledge graphs. Text is transformed into relations. The basic structure for such relations is subject–verb–object. These are two concepts connected by a relation. The two concepts can be represented as labelled nodes, the relations as labelled links. Nodes and relations (in some text called arcs) together constitute in principle the knowledge graph. The representation of knowledge by labelled nodes and labelled links between these nodes leads to structures that are usually called semantic networks (Sowa, 1987). Knowledge graphs can be viewed as semantic networks of a particular kind. One essential difference between knowledge graphs and semantic networks is the explicit choice of only a few types of relations (James, 1992, p. 98).

The construction of knowledge graphs starts with the extraction of information from texts. This is called *text analysis*. The result is a list of concepts, represented as labelled nodes, and a list of typed links between the nodes. These form the so-called author graph. The most important type of link between nodes is the causal relation. The goal of the group of scientists working on knowledge graphs was to construct graphs that represent the theory on a specific subject. So far this is identical with the methods that have been discussed.

The next step is called *concept identification*. Here the various author graphs are combined into one graph by identifying nodes with each other. When the texts that were at the basis of the graphs are about the same subject, nodes with the same label are identified. An author may use synonyms for a concept, therefore nodes with different labels should be identified. This is done by comparing the neighbourhoods of nodes so as to identify the potentially identical pairs. An index has been developed for measuring the similarity between two sets of nodes. The value this index takes, in combination with a threshold value, can be used to determine identification of two concepts. In the same way it is possible to detect nodes with the same label, but referring to a different content: the so-called homonyms. One of these nodes should be given another label.[12] What emerges now is a compiled graph which should as far as possible be free of ambiguity of language. This graph is further investigated in procedures called *concept integration* and *link integration*. The first procedure tries to find interesting substructures, the second procedure infers new links from the given ones. The result is called the integrated graph. To represent the structure of knowledge a complex relation is often necessary, namely the frame relation. This relation combines several concepts and relations into a single concept (an example of a frame is quality assessment). Concept integration aims at determining those subgraphs that are candidates for contraction into a frame. (Note: the term is used with another meaning than that generally used in artificial intelligence.) In link integration, relations are combined to deduce new relations. If relations exist between the concepts A and B as well as between B and C, there may be reasons to infer a relation between A and C. To find these new relations, path-algebra (Carré, 1979, p. 84–85) is used. Relations can be based on multiplication for the serial combination, and on addition for the parallel combination. These procedures can be represented in a flow diagram that is called the Knowledge Integration and Structuring System (KISS); see Fig. 16.2.

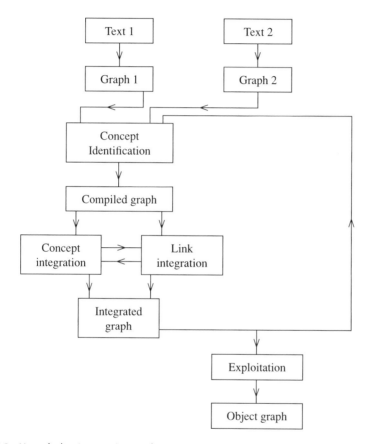

Figure 16.2. Knowledge Integration and Structuring System.

When new knowledge is added it immediately becomes clear whether this knowledge contradicts the available knowledge or augments it. This is useful in the explication process because the knowledge comes immediately in the right place, though this does not mean that it should be accepted without discussion. The new knowledge will probably have to be specified in a clearer way, or adapted because of conflicting situations, and so on. In this process it will become clear where exactly the knowledge is not sufficient, and where different views exist. In the long run it will be true for a greater part of the knowledge that agreement exists. It might turn out in the knowledge integration that relations that were not assumed do in fact exist in the available knowledge. For this reason knowledge integration might involve more than just the combining of different pieces of knowledge with which one was already familiar.

The possibilities for reducing superfluous knowledge have in part already been mentioned. Synonyms can be replaced by one concept. If in some text a concept is discussed, and in another text the definition of this concept is found, they can be related. Chains of reasoning can be replaced by shorter ones due to the use of path-algebra.

The available information about the relation between two concepts needs to be extended in two ways. A sign should be added to indicate whether a positive or a negative relation is concerned. Also, an indication for the strength of the relationship is useful. Until now, all relations have had the same weight. When this is implemented, the program offers more possibilities than present programs for "cause maps". Such programs already contain these elaborations. Many of them, however, can handle only one type of relation: the causal relation.

Concepts of two types can be distinguished: types and tokens. Tokens have a similar function as a variable in logic. Types are labelled nodes, representing generic concepts that are determined by their attribute sets. Types give schema information, whereas tokens represent arbitrary instantiations of types. A token denotes an individual that can be chosen from a universe given by the discourse. For example, "Pluto" is a token, and "dog" is a type. The choice of the individual might be restricted, and the restriction follows from the relations attached to the token.

Knowledge graphs differ from semantic networks even though both give insight in the structure of declarative knowledge. The knowledge graph has an extra facility: the facility of integration.

The methods of concept and link integration have already been elaborated. Two topics still need a lot of attention: how to transfer a text into a graph, and how to represent the information in a graph.

16.4.1. From text to graph

It has already been observed that sentences are organized according to the principle of subject–verb–object; these are two concepts and their relation. The dependency between concepts can be shown as follows (Stokman & De Vries, 1988, p. 200):

- arguments are words on which other words do not depend
- operators are words on which other words depend as arguments
- modifiers are words on which an operator or another modifier is dependent.

In a text, operators and modifiers correspond to the relations within the graph. The arguments correspond to the concepts and the frames. The relation types that can be found in the sentences are grouped as follows (Popping & Roberts, 1997).

- Similarity – records that one theme is identical to another. The relation is symmetric (abbreviations: ALIke, SIMilarity, EQUal, EQuiValent).
- Causal – denotes a cause–effect relation. The relation is asymmetric and transitive. In all methods using networks based on text the causal relation is read as "might" cause (CAUses; is Caused BY).
- Relation – indicates an ASSociation, an ORDering, an EVAluation, or a REAlization. In the first case the relation is symmetric, in the other three it is asymmetric.
- Classification – indicates transitive (is A Kind Of, Has As Kind), asymmetric (Is Property Of), or symmetric (INConsistent with or contradicts, DIStinct) classification.
- Structure – indicates a structuring. The relation is transitive (is PARt of, Has As Part).
- Affective – establishes a judgement of the subject about the object (AFFective, WILL).

The relation between token and type is denoted by ALI (alike). The token is represented by the label Q. Now an arbitrary person can be represented by Q-ALI-dog, but the individual Pluto is represented as Pluto-EQU-Q-ALI-dog. This is preferred to Pluto-AKO-dog, because the AKO-relation links an instantiation with an attribute set, and mixes up extension with intention. This is expressed by Pluto PAR dogs, and Pluto ALI dog. "Dog" is a concept of intentional nature that refers to a set of attributes, while "dogs" is a concept of extensional nature that refers to a set of instantiations. This strict distinction between "dog" and "dogs" is not always made in semantic network theory (James, 1992, p. 114).

A particular representation is the frame. A frame represents a collection of concepts and the relation between these concepts. Generally they are used to denote a process. The relations "is part of" and "is a kind of" are found not only within sentences, but also in the relation between sentences. These relations between sentences are very important in the reproduction of the coherence of a text.

Provided we have only simple sentences it is quite easy to transform them in the direction of knowledge graphs.[13] There are several systems at present that convert data collected in discussion situations immediately into relations in graphs (Carley, 1988). These systems can be extended to provide broader possibilities of application. The accent of many present systems is on representing relations between concepts. In the theory of knowledge graphs inferences are emphasized that become possible with different types of relations. This imposes higher demands on the system, but in the end it will provide more possibilities.

It has not yet been possible to represent relations between processes in knowledge graphs implemented in a computer system. Consider sentences such as: if companies make profit they will start investing. Here is implied that the process of "making profit" leads to the process of "investing". The fact that frames are not implemented in the computer program is the weak component of knowledge graphs.

16.4.2. The presentation of a graph

In this chapter the question is discussed of how to show a graph to a user to enable this user to pick the essential information from the graph. The term "presentation" is used instead of "representation" to emphasize this.

To my knowledge, little is known that contributes to the answer to this question. Experiments have been performed in which, for example, relations that need attention have been shown in a different colour to other relations. With regard to big graphs it might be useful to work with a model that contains several strata. A stratum might correspond to a classification that has been discussed before.

When looking for an answer to the question one might link up with ideas about aspects of communication of knowledge systems. Wærn *et al.* (1992, p. 219) make a distinction between three kinds of knowledge as regards the content necessary for communication:

■ *domain related knowledge* contains both an estimate of the domain knowledge of the sender or receiver and an estimate of one's own domain knowledge

■ *discourse related knowledge* includes intuitive principles for communication

■ *mediating knowledge* deals with the way in which communication knowledge can be related to domain knowledge.

With regard to knowledge graphs, it is very important to know the potential recipients. This is not always possible, though some principles can be indicated. We find them in a "user model" of the receiver. A user model is "a knowledge source in an interactive system which contains explicit assumptions concerning certain aspects of the user that may be appropriate for the communication behaviour of the system" (Wahlster & Kobsa, 1986). This model can be obtained at several levels. The system has to include the following:

■ general knowledge about the cognitive characteristics of users (the system has to know what users can and cannot do)

■ differences between users (one can obtain these by modelling stereotypes or by giving a profile sketch of individual users)

■ define characteristics of individual users during the interaction.

It will be clear that some work still has to be done before knowledge graph systems can represent knowledge that the receiver can use immediately. This, however, holds for all systems representing knowledge, though it does not mean these systems cannot be used at the moment.

16.4.3. Relation to other methods

Reference has already been made to the relationship between the knowledge graph and the model of Tsuchiya. Of course this also holds for other methods that were mentioned briefly. Some of the differences between knowledge graphs and other methods will be summarized very briefly here, even if they have already been mentioned.

It has been pointed out that knowledge graphs offer more possibilities than a causal map: on the one hand because more types of relations are permitted; on the other hand because of the possibility of concept and link integration.

Knowledge graphs are descriptive; they show a state of art. If a discussion in terms of probabilities is desired, this can be realized by using several strata. One can, for example, build a graph on the layer of empirical findings and one on the layer of theories or expectations. This last point has some similarity to case-based reasoning, where one tries to estimate the best result. Knowledge graphs do not propose a solution. The group members always have to draw their conclusions based on what is presented. They are not guided in a certain direction as they may be in some other systems. When such systems are used, a user often will not dwell on the information on which the solution was based. The complete knowledge graph is always shown. It may contain certain chains that for some reason are weak. This can be kept in mind during the interpretation, and the chains can be further investigated.

An important difference between knowledge graphs and knowledge bases is that the latter are not equipped with mechanisms for reasoning that can detect inconsistencies in a text or in knowledge. The knowledge graph affords the opportunity to relate different ways of thinking. Nevertheless, the knowledge graph can remain surveyable due to the possibility of link integration. Knowledge that is added is always confronted with the knowledge already available.

16.4.4. The application of knowledge graphs

Knowledge graphs have been developed to provide a tool for describing the state of art in a specific field of science. They can also be used for building new knowledge. In the previous section we noted the advantage that knowledge graphs have over other methods that are used today. In the context of learning they point to explanations of reason-giving knowledge, the *know-why* (Kim, 1993, p. 38). This is important for both an individual and an organization.

In the application of knowledge graphs, several different situations can be distinguished. If a field of application is more developed it will be easier to build a knowledge graph for this field, especially for the parts concerning which agreement exists. In more recent areas of application, such as process management, this will hold for only a restricted number of areas. Building knowledge graphs can be an important tool for making explicit the available knowledge and existing differences, and for comparing them more systematically. Very often process knowledge will already be available in the system, and new ideas are added. This is the way in which knowledge will be used in decision-making situations: comparison with graphs of different participants in the decision-making enables possible differences in insights to be related either to different problem definitions (the nodes in the graphs by the different participants are not identical) or to different insights (the participants have different ideas about the existence of certain causal relations, but the lines in the graphs by the different participants are not identical).

The graphs can already be used for documenting the knowledge in certain fields. Instead of texts, (protocols of) discussions with persons can be the basis for the graphs. Where the graphs have to be used in process management the theory (and technique) regarding the presentation of graphs must be further elaborated. I assume that if the graphs are used when developing critical knowledge areas, knowledge areas that are essential for the flourishing of a company now and in the future, one such graph will be at the layer of probability reasoning.

Data from projects such as "lessons learned" are well represented in knowledge graphs. Most of the possibilities exist at the tactical and operational levels within organizations. The graph one started with may contain knowledge at a strategic level, where global goals and limiting conditions are defined. This graph grows when it is filled; the concepts will be merely of the type "type". On the operational level tokens are also added.

By accepting (temporary) relations it is possible to investigate the possible effects they might have. This is a form of simulation that can help in supporting policy processes.

16.5. CONCLUSION

This contribution has tried to outline the importance of knowledge graphs as an aid that organizations could learn to use. These graphs allow the integration of knowledge that is contributed from various sources. Now knowledge can be amplified, but contrast also becomes visible. The graphs are a technical aid that can be used in combination with other forms of knowledge building. The assumption is that learning is possible where the participants in the groups allocate explicit shared knowledge.

From a mathematical point of view the model of knowledge graphs is well elaborated. Several questions regarding the way knowledge has to be transposed to graphs still need to be answered. This is also true for the way in which graphs can best be presented to ensure that all knowledge is expressed in an optimal way.

16.6. NOTES

1. It is desirable to define not only the expression knowledge, but also the notions that are related to it: data and information. Data are symbols that have not been interpreted yet. In principle

these data have no meaning for people. They acquire a meaning as soon as one needs them. Now data become information and information consists of data that are related and interpreted, and which describe a situation that was not previously known. The receiver determines whether something is information or not. Information might concern the *content* of data (qualitative) and the amount of news value of data (*quantitative*). Generally the first interpretation is used. For more details see Perrolle (1987).

2. Group decision-making systems have been developed to enable several people to contribute to decision-making. The four important components of these systems (DeSanctis & Gallupe, 1987) are: communication technology, computer technology, technology for decision-making (agenda setting, decision trees, forecasting methods, brainstorming software, voting software), and structured group methods (brainstorming, delphi method). Some investigators add computerized meeting rooms to this list.

   One of the best known forms of such systems is known as GDSS (group decision support systems). These systems are meant to reproduce the structure of the process of group decisions.

3. This and the following section rely on corresponding sections in Eherer *et al.* (1992).

4. This distinction between implicit and explicit knowledge holds for a theoretical observer. In practice there are many variables associated with shared knowledge. The participants may never know what shared knowledge the group actually possesses. Any knowledge that group members know they have in common is of course explicit shared knowledge by definition. It may be that only some members of the group actually know this; others may only suspect it, while others may not know it. These people may all be just a subset of the whole group anyway.

5. Specific declarative or factual knowledge (knowing that) is meant here. Procedural knowledge (knowing how) is not considered. Knowing how to communicate is part of this form of knowledge.

6. The working process of the group is not discussed here either, nor is the relation this has with the process of building knowledge.

7. To simplify this text, the expression "knowledge" is used where data or information is meant; knowledge is what is stored as data in some medium and can be retrieved from that medium later and (again) be used as knowledge.

8. When hypermedia are used the linearity of information is dropped; instead parts of the information are linked. This information can be stored in different media: text, drawings, pictures, audio, and video. Where hypertext systems are involved only the textual content is considered. Hypertexts consist of parts of text, called nodes, and the relations between these nodes, the links. The total of nodes and links constitutes a network. Many hypertext implementations allow a specific meaning to be given to the links (association, sequential, structural). Some sets of nodes and links, called composites, are treated as nodes. Now it is possible that links start in composites, but it is also possible that they end there.

9. The prototype of a hypertext system that can be used here is described in Eherer *et al.* (1992).

10. The computer can only register who has opened the record containing new contributed knowledge. The computer cannot control what the group member is doing with this knowledge. The amount of time a record has been open can also be registered, but this does not give the necessary information concerning how the knowledge was "obtained".

11. For example, in 1994 a plane crashed on a suburb of Amsterdam. The pilot had reported that "they had *lost* a motor". This was interpreted as "a motor doesn't work any more", and did not seem that serious. The reality was that "a motor had broken off", and that was more serious (*De Volkskrant*, 27 January 1996).

12. A very tiresome inconsistency is the one resulting from a change in the content of a notion in time.

13. Generally speaking, sentences are very difficult to code, since one has to be aware of all kinds of semantic complexities. For more details, see Roberts & Popping (1996).

16.7. REFERENCES

CARLEY, K. (1988). Formalizing the expert's knowledge. *Sociological Methods & Research*, vol. 17, 165–232.

CARRÉ, B. (1979). *Graphs and Networks*. Oxford: Clarendon Press.

DAFT, R.L. & WEICK, K.E. (1984). Toward a model of organizations as interpretation systems. *Academy of Management Review*, vol. 9, 284–295.

DESANCTIS, G. and GALLUPE, R.B. (1987). A foundation for the study of group decision support systems. *Management Science*, vol. 33, 589–609.

EHERER, S., ERKIÖ, H., LEWE, H., LUDWIG, B., MYRSETH, S., POPPING, R. & TONG, X. (1992). *Information technology support for group knowledge development*. Working document of COST 14 Co-Tech working group, 1. September.

JAMES, P. (1992). Knowledge graphs. In R.P. VAN DE RIET & R.A. MEERSMAN (Eds), *Linguistic Instruments in Knowledge Engineering*, Amsterdam: Elsevier. 97–117.

KIM, D.H. (1993). The link between individual and organizational learning. *Sloan Management Review*, vol. 35, No. 1, 37–50.

KRAEMER, K. & KING, J. (1988). Computer-based systems for group decision support: status of use and problems in development. *Computing Surveys*, vol. 20, 115–146.

LEVITT, B. & MARCH, J.G. (1988). Organizational learning. *Annual Review of Sociology*, vol. 14, 319–340.

McGRATH, J.E. (1984). *Groups: Interaction and Performance*. Englewood Cliffs, NJ: Prentice-Hall.

PERROLLE, J.A. (1987). *Computers and Social Change. Information, Property, and Power*. Belmont, CA: Wadsworth.

POPPING, R. & ROBERTS, C.W. (1997). Network approaches in text analysis. In R-KLAR & O. OPITZ (Eds), *Classification and Knowledge Organisation*, Heidelberg: Springer, 381–389.

ROBERTS, C.W. & POPPING, R. (1996). Themes, syntax, and other necessary steps in the network analysis of texts. *Social Science Information*, vol. 34, 657–665.

SOWA, J.F. (1987). Semantic networks. In S.C. SHAPIRO (Ed.), *Encyclopedia of Artificial Intelligence*, Part II. New York: Wiley, 1011–1024.

STOKMAN, F.N. & DE VRIES, P.H. (1988). Structuring knowledge in a graph. In G.C. VAN DER VEER and G. MULDER (Eds), *Human–Computer Interaction: Psychonomic Aspects*. Berlin: Springer, 186–206.

TSUCHIYA, S. (1993). Improving knowledge creation ability through organizational learning. In: J-P.A. BARTHÈS (Ed.), *Proceedings ISMICK 93*. Compiègne: IIIA, 87–95.

WÆRN, Y., HÄGGLUND, S., LÖWGREN, J., RANKIN, I., SOKOLNICKI, T. & STEINEMANN, A. (1992). Communication knowledge for knowledge communication. *International Journal of Man Machine Studies*, vol. 37, 215–239.

WAHLSTER, W. & KOBSA, A. (1986). *User Models in Dialog Systems*. New York, Heidelberg: Springer.

WILSON, P. (1991). *Computer Supported Co-operative Work: An Introduction*. London: Intellect Books.

PART SIX

Conclusions

CHAPTER SEVENTEEN

Final discussion and conclusions

YVONNE WÆRN

17.1. SUMMARY OF CONCEPTS AND MODELS

It can be seen that our examples vary widely, that different concepts are used in different contexts, and that there are some crucial entities to consider in the co-operative handling of dynamic situations. To summarize, it seems necessary to consider the concept of dynamics, particularly with regard to the role of time, the concept of control and the concept of co-ordination.

17.1.1. The role of time

In most of the chapters, the idea of a "dynamic system" has been taken as self-evident, and the role of time has not been problematized. The role of time is indeed central to the concept of a dynamic system, in two respects. First, the dynamic system changes over time. Secondly, if we want to control the change, it is necessary to act before it is too late. It may even be said that the point of time for acting is important. Sometimes correct timing rather than hasty action, may be crucial.

To a certain extent it can be claimed that all systems human beings want to control are dynamic, and the only discriminating feature between systems here called "dynamic" and systems considered to be "static" is the pace of time. Business systems as well as environmental systems may change their states slowly, whereas emergencies change their states faster. The chapters here have all been concerned with the fast to moderate paces of time. To some extent, however, "pace" is not absolute but should be related to the actions taken to control the system. The spontaneous system change may be considered to be slow, when actions can easily change the system state. A disease that may be countered by a medicine is one example of a dynamic system which is developing at a medium pace. Here, there may be ample time to diagnose the disease, whereas the insertion of the medicine at an appropriate time is essential. In other, more slowly developing systems, such as environmental changes, we may not have the proper understanding or means of managing the system, and thus the pace may be too fast for our handling of them (greenhouse effects, overpopulation, etc.).

Thus, the role of time is related to the time taken for us to get information in order to diagnose the system state, to act on it and to make any sense of the feedback. If our activities (be they concerned with planning, information-seeking or actual actions) are slower than required by the system dynamics, there are some different ways of handling the situation.

First, some activities may be made more efficient by finding new and quicker procedures. It has been suggested that human decision-making in natural situations is concerned with recognition rather than conscious deliberation of possible alternatives (Klein, 1993). This means that previous experience with similar situations is crucial for relevant actions on new situations. Only when the actors consider that there is sufficient time before action has to be taken will they proceed to a more involved information search in the environment or in the long-term memory (see Cohen *et al.*, 1996).

Second, each action may be speeded up. However, there is always a limit to the possible pace of acts, whether a human being or a machine is involved. For humans, skill training is one important way of achieving a higher pace. When the limit of human acts has been reached, other means of handling time requirements must be found. The most obvious consist in distributing activities over several people or in using artifacts. When the task is easily divided into several, independent tasks, the advantage of distributing activities is apparent. Artifacts as well as people may perform some of the sub-tasks, and the trick lies in finding the best division of labour. However, the division of tasks will suffer time lags as soon as task results have to be communicated between participants (be they humans or machines).

It seems useful for conceptual purposes to differentiate between different kinds of actions, involving time limits of different types. For our present purposes, the distinction between "physical", "conceptual" and "communicative" actions is crucial. Further distinctions may of course be made, as is evident from the human factors literature, where distinctions between various kinds of senso-motor actions are crucial, or in the cognitive psychology literature, where various kinds of mental actions have been timed.

For present purposes, dealing with physical dynamic systems, physical actions involve actions in the physical world, such as moving trucks, spreading water on a fire or changing the direction of a vessel. Conceptual actions involve mental actions, such as planning, diagnosing and interpreting feedback. Communicative actions involve transferring data, interpreting data and negotiating the meaning of data. There may be different means of speeding up these various types of action. Physical actions may to some extent be made quicker if they are performed by machines rather than by human beings. There is inconclusive evidence as to whether or not conceptual or communicative actions take less time through automation. The reason for this is that these kinds of action are less well understood and require more consideration of the context, a consideration which seems to be easy for human beings but is still difficult to realize in an automaton. It also seems easier to divide physical actions into part tasks, such as different localities or different object parts, than to do the same with conceptual or communicative actions. Thus it may be easier to allocate physical actions to different people or artifacts than to distribute conceptual or communicative actions.

One of the chapters in this book exemplifies the role of time in distributed dynamic decision-making, i.e. chapter 11 by Berndt Brehmer. The experimental variation consisted in having both the system to be controlled (here a forest fire) and the controlling system performing (simulated) physical actions at a slower or a quicker pace. The effect on the performance as a whole was observed. It was found that the quicker pace for both the controlled and the controlling system led to more forest being burned down than the slower pace. Thus it can be claimed that the conceptual and communicative actions could not be made quick or efficient enough, even though there was more total time available.

This finding indicates that conceptual and communicative actions cannot be performed independently of the physical activities. Although it might be possible to think and communicate while moving, every new state has to be considered so that the allotted time still does not suffice. An interpretation of this effect is given in the idea of control, covered by Erik Hollnagel in chapter 4, and to be considered further below.

17.1.2. Control

The next important concept is control, or controlling. In this concept lies a normative value of controlling for a purpose. In emergencies, the purpose lies in getting the system to return to normal (no fire, no sickness), in navigation the purpose lies in having the vessel follow a certain track, in industrial processes the purpose lies in avoiding or preventing emergencies as well as in obtaining as efficient a process as possible.

We suggested that control was dependent on "situation assessment". Situation assessment, in turn, comprises both perception and evaluation of the situation currently at hand and a prediction of the possible outcomes of actions upon the system. Chapter 7, by Leena Norros and Kristiina Hukki, indicates that situation assessment and in particular predictions can indeed be supported by providing information. The finding that the value of information is greater for novices than for experts complies with the general idea of competence and level of control suggested by Erik Hollnagel.

We also saw that in order to cope with the changes of system states, it was necessary to plan actions in advance. Planning is to some extent incompatible with adaptation to current circumstances. When handling a dynamic system, it is necessary to be attentive to its current state, and at the same time to know what to do in different states.

Planning is, of course, related to time, as is shown by Erik Hollnagel in chapter 4. If a plan can be created which covers both prerequisites of actions and possible side-effects of actions, time may be sufficient to counter the dynamic changes of the system. However, this kind of planning is seldom possible, for two reasons. First, the knowledge of the system may not be sufficient to enable the creation of tactical or strategic plans. This lack of knowledge may lie in a single individual in a decision position or in the team of people who are to handle the situation, or more generally in the total, accumulated knowledge of such situations. Secondly, the situation may be developing in a new and quite unexpected way. In such cases, control has to rely less on planning and more opportunistic or even scrambled actions will then occur, with the result that the time available will not be sufficient for control to be satisfactory.

17.1.3. Co-ordination

Many of the chapters of the book are concerned with the concept of co-ordination. Since most previous research relating to the control of dynamic situations has dealt with individual decision-making, technical control or the devising of instruments for control, it seemed appropriate to direct attention to the role of co-ordination between people.

Co-ordination was here covered in three different ways: through institutional task allocations (in chapters 3 and 5), through the spontaneous distribution of information (in chapters 5, 6, and 10) and through the provision of a "collective memory", here covered in chapters 9 and 13.

It was suggested by Rob Stammers (in chapter 3) that a task analysis can be used to propose a beneficial task allocation and information distribution among people involved in a common management of a dynamic situation. Institutions built to manage dynamic situations must of course provide such general rules in order to be efficient.

In the air traffic control example, one institutional task/role allocation conforms to the horizontal integration concept (see chapter 2). One role was concerned with planning, another with actions. One controller took care of all planning, for all aircraft, whereas the other took care of all communication with the aircraft. As was shown in chapter 3, this kind of role/task allocation gave rise to the planner having a low workload at all times. On the other hand, the other controller had a very high workload on many occasions. Thus, a hierarchical task organization may not always be beneficial either for individuals or for the system as a whole.

The other example conforms to the vertical integration concept. One controller dealt with all departing aircraft – both their planning and communication requirements – while the other controller dealt with all aspects of incoming aircraft. Thus, the intra-task organization favoured the integration of all activities concerned with arrival and departure. These two part tasks were fairly independent, and there were just a few cases where an arriving aircraft did not land and thus suddenly turned into a departing aircraft. In that case, the two persons had of course to co-ordinate their actions in a way not foreseen by institutional rules.

In chapter 5, Henrik Artman shows that even a traditional, very strict institutionally-ruled organization such as the military may allow for spontaneous, unforeseen task allocations, particularly when new technology is introduced. Here, the degree of freedom was afforded by the task of information distribution. It may be easier to overrule institutional norms concerned with communication than those concerned with decision-making and physical actions, simply because the former actions are not as well defined as the latter. Spontaneous ways of distributing information may not always be efficient, however, as is indicated by Henrik Artman's studies presented in chapters 6 and 10.

Spontaneous communication is characteristic of local co-ordination. For co-ordination purposes, it is necessary to consider *what* is (and has to be) communicated, *how* the content is communicated, with *whom* and *when* communication takes place.

In designing information systems, research has been largely concerned with *what* is communicated. In particular, different display designs have been considered, and different kinds of information to support various decisions (see chapter 7, by Leena Norros and Kristiina Hukka, chapter 9 by Peter Svenmarck and chapter 14 by Esa Auramäki and Mikko Kovalainen).

A new approach to the question of communication content is presented in the study by Peter Svenmarck in chapter 9. In line with the idea that situation assessment in a dynamic situation requires a predictive element, it was suggested that people might benefit from knowing each other's intentions and not only the actual actions. The results indicated that a common information display might reduce the need for actually communicating intentions. Thus, the information of intentions did not actually increase performance.

The question of with *whom* communication takes place is to some extent covered in the study by Henrik Artman, presented in chapter 10. Here it transpires that participants in a team who got the same kind of information from an external source did not arrive at the same situation assessment. However, when information was communicated from one person to another, their situation assessment was more alike. In this particular case, then, direct communication between two persons affected their interpretation of the situation in a convergent way, whereas access to a joint information source made their interpretations more divergent. It is impossible to say what is most efficient in a dynamic situation. A convergent situation assessment is more useful when it is correct, whereas divergent ones may be more useful if one or both deviate from the actual situation and a discussion of the different perspectives can be performed within the given time-frame.

In the chapters above there is only one little hint concerning the question of *when* to communicate, which is in the study of the emergency control centre presented by Henrik Artman and Yvonne Wærn (chapter 6). Here it was found that the team had the habit of "talking aloud" to the room, a habit which has also been described in several other studies concerned with control rooms (see Heath & Luff, 1992; Heath, *et al.*, 1993). Talking aloud to the room relieves the speaker from consciously having to think about when, how and to whom to speak. This kind of sharing of information is useful when other participants need the information left "in the air". It is one of the practices which supports the development of "cognitive empathy", i.e. a feeling of when and how to attend to others' needs. It also seems to be the case that team members can disregard information when they themselves are very busy. However, the information offered may also be interpreted in a context different from the one intended, as was evident in the second example of chapter 6. In this particular case the reactions were not helpful, and it was suggested that "cognitive empathy" was lost. It can be said that the time point was not the right one either for listening to the comment or for reacting to it.

17.2. THEORETICAL IMPLICATIONS

The nature of dynamic systems, the requirement for control and the demand for co-ordination have certain theoretical implications, the first of which is related to the role of context and the second to the role of communication.

First, it is apparent that the changing nature of the dynamic system precludes any formulation of control that relies on fixed procedures or long-ranging plans. Therefore, traditional cognitive science approaches which rely on plans or sequential processes have been criticized. Instead, it is apparent that control of such situations has to be context-sensitive and open to adaptation to changes in the situation. At the same time, however – as was pointed out by Erik Hollnagel in chapter 4 – we still have the need for "mental" concepts such as "constructs" or "competence". Control by situation only would lead to "scrambled" actions, which would never keep up with the changing situation. The model of contextual control seems to be a good candidate for understanding the control of dynamic situations.

The levels of control relate to the interaction between competence and situation demands. If the competence includes strategical or tactical plans which comply with the spontaneous development of the dynamic situation, the requirements of the situation can easily be met within the time allotted. If the situation develops in a way that cannot be covered by any plan, a lower level of control has to be used, with the ensuing difficulty of meeting the time demands.

Second, the complex and changing nature of the dynamic system precludes any formulation of a theory which takes only the individual mind into account. At the same time, organizational theories are not relevant either, since they work with too crude a grain to be useful for state-to-state actions. A prescriptive co-ordination theory cannot work, since the dynamic situation will require distributions of tasks and information according to the current task load of the participants concerned. Thus, co-ordination must rely mainly on communication.

A communication theory that is to be used in these contexts has to consider function rather than communication structure. On a general level, the main functions consist in the

forming of a shared situation assessment (including perception and prediction), an acceptance of the tasks allocated, and an allocation of new tasks when necessary.

Communication has its costs, however. It has repeatedly been found that communication between people decreases their joint performance (Rönnberg & Andersson, 1996).
Co-ordination losses, motivational effects and cognitive factors contribute to the lowering
of efficiency. An important factor also lies in the relationship between the participants of
communication. It has been shown that people who know each other well communicate
more efficiently than people who do not know one another (Andersson 1996).

Communication is, of course, an interactive activity, and taking account of the participants involved in the communication is as important as consideration of the situation
of concern to the communication between them.

It must therefore be noted that communication cannot be considered to consist merely
in the transfer of information. Even though there is a "sender", this sender has to consider
the possible receivers in selecting data to "transfer" as well as in formulating a message.
On the "receiver" side, the message is interpreted not only with respect to the receiver's
current knowledge of the situation, but also with respect to the knowledge of the sender.
The meaning of the message can therefore never be derived from its form, but has to be
considered as derived not only from the knowledge context, of which both senders and
receivers form a part, but also from the situation in which both reside.

17.3. LEARNING/TRAINING ISSUES

It is obvious that there is a lot to learn and to train in dynamic situations: the behaviour
of the target system, the task/role allocation to be used, and the co-ordination of information, planning and acting. We find two main conceptual frameworks to be useful for understanding the issues of learning and training, one concerned with different knowledge
"levels", the other with learning.

17.3.1. Knowledge levels

An important insight into both action and learning lies in the suggestion that human
knowledge can be considered to be available at different levels (Rasmussen, 1985). Here
we will follow Rasmussen's suggestion, adapted somewhat to our particular purposes,
in Fig. 17.1.

Fig. 17.1. can be regarded from different perspectives. On the one hand it may be
conceived as requirements posed by the environment on people. A "routine" procedure
requires knowledge at a skill level, where the skilled person observes the situation and
acts according to the requirements of the situation. A rule-based procedure consists in
instructions such as "if the situation is X, then perform Y and Z", which corresponds to
requirements on the rule level. Finally, a new problem requires the knowledge level,
where the various alternative routes may be considered (here denoted as "problem space")
and where a mental search of the best path is performed (here denoted as "search").

On the other hand, people may be characterized by the level of knowledge they possess
with regard to a particular task. If people have not got the prerequisite skills for performing routinely, they have to resort to a rule-based or knowledge level. If they find
applicable rules, they may use these whether they are relevant in the particular case or
not. However, if they apply general knowledge (on the knowledge level), they may solve

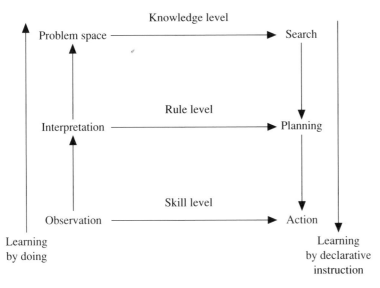

Figure 17.1. Knowledge levels and learning/training issues.

problems on a general level and apply this solution to the current situation. In both cases, unskilled people will take much longer to perform their tasks than will skilled ones. They may also err to a greater extent and have less opportunity to recover from their errors.

17.3.2. Learning issues

Now, as to learning, two different approaches may be considered, here to be called "experiental" and "instructional". "Pure" experiential learning starts at the observation and action level. People are then supposed to build their own rules and knowledge on the basis of their experiences (see Auramäki & Kovalainen, chapter 14). The "pure" instructional approach to learning starts at the knowledge level and proceeds downwards towards observations and actions. This is the course of learning suggested by Anderson (1980). In a real-world setting, none of these "pure" approaches are taken.

"Pure" experiential learning suffers from the drawback that learners do not know what to attend to, that they have difficulty interpreting both the situation and the feedback from the situation, and that they do not know what kinds of alternative actions they may take (see Wærn, 1992). It is thus fairly evident that learners will have difficulty forming knowledge on both the rule and the knowledge level. They may, however, be able to react efficiently whenever the new situations comply with a situation they have already learnt (and remember).

An important educational strategy for experiential learning lies in selecting examples in order to restrict the learners' attention and interpretation possibilities. The learning situation is "scaffolded" so that the learner is trained on only one part of the task at a time.

It is also obvious that good teachers will not only present relevant situations to the learners, but will also talk about these; this facilitates declarative learning, from the top downwards, and is what happens in the "briefing" and "debriefing" undertaken in training situations. In the "organizational memory" systems, the idea is that both declarative knowledge and procedural knowledge are essential if "organizational learning" is to take place (see Auramäki & Kovalainen, chapter 14).

Independent of the approach to learning, learning must be related to some content. In chapter 12, John Dowell and Walter Smith analyzed some requirements for the training of co-ordination in emergency management and applied these to the opportunities offered by different training environments. In particular, characteristics of planning, action, communication, role and task knowledge were suggested. This kind of cognitive engineering is an important step towards designing good training for controlling dynamic situations.

A somewhat different approach is taken by Rego Granlund in chapter 13, where a full-scale simulation of a complex dynamic environment is considered. Here the analysis showed that it is not enough that the environment is realistic, it should also enable the selection of tasks to afford "scaffolding". Further, the insight that knowledge may exist and be usable at different levels makes it necessary to consider the ability to provide feedback at different levels.

17.4. COMPUTER ARTIFACTS

A device as versatile as a computer can be used as an artifact in various information-processing tasks. As such, it will at some level of detail change the actual processing in carrying out the task. So, for instance, we may communicate face to face or via letters, telephone or e-mail, but when the actions with the artifacts are considered, the process of "communicating" varies with these different circumstances. In that respect, the term "support" may be a little misleading. Computers "support" communication as much or as little as ordinary letters or the telephone. What happens when using computers is that new tasks are enabled (storing and retrieving, for instance) and that the actual details of communicating are changed. Thus, computers can be regarded from a task point of view, in which there will be changes in subtasks related to the introduction of a computer for a certain task. They can also be considered from a technical point of view, where they enable people to perform new tasks which are enabled by the technology itself. Further, people may create new uses for the artifacts, just as all technology has been put to unexpected uses.

In our studies, some different kinds of computers as artifacts have been presented. They can be divided into collective information sources, information displays and learning-oriented supports.

17.4.1. Collective information sources

Collective information sources hold information about the situation, its prerequisites or its possible management, and they are intended for use by several people. The idea is that people should be able to share experiences with one another as well as provide information about current events. A common term for describing such sources is "organizational memory" (see Argyris, 1993), a term which indicates the enterprise and business perspective used in talking about collective information sources. It was suggested in chapter 2 that such an organizational memory may concern long-term knowledge as well as the short-term information which changes during the course of a case. We are of course aware of criticism voiced against the concept of "organizational memory" (see Bannon & Kuutti, 1996). However, in a work setting, the need for some kind of storage of information has to be met, and in this book some of the possible solutions have been presented.

There seem to be different approaches to the storing of information for long-term use versus short-term application. For long-term storage, formal approaches have been favoured, exemplified above by knowledge-based systems (chapter 15) and knowledge graphs (chapter 16). For short-term storage, a more informal storage has been suggested, in terms of natural language annotations. Let us consider some of the advantages and drawbacks of both these approaches.

The formal approach may only be feasible for long-term storage. Knowledge-based systems require a prolonged period of "knowledge acquisition", which hitherto has mostly been performed in co-operation between an "expert" and a "knowledge engineer". Although methods are now emerging which enable the experts themselves to represent their knowledge in a computational form, the work involved is still quite complex. As long as the same experts are available, new knowledge may be added to the old one, provided it does not conflict with the knowledge already stored. If new, revolutionary knowledge is developed, the knowledge base also will have to be redesigned and this revision may take as long as the original construction.

As here presented, knowledge graphs are based on text, a familiar form of expression for most experts. The graph is built on the currently available information, and new information may imply that a quite different knowledge structure has to be derived from the old nodes combined with new ones. This may be handled by an iterated integration of nodes. A problem arises when, for whatever reason, available information turns out to be no longer correct.

The formal approach offers some advantages which do not apply to informal approaches. The search for knowledge which is applicable to the current problem is facilitated through the very construction of knowledge bases. Whether these require input of data (expert systems) or a suggestion put forward by the user (critiquing systems), the solution (or comment) is derived directly from the knowledge base and does not need any involved search by the user. Also, knowledge may, in principle, be "reused" in various contexts, such as problem-solving, advice-giving or educational contexts. It may also be possible to propose such systems as "knowledge agents" who, together with the user, co-operatively solve a problem. Adaptation to different kinds of knowledge possessed by users is a further possibility offered by such systems.

So, to conclude, formal systems are effective for routine use in non-changing conditions. They are modifiable when minor changes are introduced into the system, but inflexible when the information structure changes radically. In the latter case, there is the risk that wrong solutions may be derived from the systems, if indeed the user input is accepted.

Informal approaches, where people themselves write annotations in some kind of system, are flexible at the input stage. People can express themselves as they want to, and knowledge acquisition offers no problem. However, this flexibility at the input moment is outweighed by the complexity of the information when people want to retrieve it. If no structure is given to the input, it will be very difficult to retrieve information. The output will be difficult to overview, and there will be redundancies and inconsistencies, if the information base has been allowed to grow in an uncontrolled way, as is most often the case.

In practice, the informal kind of "organizational memory" has been subjected to similar critique as the formal one. The main thrust of the critique is that we should not talk about "knowledge" but rather about "knowledge creation", not about "memory" but rather about "remembering". The dynamic nature of knowledge creation and use should not be lost in the static language of "storage" (see Bannon & Kuutti, 1996).

Thus, for the future, we may want a collective information store which combines the advantages of natural language input with the advantages of inferences and control offered by a formal representation. Further, a simple way of retrieving data is desired, as is also a structured way of surveying the information gathered. It is important, moreover, to ensure that the user can judge the adequacy of data retrieved, which means that some explanatory facility is also desirable (see Southwick, 1991; Wærn et al., 1995). Such a store will meet at least some information needs when the context and use of information do not differ too much or when the information needed does not change too much over time. We still lack a suitable mechanism for working on the revision of information in new contexts, as well as on the need for the restructuring of information.

17.4.2. Learning-oriented support

In this book, a particular kind of learning-oriented support is analyzed, i.e. one concerned with simulations. We will not discuss here the usefulness of simulations *per se* from an educational point of view, since this has not been considered in the book. A good overview is found in Gestrelius (1993), unfortunately only in Swedish.

We can note, however, that offering a simulation environment for learning the complexities of managing a dynamic process is a problem which requires a lot of consideration. First, *what* should be learnt has to be considered, and we cannot yet claim that the goal of learning is made clear and explicit in the real life situations which have been studied. Vague goals of "co-operation" in "learning the dynamics of reality" have been offered, but these are difficult to compare to actual performance. A cognitive engineering analysis is needed along the lines, exemplified here by chapter 12, by John Dowell and Walter Smith.

Secondly, the simulation is in itself complex. It does not seem feasible to automate the presentation of a dynamic situation in all its complexity. Instead, having people role play has been used in some full-scale simulations, notably in military and rescue training contexts. People serving as role players need support in order to cope with their tasks adequately. Rego Granlund considered such needs in chapter 13.

However, it may be the case that some learning can be advanced in a simpler environment. Rego Granlund suggested one such, i.e. a microworld. By constraining situations to factors which are considered essential, it is easier to automate the presentation of the situation. It is usually considered to be advantageous from an educational point of view to train one part of a complex situation at a time (see Carroll, 1990).

17.4.3. Dynamic information displays

One particularly common artifact in the handling of dynamic systems consists in displays which show various aspects of the current state of the system. Much work within cognitive engineering has been concerned with proposing and assessing the functionality of such displays.

In this book, Leena Norros and Kristiina Hukki (chapter 7) presented two different kinds of dynamic displays to be used in navigating big vessels in narrow waters. One was concerned with predicting the ship's future sweep. The need for prediction in situation assessment has already been discussed, and this kind of display would therefore be expected to facilitate this activity. The assessment of the predictor display supported this suggestion. In particular, inexperienced navigators gained more from the display, which indicates that experienced navigators by themselves make predictions similar to those offered by the predictor display. In narrow sounds, where more attention has to be paid to small movements of the ship, both inexperienced and experienced navigators were aided by the predictor display.

The researchers also made a study of another kind of information device aimed at integrating various kinds of information, such as the hydrographic situation and the traffic situation as well as the movement of the ship. This study did not show any clear evidence of a better performance due to use of the system. The conclusion can be drawn that information systems should not be considered as some kind of *deus ex machina* solution to all kinds of tasks. The difference between the two types of information technology solutions suggests that it is more important for human controllers to obtain predictions of the course of the dynamic system than to obtain an integrated conception of the current situation state.

17.5. FURTHER DEVELOPMENT

We have found three main ways in which the problem of co-ordinating process management has been approached, namely the field study approach, the experimental approach and the system design approach. We propose that these different approaches may be necessary in the future, but that a better adaptation of the studies to one another might be performed. Observations from a field study might be further analyzed and investigated in a systematic experiment, as was exemplified in chapters 3, 5 and 10.

We suggest that observations from experiments should be further investigated in follow-up field studies. In this way, it might be possible to replicate and refine interpretations from one context to another. The field studies give an ecological context to the observations, whereas the experiment enables us to study decontextualized effects of variations observed in the field study.

Several studies and models show that it is possible to generalize to some extent over different contexts, whether in terms of situation assessment, in terms of the level of control used or in terms of the co-ordination rules and communication practices. There is a need for many more detailed studies of different contexts to support the various suggestions as to general (decontextualized) effects, as well as to very specific context effects. The most probable outcome is that there will be a range of contexts within which similar models or rules are valid. We do not yet know anything about relevant contextual constraints and their corresponding models.

The lack of knowledge of relevant contexts also affects the conclusions to be drawn from the suggested computer artifacts. Since they change the human task at some level, the use of the artifacts should be more systematically related to both field observations and experimental studies. At the moment we know that it is technically feasible to design the artifacts studied here, but we know very little about their effects in actual use.

We also see that several aspects have to be further investigated, and we will merely hint here at the observations on flexible task allocation and situation assessment.

Several previous studies in this field have focused on task allocation, where mostly institutionalized rules or experimental variations have been investigated. In the chapters presented here we found that task allocation may be changed during the handling of a dynamic situation. This means that we have to investigate how people observe the needs for changing task allocation and how they cope with this need. Some hints on this situated task allocation appear in chapters 5, 6 and 10. One of the observations led to the concept of "cognitive empathy", which can be seen as a precursor to flexible task allocation. Since all these observations were made in particular situations where people were co-located, it is difficult to generalize to other possible situations. It might be asked, for instance, if and how people manage this kind of flexible task allocation in situations where they are distributed or where the complexity is higher than in the current examples.

As to common situation assessment, we still know very little about how it is performed and what factors might facilitate it or make it more difficult. As we have already noted, there are two sides of the coin, one concerned with the dynamic situation *per se* and its assessment, the other concerned with co-ordinating the various situation perceptions. This co-ordination does not require a joint situation assessment, but rather a distributed one. Since distribution takes time, crucial questions arise as to the role of artifacts and communication in this process. Some insights have here been gained from field studies, for instance by Hutchins (1990, 1995a, 1995b), but there is much more to be learned about these processes.

Although the analyses and studies have theoretical implications, as discussed above, it should not be assumed that a theory of distributed dynamic process management is certain to be constructed. There is, after all, no sense in expecting the emergence of a theory of emergency or industrial plant management. Instead, the cases treated here should be regarded as special cases of how human beings adapt to external circumstances.

Candidate phenomena to be included in such a theory are flexible task distribution, artifact creation and the creation of conceptual constructs. These in turn need to take account of co-ordination and communication, the nature and role of artifacts, and as cognitive issues. This book is but a small contribution to an integrated analysis of these theoretical needs.

17.6. REFERENCES

ANDERSON, J.R. (1980). Acquisition of cognitive skill. *Psychological Review*, vol. **89**, 369–406.

ANDERSON, J. (1996) *Two is one too many: dyadic memory collaboration effects on encoding and retrieval of episodes*. PhD Thesis. Linköping Studies in Education and Psychology, no. 47, Linköping University: Department of Education and Psychology.

ANDERSON, J. & RÖNNBERG, J. (1995). Recall suffers from collaboration: joint recall effects of friendship and task complexity. *Applied Cognitive Psychology*, vol. 9, 199–211.

ANDERSON, J. & RÖNNBERG, J. (in press). Cued memory collaboration: effects of friendship and type of retrieval cue. *European Journal of Cognitive Psychology*.

ARGYRIS, C. (1993). *On Organizational Learning*. Cambridge, MA: MIT Press.

BANNON, L.J. & KUUTTI, K. (1996). Shifting perspectives on organizational memory: from storage to active remembering. *Proc. 29th IEEE HICSS, vol. III, Information Systems – Collaboration Systems and Technology*, 1996. IEEE Computer Society Press, Washington, DC, 156–167.

CARROLL, J.M. (1990). *The Nurnberg Funnel. Designing Minimalist Instruction for Practical Computer Skill*. Cambridge, MA & London, UK: MIT Press.

COHEN, M.S., FREEMAN, J.T. & WOLF, S. (1996). Metarecognition in time-stressed decision making: recognizing, critiquing and correcting. *Human Factors*, vol. **38**, 206–219.

GESTRELIUS, K. (1993). Pedagogik i simuleringsspel – erfarenhetsbaserad utbildning med över-inlärningsmöjligheter. *Pedagogisk Orientering och Debatt 100*. Lund University, Sweden.

HEATH, C.C. & LUFF, P. (1992). Collaboration and control: crisis management and multimedia technology in London Underground line control rooms. *CSCW Journal*, vol. **1**, Nos 1–2, 69–94.

HEATH, C.C., JIROTKA, M., LUFF, P. & HINDMARSH, J. (1993). Unpacking collaboration: the international organisation of trading in a city dealing room. *Proceedings ECSCW 1993*, 13–17 September, 155–170.

HUTCHINS, E. (1990). The technology of team navigation. In J. GALEGHER, R.E. KRAUT & C. EGIDO (Eds), *Intellectual Teamwork: Social and Technical Bases of Collaborative Work.* Hillsdale, NJ: Erlbaum.

HUTCHINS, E. (1995a). *Cognition in the Wild.* Cambridge, MA: MIT Press.

HUTCHINS, E. (1995b). How a cockpit remembers its speeds. *Cognitive Science*, vol. 19, 265–288.

KLEIN, G. (1993). A recognition-primed decision (RPD) model of rapid decision making. In G. KLEIN, J. ORASANU, R. CALDEWOOD & C.E. ZAMBOK (Eds), *Decision Making in Action: Models and Methods.* New Jersey: Ablex, 138–147.

RASMUSSEN, J. (1985). The role of hierarchical knowledge representation in decision making and system management. *IEEE Transactions on Systems, Man and Cybernetics*, SMC-13, No. 2, 234–243.

RÖNNBERG, J. & ANDERSON, J. (1996). Recall in individuals and groups.

SOUTHWICK, R.W. (1991). Explaining reasoning: an overview of explanation in knowledge-based systems. *The Knowledge Engineering Review*, 1–19.

WÆRN., Y. (1992). Varieties in learning to use computers as tools. *Computers in Human Behavior*, vol. **9**, 323–339.

WÆRN, Y., HÄGGLUND, S., RAMBERG, R., RANKIN, I. & HARRIUS, J. (1995). Computational advice and explanations – behavioural and computational aspects. In: K. NORDBY, P.H. HELMERSEN, D.J. GILMORE & S.A. ARNESEN (Eds), *Human–Computer Interaction.* Interact '95. London: Chapman & Hall.

Index